EVERYTHING®

ONLINE GENEALOGY BOOK

Use the Web to discover long-lost relations, trace your family tree back to royalty, and share your history with far-flung cousins!

Pat Richley, a.k.a. Dear MYRTLE

Adams Media Corporation
Holbrook, Massachusetts

An Everything® Series Book.
Everything® is a registered trademark of Adams Media Corporation

Published by Adams Media Corporation
260 Center Street, Holbrook, MA 02343 U.S.A.
www.adamsmedia.com

ISBN: 1-58062-402-2

Printed in the United States of America.

J I H G F E D C B A

Library of Congress Cataloging-in-Publication data
available upon request from the publisher.

Illustrations by Barry Littmann

This book is available at quantity discounts for bulk purchases.
For information, call 1-800-872-5627.

Introduction

Are you intrigued by the contents of Great-Grandma's trunk in the attic? Do you enjoy tromping though the cemetery behind the ivy-encrusted stone walls of the churchyard? Are you wondering what's behind that peculiar smile in that old tintype of Great Uncle Zebulon?

If so, then you've got the bug—the genealogy bug!

Maybe it was Alex Haley's *Roots* that got us going. Or, maybe it's what makes both the History and Biography cable channels so popular. Then again, maybe the change of the century is giving us reason to reflect on the past. Whatever the reason, people just plain get hooked on climbing their family trees. In the last four years, I've noticed it's not just the gray-haired retirement set anymore. Younger folks are getting into the hobby every day. Actually, "hobby" is a misnomer— genealogy is more of an obsession. Once the genealogy bug has bitten you you'll find yourself staying up late searching for just one more clue!

Thousands upon thousands of people are doing genealogy—tracking down information about parents, grandparents, and ancestors. Researchers constantly use the family records sections of public libraries. Libraries contain hundreds of thousands of books about particular families or genealogical lines. Computer nets buzz back and forth between genealogy Web sites. Magazines and television programs focus attention on genealogical activity. Among thousands of genealogy organizations in America's counties, many meet regularly and publish local guides to old cemetery, court, and church records. Boy Scouts can earn a Family History merit badge. Thousands of family organizations operate at national and local levels. Most large libraries have family history reference sections, genealogy reference specialists, and guidebooks for the beginning genealogist.

Some high school and college history classes ask students to do simple genealogy exercises designed to let students see their families' situations as immigrants coming to America or during major events like the Great Depression, the influenza epidemic of 1918, or the Civil War.

The Definition

The word "genealogy" is derived from the Greek, meaning the tracing of the descent of family and individuals. Genealogies are often referred to as family trees and sometimes pedigrees.

The word pedigree is derived from the French meaning crane's foot. In early British genealogies, a three-line mark resembling a crane's foot was used to show lines of descent—thus the word pedigree.

Regardless of what term is used to describe genealogies, they have existed since very ancient times, and all cultures have some form of genealogy.

Because of widespread interest in family history, scores of professional genealogists make their livings by searching for genealogy information for clients who hire them. Because of genealogy interest, publishers have produced scores of important handbooks and guidebooks designed for beginners and specialists, for genealogy research in general, and for very specific genealogy research problems such as Jewish genealogy, adoptions, immigrants to Canada, and Native American research.

Several large urban and university libraries are recognized as being important genealogy research centers, serving a very interested public, including:

> Allen County Public Library in Ft. Wayne, IN
> National Archives in Washington, D.C.
> Family History Library (Mormons) in Salt Lake City, UT
> New England Genealogical and Historical Society
>   in Boston, MA
> Newberry Library in Chicago, IL
> New York Public Library in New York, NY
> Sutro Public Library in San Francisco, CA

Introductory genealogy classes are available in virtually every state. Many libraries, local genealogical societies, and community education programs offer these. Or, you can visit one of the LDS Church's thirty-five hundred family history centers and receive beginning instructions there.

Why Do People Get Started?

Curiosity, often fed by the urge to know one's identity but sometimes acting on its own, causes people to think about their past family members. A woman visits Ellis Island and wonders who in her own family were the immigrant ancestors, where they came from, and when they arrived in America. A man walks by the Gettysburg battlefield monument and wonders if one of his ancestors fought in the Civil War. Or, a person inherits a faded photograph of a great-grandparent and, looking into that person's eyes, wonders where and when that person lived and what life was like for that ancestor.

Interest in genealogy strikes people in every walk of life, every social class, across all ethnic groups, young and old, male and female:

- Among those of western European descent, some take pride in discovering that their family way-back-when had a family crest or coat of arms.
- Descendants who find they had a Scottish family with its own tartan like to have a blanket or tie or goblets featuring the tartan design.
- Descendents of *Mayflower* passengers join a *Mayflower* organization.
- Many people brag about Native American ancestry they might have.
- Famous African-American author Alex Haley, who wrote *Roots*, enjoyed telling audiences about his Irish ancestry as much as about his African forbears.
- Many families of Asian descent inherit a reverence for ancestors that requires that they know and tap into genealogies extending back centuries.

Forty million people can't be wrong. The best place to begin your family history research is the Internet. The big genealogy Web sites, such as FamilySearch, are getting big numbers—40 million hits a day—the kind any dot.com marketing guru would be proud to claim. There's a lot of excitement about genealogy!

A Day in the Life

Let me tell you about a typical online research day for me. Plus or minus a few telephone calls, this is what it's like:

DearMYRTLE is a nom de plume for my online activities. In "real life" I serve as a computer instructor at Manatee Technical Institute in Bradenton, Florida. I've been online since 1985, back

then using a Commodore 64 and signing on to Q-Link (the grandparent of America Online. (Those were the days of really, really slow 300 baud modems!) In 1995 I began writing the DearMYRTLE column for the Genealogy Forum on AOL. With the expansion to the Web, the Genealogy Forum and DearMYRTLE's columns can be enjoyed by online researches who might not sign on with AOL.

I was trained in genealogy at the Washington, D.C. Temple Family History Center. I've done extensive research at the National Archives, Library of Congress, Daughters of the American Revolution Library, as well as local and state libraries and archives in the localities where my ancestors once lived. Since my children have all moved to Utah, I have a built-in home for my annual research trips to Salt Lake City. I've spoken at National Genealogical Society Conferences, Everton Genealogy Seminars, and other seminars throughout the United States. I volunteer as the instructor of my local Manasota PAF Users Group, where we talk about all sorts of genealogy software, research techniques, and Internet sites.

As you can imagine, I get a lot of e-mail from inquiring genealogists. I regret not being able to answer each e-mail or message board posting personally, but I do read them, and use them as the basis for nearly every column I write. My Web site has articles discussing great ideas for getting started in online genealogy, organizing what you've got, and continuing with your research beyond family legends. If you'd like to see my site, go to *www.dearmyrtle.com*.

- My newly discovered cousin in Abilene, Texas, notified me by e-mail that she had posted seven new family portraits to the Froman family Web site at MyFamily.com.
- Uploaded a copy of my compiled genealogy to a private Web site to share the info with my cousins. This will save them hours of typing in the names on their own.
- Reading the online Ancestry Daily News, I discovered that the National Genealogical Society (NGS) and Federation of Genealogical Societies (FGS) are working to forestall the

closing of vital records access in Iowa (where I still have a lot of research to do).

(And this was all before 10 a.m.!)

- Printed out a research outline from FamilySearch.org about tracing immigrant ancestors. I really need help with my eastern European ancestry.

- Printed the scanned image of a certificate of marriage for Charles C. Todd and Ruby E. Collins on December 24, 1889.

- Browsed through USGenWeb's site.

- Ordered two genealogy books from amazon.com (and saved $15.43).

- Found a source for acid-free tissue paper and archival-quality boxes to safely store my grandmother's lace doilies and the family Bible.

- My grandson's birthday is tomorrow, so I send him an animated, musical online greeting card from *www.bluemountain.com.*

- Read a neat article about the Battle at Hatcher's Run in 1863. "Bits of Blue & Gray" is a monthly column that chronicles personal histories of ancestors who served in the Civil War.

- Printed out an 1875 map of Ogden, Utah, by E. S. Glover, published by Strobridge in Cincinnati, part of the Library of Congress, American Memory project, which I found a link for on Utah GenWeb. I'll use this to pinpoint where Mary Ann (Hoopes), widow of David Dutton Yearsley, had settled following his death at Winter Quarters in 1849. The printout will fit neatly in a top-loading sheet protector, and I'll file it in the Yearsley notebook.

If these are the sorts of things you'd like to learn more about doing on the Web, keep reading.

Just E-Mail!

Thankfully, we don't have to rely on "snail mail" when writing to family members. Electronic mail has pushed us into the 21st century at lightning speed. I can send a note to my father in Seattle from my home in Bradenton, Florida and he receives it in about 20 seconds. Even the best mail carriers can't compete with this. Now, if I could just learn to type better . . .

CHAPTER ONE

Getting Started in Online Genealogy

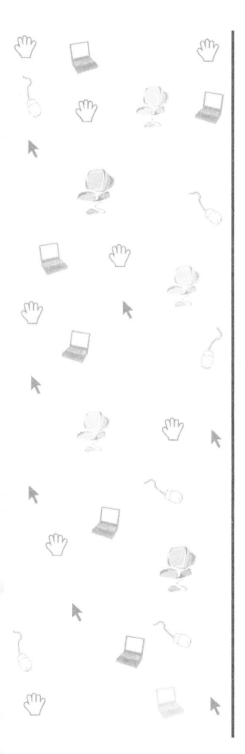

Before Going Online, Examine Your Family Tree

Let's resort to the old fashioned way of writing down the facts before getting online. Take a closer look at your lineage. "Family tree" is a term applied to one's genealogical past. A tree has a main trunk with branches that extend out indefinitely. The family tree image is a nice one, implying a branch, and then branches from that branch, and then new branches and twigs as the family grows and spreads. But the family tree image provides a limited view of the family. Three other descriptions seem more useful to show what the genealogy patterns are.

1. *An upside-down triangle or pyramid with the point at the bottom and base at the top.* This is the most popular approach people use when doing genealogy. Not counting remarriages, a person typically has two parents, four grandparents (two couples), eight great-grandparents (four couples), 16 great-great-grandparents (eight couples), and so on backward in time. From you (at the bottom point) working upward, this forms the upside-down triangle, this upside-down pyramid describes an ancestral family—your ancestors back four generations from you.

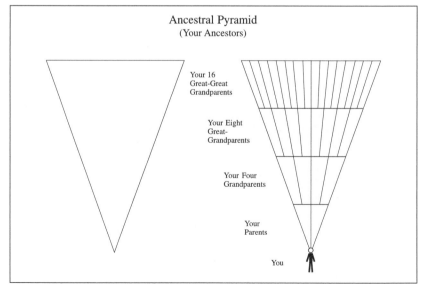

Ancestral Pyramid
(Your Ancestors)

Your 16 Great-Great Grandparents

Your Eight Great-Grandparents

Your Four Grandparents

Your Parents

You

2. *A rightside-up triangle or pyramid with the point at the top and the base at the bottom.* This describes a family coming down through time from one common set of ancestors. Its point is one set of great-great-grandparents, and then as the pyramid widens it includes all their children, then widens to include all their children's children, and so on down to the big base at the bottom—all the living descendants of that couple. This rightside-up pyramid describes a descendent family, or all the descendants from one common ancestor.

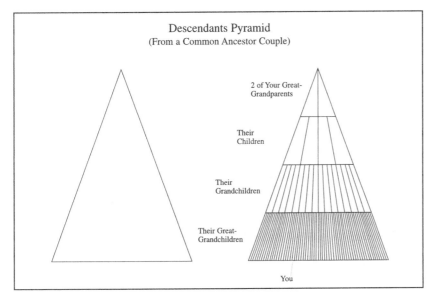

Descendants Pyramid
(From a Common Ancestor Couple)

2 of Your Great-Grandparents

Their Children

Their Grandchildren

Their Great-Grandchildren

You

3. *The Christmas tree with one triangle sitting on top of another triangle just like it.* This is the direct-line family. It starts with a couple at the top and branches out to show their children, one of whom is the direct line to the present, but—to keep it from becoming too big and too wide—it continues down to only the children of the child who is the direct-line ancestor. Then, that child is dealt with as a married person with children—like the tip of the next pyramid down—so another set of branches flares out from the trunk. But that next generation, again shows only the direct-line child, his or her spouse, and their children.

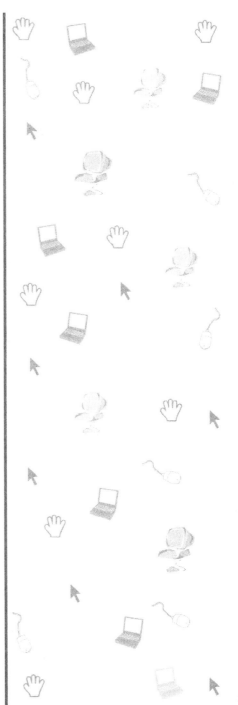

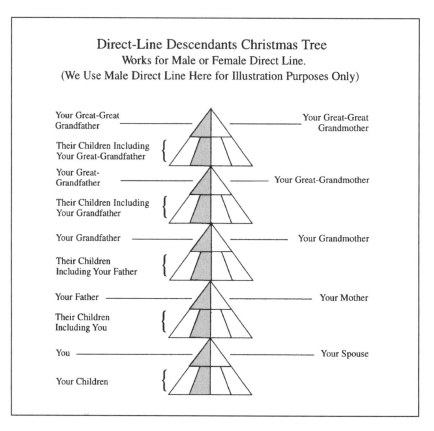

Direct-Line Descendants Christmas Tree
Works for Male or Female Direct Line.
(We Use Male Direct Line Here for Illustration Purposes Only)

Your Great-Great Grandfather — Your Great-Great Grandmother

Their Children Including Your Great-Grandfather

Your Great-Grandfather — Your Great-Grandmother

Their Children Including Your Grandfather

Your Grandfather — Your Grandmother

Their Children Including Your Father

Your Father — Your Mother

Their Children Including You

You — Your Spouse

Your Children

In real life, most of us can only "handle" in our minds the Christmas-tree version of the family. That is, as children we know our brothers and sisters and parents—our own little triangle or pyramid. And we know uncles and aunts and first cousins. So, we tend to be able to account for two generations. But, even though we know a third generation, our grandparents, we usually do not know all of their brothers and sisters, and their children and grandchildren. That is, it's great if we know our uncles and aunts and first cousins, but please do not expect us to know all of our great aunts and great uncles, and those more distant cousins. Those become too distant in relationship and distance for us to pay much attention too.

When we marry, our children will "inherit" two of these Christmas-tree versions of the family, one for their father's family and one for their mother's. When we become parents, and then grandparents, we keep track of our children's children. But very likely, our grandchildren will not know all of our brothers and sisters, or those who are our own nieces and nephews.

Upside-down and rightside-up triangles and Christmas trees? Where all these diagrams lead is here:

The direct-line family becomes the trunk of the family tree that we try to identify first, when doing genealogy research.

Each ancestor or descendant, no matter which way you want to research, is a blank. So to "do" your genealogy, you will have to try and fill in as many blanks as possible. For each person, the basic information to find is what we call *vital information*. In other words, we need to unearth key facts about each person's life—birth, marriage, and death information:

- Full proper name
- Day, month, year, and place of birth
- Day, month, year, and place of marriage
- Full information about spouse(s)
- Day, month, year, and place of death
- Full information about every child from each marriage

Family History is Genealogy—and Much, Much More

Genealogy is one way to find, preserve, and share family heritage. But, the family's heritage is furthered through doing other projects in a range of other non-genealogy activities. Many families do several of these other activities automatically, just because they seem to be good things to do. Among the common activities are:

- Writing the life story of a relative
- Tape-recording the life story of a relative
- Writing one's own life story, or parts of it
- Sending and receiving family letters

- Keeping a personal diary or journal
- Making scrapbooks for oneself or for another family member
- Taking, storing, displaying, and sharing photographs, slides, and videos
- Taking proper care of old family records, documents, and objects
- Holding family reunions
- Taking trips to sites important to their ancestors' lives.

A Revolution in Genealogy

The Internet, or information superhighway as it is called, is an invisible telecommunication web of electronic lines and connections that link together many sites of information. Even if you have no previous hands-on experience with the Internet, you probably know people who use it. Millions of Americans with computers are linked to the Internet.

The Internet, via the World Wide Web, is able to bring the world to your desktop computer. This ability is revolutionizing how we research genealogy—making the process faster, less costly, and easier than the old, standard methods of research—which involved a lot of snail mail and a lot of wading through dusty old files and papers! The Internet links together libraries, genealogists, and data-bases—and you on your home computer. For those with access to computers, the Internet is making genealogy know-how and source-materials available to more people than was happening before the age of cyberspace. If you don't own a computer, you probably can use one at a public library that is already connected to an Internet server.

Tons of genealogy-related material is "on the Net." However, don't plan on finding your genealogy already done for you—thinking that all you have to do is click a "Print" button to get it. Rather, expect the Internet to show you where and how to research partic-ular kinds of records, and allow you to look at the records that are computerized.

To look, scan, or "surf" the Internet, you need to subscribe to an online service. America Online, CompuServe, and Prodigy are the best known, but there are dozens of national and local Internet service providers (ISPs) you can join for a monthly fee. To connect your computer to their service, you need a modem and a telephone line that plugs into your computer.

Once connected, you can then access the World Wide Web. The Internet is much like a phone system for your computer screen—you type in a Web site address (URL) and your Internet service provider connects you to that Web site. Once there, the site has a home page that tells you what to do and how to view information files available for you at that site.

To journey into the world of the Internet and become involved in remote accessing of information from your home computer is an exciting experience of discovery. A few genealogy Web sites have become established as the best ones at which to begin a genealogy search. They have menus of the best Web sites to be consulted and group these by category and/or location, such as adoption records, county records, vital records, Jewish records, libraries, surname files, census indexes, etc.

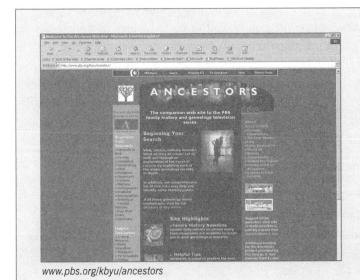

www.pbs.org/kbyu/ancestors

Practice with PBS

One genealogy site was developed to work with a PBS 10-part genealogy how-to-do-it series called *Ancestors*. You can access this Web site at:

www.pbs.org/kbyu/ancestors

Each site on the World Wide Web will offer you connections to a dozen other sites that contain information. You can go to site after site, and no two sites will suggest the same list of next sites for you to check. Experiment with going to one site, learn from it, and then go to another one it recommends—and then do the same thing again from that next site. Your browser has a wonderful "back" command which lets you instantly go back to the previous file, and back to the one before that if you want, so that you can go backward through the same Web connections you came forward on.

Many Internet sites have a FAQ—Frequently Asked Questions—file that provides valuable help to "newbies" on that site. Also, the Internet will let you "chat" with others who have similar interests or are doing the same surname searches as you are. You can visit with others on any number of "message boards" and in "chat rooms."

Records Available on a Computer

Thousands of valuable records, or databases, are computerized and available on palm-sized CD-ROM disks. Personal computers can have drives that let you look at 3.5" disks, perhaps the old 5¼" floppy disks, and CD-ROMs—like the music CDs you buy in a record store. With a CD-ROM drive in the computer, you can look at incredibly huge collections of records valuable to family history research. We are just at the beginning stage of this information revolution. Month by month the amount of files available for research mushrooms.

Ancestry, a leading genealogy firm, has a slogan that it produces three new genealogy databases for computer users every business day. Examples of the types of records being indexed and then published on CD-ROMs and the Internet are these recent databases from Ancestry:

Early Quaker Records of Virginia
Massachusetts Town Vital Records
Boston Births, Baptisms, Marriages, and Deaths, 1630–1699
Boston Births from 1700–1800
Virginia 1790 Census

E-Mail: A Research Basic

Electronic mail, or e-mail, is a wildly popular service on the Internet and the major online services. So popular, in fact, that some people have turned away from all other forms of communication, such as regular mail—disdainfully called snail mail due to its pace of delivery—or even the telephone. It's easy, fast (usually, though sometimes messages are delayed just like snail mail), requires no paper, postage, or pen, and can be done at any hour. Your e-mail address is the name you have chosen or have been assigned by your ISP or online service.

In genealogy research, e-mail can't completely replace the old-fashioned art of letter writing, but it's certainly a dynamic tool that you'll use all the time. There is a danger, however, in totally trusting information you obtain via the Internet or even from CD-ROMs. Misinformation gets posted just as easily as the facts do. Errors, once placed on the Internet and copied, can spread quickly. What is circulated in written form seems to carry the ring of authority. But, like people who spray graffiti on buildings or the computer villains who take delight in creating viruses to cause computer users great aggravation, a few in genealogy circles maliciously post false genealogy information on the Internet to harm genealogists.

Remember, if you bookmark a Web site, you never need to type its long, complex address again. You can find it in one click. No spaces are used between parts of an e-mail address, and every letter, number, or punctuation mark must be typed exactly to reach the person. Generally, e-mail addresses are lowercase—MarySmith is the same as marysmith—but sometimes addresses at companies or organizations are case-sensitive, meaning a capital letter really counts.

If you are corresponding with someone within the same online service, you can leave out the domain name. This means that America Online members can delete the "@aol.com" among themselves, and CompuServe members can delete "@compuserve.com," or "@cs.com" but the ending must be included if they are sending mail outside their online service. Otherwise, the mail will not arrive.

What's a Uniform Resource Locator (URL)?

The long addresses for Web sites follow a format: for example, *"http://www.xyz.com"* is the Internet address, or URL (uniform resource locator).

You must type the URL EXACTLY the way it appears—no matter how weird it looks—including every bit of punctuation, the whole string of letters, or sometimes numbers and capital letters in the middle. Most URLs are entirely lowercase, but if one includes capitals, it means the host computer is case-sensitive. This is probably the single main reason for people throwing up their hands in despair and complaining they can't find anything on the Internet.

E-Mail Programs

If you have a browser, you may have a built-in e-mail program. If not, or if you prefer a different e-mail program, you can download one free from the Internet or buy one. If Internet Explorer is your browser, Outlook Express is your e-mail program. If you have Netscape Communicator, Netscape Messenger is the name of its e-mail component.

You can send e-mail to groups or individuals. You can also keep track of people's e-mail addresses in an address book, so you don't have to keep looking them up on scraps of paper or on business cards. You can save messages you have received or sent, print out e-mail on paper, include part of an e-mail message in your own message, and, of course, discard e-mail.

There are many things you can do to organize your e-mail, which is very important when you're doing online research. It can be stored in different named folders (by subject, sender, or date), filtered by priority (high priority, automatic deletion, etc.), and displayed grouped into threads (messages on the same subject). You can also encrypt your messages for privacy reasons if you wish. You can ask your program to check for new mail at regular intervals.

Messages can be sent in plain text or in HTML (great for sending Web pages), and you can change the look of your mail from drab to creative—boldface or underline it, pick a different or bigger printing font, use color, or include art—with the popular browsers. Most e-mail programs show URLs named in a message as hyperlinks, so you can instantly get to that site, which is very handy. For instance, someone can send you the URL for a site on your surname; you simply click on the link and you're there.

Other Mailers

Eudora, named after the writer Eudora Welty, and Pegasus are the names of some popular stand-alone e-mail programs. Some people prefer to use these even though an e-mail program is included with their browser. Both can be downloaded from the Internet (Eudora from *www.eudora.com*, Pegasus from *www.download.com*), obtained from your ISP, or purchased. The

Watch Your Netiquette

Once you get up to speed in your online genealogy research, you're going to be sending and receiving a lot of e-mail—and probably doing a lot of posting to message boards, chat rooms, and mailing lists. When you do, there are a couple of basic rules of Internet etiquette to keep in mind:

1. Always fill in the subject line of your e-mail message. The new correspondent will not know who you are and is likely—especially in this time of virus alerts—to dump your message in the trash bin without reading it. Another reason to add a subject line is to help your recipient, who is doubtless doing genealogy research as well, to file your message in the proper folder.

2. Don't type in ALL CAPS. It reads as if you're SHOUTING!

3. And an important security note: Never give your residence address to anyone you've just "met." Communicate strictly via your e-mail address until you are confident the other person is legit.

free version of Eudora, Eudora Light—which can be downloaded—has fewer features than Eudora Pro, its for-sale version. Popular features of Eudora Pro include its compatibility with many different mail programs and its ability to let you pick up or send mail from several different e-mail accounts, each for a different function, without restarting the program, which Eudora quaintly calls "multiple personalities." Other handy features are its ability to sort messages into folders by subject or sender automatically, as soon as they arrive, and understand "nicknames," which you can type instead of the recipient's e-mail address (or addresses for a group of recipients). Users who send and receive a lot of mail like such efficient mail management features.

Eudora can only be used with an ISP account, not with commercial online services, such as America Online or CompuServe, which have their own private mail systems.

Different e-mail programs announce that you have mail in different ways. You may hear a cheery computer voice say, "You've got mail!" You may hear a song announcing a mail delivery. You may hear a horn blow and a picture of a mailman with a letter (if you have Eudora on a Macintosh). You may see a red light and hear just a ping sound (if you have WebTV).

Mail sometimes gets returned with a message that says "undeliverable." This is due either to a wrong e-mail address (just like the real post office) or because the person's mailbox is full. Check the address carefully and try again.

The higher the number of the version, the more recent a browser is and the more features it has. For example, 5.0 is more advanced than 4.0; 4.5 surpasses 4.0. You don't have to have the absolute latest version of a browser, but you will be able to do more with it. Many Web pages note they can be seen best with a certain browser or version: "Netscape and Internet Explorer 3.0 or better."

How to Attach Files

In genealogy research, you'll often want to send something along with your e-mail message. This can be an article, photo, or GEDCOM file (a special genealogy file of your family tree) as long as it is in the form of a computer file. Of course, the recipient's computer has to have the proper software to read and play the file, if not, it will appear as a large unreadable file of gobbledygook.

To send a file attachment, you generally create the e-mail message first, then give a command noting a file will be attached, choose the file name, then send both. For example, in Netscape Communicator, after writing your message—maybe something like "Article on 1890 census attached" or "The enclosed photo may be of interest"—click "Attach," click "File" (your other choices are to send a Web page or your address book card), click the name of the file, then click "Open." End by clicking "Send."

How to Open an Attached File

Click the e-mail message that has a file you want to open (it should have a subject like "article attached" so you know to look for an attachment, unless you are expecting it), then click the file name, which appears below the sender's message. Click "Open it," then "OK" in the box warning you of possible security hazards, and the attached file appears. If you clicked "Save it to disk" instead, click "Save" and note the location where the file will be stored for future retrieval.

The warning appears, by the way, because some unkind people sometimes send a file attachment with a virus that can mess up your computer. Thus, you should only open attached files from people you know, and when you've protected your computer with anti-virus software. Norton (*www.norton.com*) and McAfee (*www.mcafee.com*) are popular choices.

The Browser: Your Essential Tool

Browsers are software programs that scan the Internet to locate Web pages and show them on your screen. They also respond to commands to perform many other tasks. The most popular browsers, Netscape and Internet Explorer, are workaholics: they handle e-mail, read newsgroups, create Web pages, find people and businesses, connect you to search engines, send customized news and information, and let users work together easily by sharing documents.

Scroll on Down

When you want to see more of a Web page than what is shown on your screen—some are quite long—press your scroll down key (or scroll up to reread what you've already seen). If you want to move more slowly, click the down arrow on the bottom right of your screen to read more (or click the up arrow to reread). To scroll faster with your mouse, click the vertical box above the down arrow for more, or click the vertical box below the up arrow to reread. Many Web pages also have links called "next" or "continued," or arrows, which you can click to take you to the next page.

Point and Click: Links

When all is said and done, all the thousands of words written about how to get around on the Internet—all the technicalities and high-sounding gobbledygook—can be boiled down to three little words: point and click.

This means that when you see something that looks interesting—words, a picture or a button—move your mouse so its cursor rests on it, then click. If the interesting word or picture is a link, you'll suddenly be transported to another place, either on the same Web site or a different site. You're here, next thing you're there.

You know it's a link because if it's a word or phrase, it's underlined. Links are generally blue, in contrast to the generally black text (if the colors are different, it's still fairly easy to tell the link apart from the rest). Your cursor will suddenly change to a pointing hand, and the Internet address of the new location will appear at the very bottom of your screen. Buttons that say "e-mail us," "next," "search," or "register here" are generally links. Pictures that are links have borders; often, they tell you to "click to see a larger image," "click on the map to locate a county," or something similar.

Before you know it, you're navigating the interface—computer talk for moving around and interacting with the screen you're viewing. Some interfaces are easier to travel than others, depending on how well they were designed.

What the Big Online Services Offer

The online giants—America Online, CompuServe, Microsoft Network, and Prodigy—provide access to the Internet and content to subscribers only. For the genealogy forums of those private domains, this is fast changing. For example, you must belong to AOL to visit with the 140 hosts in the six Genealogy Forum chat rooms, but most of the articles and newsletters provided by the staff are available on the Web at: *www.genealogyforum.com*.

Here are how the other services match up:

- *CompuServe*—There is a genealogy department on CompuServe, with private message boards, but you must subscribe to the service to participate.

- *Microsoft Network*—Same things. There is a genealogy department on MSN with private message boards, but you must subscribe to the service to participate.

- *Prodigy*—There is a genealogy forum on Prodigy, however, all the links take you out to the well-known site Genealogy.com. Just shorten the trip and bookmark *www.genealogy.com*, where your postings will reach a wider audience.

CHAPTER TWO

Gonna Find Her . . . Searching

How Genealogists Use Search Engines

The problem with regular search engines is that as a family historian, you'll get too many hits and they won't be genealogy specific.

For genealogists, a search works better if you go to the top five or six genealogy sites, and look for info on an ancestor by name or locality. Several are free, and some require membership fees. The granddaddy of them all is located at *www.familysearch.org*. Once you get there, click the "Search" tab, and enter the name of your ancestor in the screen provided. The FamilySearch search engine will look through its extensive files and provide hits from:

- Ancestral File
- IGI International
- Genealogical Index
- Pedigree Resource File

The Mechanics

A search engine is a software program that searches for topics, words, or phrases on the Web or in newsgroups and displays them as links for you, usually with descriptions.

To start the engine, click your browser icon to launch your browser and type the Internet address of the search engine you want, or pick one from the dropdown list of the "search" icon on your browser.

Type words or phrases that describe what you're looking for in the search box, then click Search (or hit the Enter key). A page will soon appear that lists links to the pages that match your words or phrases and short descriptions. If a list of subject areas appears, click on whichever subject seems appropriate and pages that list subcategory areas will appear. Again, click on whichever link seems closest to narrow the search down to what you're looking for. Results the search engine thinks are closest to your request appear first. The results are called "hits."

Pinpointing Your Search

For genealogists, a search like this can work to some degree. But if you want to search the surname Concord, for example, you'll get thousands of hits—for Concord grapes, for towns named Concord, even pages about supersonic transportation to Europe (part of the word is Concord).

How do search engines work? During the off-peak hours, search engines "crawl" the Web, cataloging key words on Web pages. When you happen to specify one of those words in your Search box, the page will show up as a hit. The page you seek could be buried as item 13,867 in a hit list of 100,000 total. To avoid this, you must modify your search words to narrow the hit list.

Here are some tricks to improve your searching. Narrow your search by using terms like "AND," "OR," and "NOT" so you won't be swamped by a huge list of results. Using "AND" means both words should be included in the search. "OR" means either word can be included, so you'll get a bigger list. "NOT" before a word means the next word should be excluded from search results.

For example, if you're looking for Venice, California, type in "Venice AND California," which means both words are required to appear in the search results. If it's Venice, Italy, you want, type "Venice AND Italy." Use "OR"—"Venice OR California"—only if you want a massive list of all the Web pages that include either city plus the state of California. If you want the city in Italy as well as the California beach town, just type "Venice."

Putting phrases—words that must go together in order—in quotes also works. For example, "streets in Venice" should turn up only pages listing this phrase; the phrase without quotes will turn up many more pages with the words streets and Venice. Plus and minus signs before words—no space in between—also work the way "AND" and "NOT" do in some search engines. For example, "Venice+California" or "Venice–Italy" will both turn up the California town.

Type your words or phrases in lowercase, unless they are proper names starting with capital letters. A search for Rock Hudson should serve up vitals on the actor; lowercase, it will turn up hits on the Hudson River, rock music, and rock climbing.

Using a wildcard—placing an asterisk or another symbol after a word—means you welcome results with different word endings. Typing "gold+" means golden, goldfinger, and goldfinch are all acceptable. You'll get everything from James Bond movies, birds,

Let the Search Engines Do the Searching

Here are the online addresses for the best of the Internet search engines:

Google	www.google.com
Northern Light	www.northernlight.com
Yahoo!	www.yahoo.com
AltaVista	www.altavista.com
WebCrawler	www.webcrawler.com
Excite	www.excite.com
Lycos	www.lycos.com
HotBot	www.hotbot.com

the precious metal, and companies and people whose names begin with "gold" or "golden."

Comparing Different Search Engines

The many different search engines—Yahoo!, AltaVista, Web Crawler, Infoseek, Excite, Lycos, Google, HotBot, and Northern Light— all have their fans. Each has its own distinctive features, and some are better for certain searches than others.

There are two main types of search engines. The first, called the index type, scours the Internet for the same words or phrases you're seeking by using an automated computer program, and tends to return an enormous list of matches. The second, the directory type (such as Yahoo!), consists of broad subject areas where employees have organized the contents into smaller categories.

Search engines vary in terms of how they display results, how many pages they cover, how they index, and extra features they offer, such as searching newsgroups as well. Each offers detailed advice on how to best use its specific service—click the "help," "tips," "options," "advanced search," or similarly named button near the search box.

That's the most important tip on getting good results from search engines: read the search engine's own help and tips sections for clear advice on how it works. Because search engines are owned by different companies, they don't work exactly the same way.

Genealogy Web sites have their own internal search functions, so you can easily look through the databases on their sites. Often, their rules and tips are posted as well. You'll doubtless prefer to use them— there's no chance they'll confuse the surname Concord with the airplane!

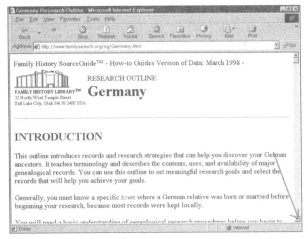

www.familysearch.org/sg/Germany.html

Edit > Find in Top Window > *Jewish*

The Fabulous "Find" Option

So you've clicked on a link that takes you to a large, complicated Web document, and you can't seem to find the reference to your ancestor? What do you do now?

If you already know about this indispensable computer feature, then skip to the next section. But if you'd like to make your computer search every word on a Web page and find the word or words you specify, keep reading.

Let's say you've located the SourceGuide's Germany Research Outline located at *www.familysearch.org/sg/Germany.html*. (Actually, I recommend printing out these guides, as you'll more than likely use the information to plan research strategies; even in this high-tech society, I think there is a place for the printed page.) But since this particular research outline comes to some 78 pages, maybe for the moment you'd like to "browse" through this document to decide if it's worth it to print it out.

You could elect to use the scroll bar on the right side of your Web browser. But you'd still have 78 pages to scroll through. Much easier is to let your computer do the walking by using the find option. Here's how you do it in AOL 5.0:

AOL's "Find in Top Window"

1. Bring up the Web page you want to work through. (In this case the Germany Research outline)
2. Click "Edit" on the AOL menu bar.
3. Select "Find in Top Window."
4. Type in the word you wish to search for. In this case I've typed in the word *Jewish*. (Although a better search word would be "Jew" as it would find Jew, jew, jewish, and Jewish.) Notice that I am not recommending the "Match Case" option, which would specify a search for upper or lower case letters. If someone had made a typo on the page and inadvertently spelled my search word with lowercase letters, the find option wouldn't find it.

5. Click the Find button, and AOL's browser looks for the first occurrence of the word *Jewish* in the document. After several brief references to Jewish records, I find a major section titled "Jewish Records." I discover that there are over two-thousand microfilms of German Jewish vital records of birth, marriages, and deaths at the Family History Library in Salt Lake City, Utah.

6. Each time you click the Find button, you'll be taken to the next occurrence of your search word in the document you've called up.

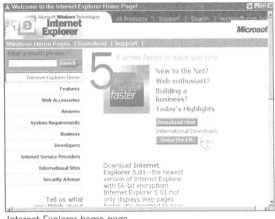

Internet Explorer home page

FIND menu prompt

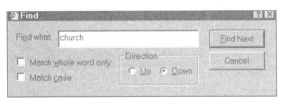

FIND > *church*

Internet Explorer's Find Option

I often sign on to the Internet with AOL, then minimize it, and use Microsoft's Internet Explorer (IE) to go on the Web. Why? IE just looks at Web pages a little better than AOL, specifically when it comes to recently changed Web pages. AOL looks at "cached"—or previous visit versions of pages—and it sometimes takes 20 minutes before the page actually brings up the new data. Basically, I use AOL as the access number, and IE to look at Web pages.

There are also a few more search capabilities in IE. As in AOL, in IE you type in the word you are looking for, and have the option to "Match Case." But in IE, you can reverse the search direction by choosing "Up" or "Down" before clicking the "Find Next" button. Say you've already browsed through half of a lengthy document (page) and you want to change your search word. You can backtrack by choosing "Up." The Find option will then ask whether you wish to search the rest of the document. Click again to get to the next occurrence of the specified word until eventually you are at the end of the Web page.

As a matter of course, I use the Find option on every page, even if I feel I've read most of it. I just don't want to miss something important to my family history because I might have scrolled by a paragraph or two too fast.

Before Beginning . . . The Five Steps
Step 1: Write Down What You Already Know

Most people grow up knowing who their parents and grandparents are. (Adoption situations are discussed in chapter 8.) They know relatives who were alive during their lifetimes and with whom they have had some contact. And, usually, they have heard about a few relatives who lived before they were born.

So, start your genealogy adventure by making a chart called a pedigree chart. Start with yourself and write down your own vital information on the first line at the left. Then, write down what vital information you know about your parents. Next, fill in all you can about your grandparents, and then for any direct-line relatives behind them in time.

After you have filled in as many blanks as you can on your chart, see what you can do with a family group chart. List the vital information for an entire family unit—father, mother, and each child in birth order from first to last. So, for your own immediate family, record what you know. If you are married and have children, do a chart listing everybody in your own family unit and their birth, marriage, and death dates and places (including county). Or, if you are single, fill out a family group chart for your parents. On that chart you will be listed as their child, along with any brothers and sisters you have.

You will see gaps in what you have. That's OK. Everybody who starts doing genealogy faces gaps. Those gaps are what you try to fill—they are what drive your searches for information.

Step 2: Draw Information from Records in Your Home

Few of us can recall details of date and place too well. So, you'll need to find some records that contain the information you can't remember or were never told. After you write on the charts what you know, the next thing to do is to rummage through the house for more information. Look through scrapbooks and photo albums,

Caesar's Pedigree

During the time of the Roman Empire, genealogies of pedigrees were common at the courts of the Roman emperors and in the halls of the Roman patricians. There was a tendency to assume identity of blood from identity of name and claim a semidivine descendent. Julius Caesar, for example, was supposed to have descended from the Roman goddess of love, Venus.

closets and drawers, attics and basements, to find any records that contain genealogy information about your immediate family.

Some families record birth, marriage, and death information in the family Bible (although keep in mind those facts may not be accurate!). Often, a family has saved a marriage, birth, or death certificate; a will; or some obituary notice. Scrapbooks can be good sources of vital information, especially birth and wedding announcements, citizenship certificates, and copies of obituaries. Family pictures can be helpful, too. A wedding photograph of the grandparents, for example, might have the wedding date and place written on the back of it.

When you find new information in the records in your home—names, dates, and places—add it to your charts. Your goal is to find out full names and dates.

Step 3: Ask Relatives

After you have recorded what you know and scoured the records in your home for information, it is time to look outside your house—but not beyond your own family. The next step is to contact relatives and ask them for genealogy details you need. In many families there is one person who seems to be the family historian, the one who everyone believes has the most information about the family's genealogy and records. If your family has such a knowledgeable person, contact him or her and get the facts!

Contact others, too—parents, brothers and sisters, uncles and aunts, grandparents, and other relatives—and ask them for details needed to fill in the blanks. This can be done by visiting them in their homes, talking to them on the telephone, or writing/e-mailing them.

Sometimes a genealogy interview in their home works well. If you have a relative who knows a lot of the family's genealogy facts, visit and record what he or she remembers. Take a tape recorder with you; record the oral genealogy information on tape. (Don't videotape—at least during your first visit—videotaping can be intimidating.) Ask specific questions. If your relative can't be precise about dates, you can help him or her approximate the time setting

A Guide to Abbreviations

Genealogy charts sometimes include abbreviations beside certain lines to be filled in. These abbreviations' meanings are:

b. = birth
m. = marriage
d. = death

Some charts also add these abbreviations:
bp. = birthplace
mp. = marriage place
dp. = death place

When writing the day, month, and year on charts, place the known month between the date and year. In the U.S. 3/10/1943 would be March 10, 1943, but in Europe it would be 3 October 1943.

4 Apr 1943   31 Dec 1887   20 June 1911

Use the full names of cities, towns, counties, states, and foreign countries.

by asking questions like, "Was that before or after Frank went into the army?" or "Did they marry before her mother died?" or "Do you remember who else was at their wedding?" Answers can help you narrow down the needed date, to help you when you search government marriage records. Also ask them who else they think you should contact about genealogy details.

For best results when contacting any relatives, ask for specific details: "Aunt Rosa, I need to find out when and where your dad's parents died." "Grandpa, do you know the full names of your grandparents?" "John, do you remember in what town Mom and Dad were married?"

Likewise, when writing to a relative, be specific. Tell them what information you need. To make it easy, send them a pedigree chart filled in with what you already know but with spaces marked with a highlighter where you need information. Be sure to include a self-addressed, stamped envelope with extra postage. You need to make it as easy as possible for them to mail it back to you. It is typically useful to follow up your mailing with a phone call to be sure they received your letter and to encourage them to respond.

What kinds of records should you ask about? Find out if they have any genealogy lists, a family Bible with genealogy items recorded in it, certificates, scrapbooks, clippings, photographs, diaries, letters, and written biographical sketches about family members.

Ask them to send you copies of what you need. If you must borrow these items, be sure you give the relatives a list of what they are loaning you, and you keep a copy of the list, too. (Then, be sure to return everything as soon as possible.)

When tracking down details about people in your grandparents' generation or before them, you need to find relatives who descend from those same people—distant cousins you do not yet know. Your older relatives usually can identify a person or two in these distant families whom you can contact.

Ask relatives if they know where family members in previous generations are buried. Then, try to visit the cemeteries and record information from the family headstones or from the sexton's record books.

Step 4: Create a Note-Taking and File System

No file system is easier than using manila folders. When you find more information about various relatives, create a folder for your mother's side of the family and another one for your father's side. In time you will have a file folder for each family unit or married couple on your family tree. (If a man was married three times, you might have three folders for him, and the same for a woman who married more than once.) Into the folders place such items as your family group chart; notes you copy from family records; notes you write down from telephone inquiries; photocopies of obituaries, certificates, letters, and family info from the family Bible; and photographs.

You may not want to make separate computer folders to complement each paper folder. However, you're always going to have paper records, so paper folders are still necessary. Give computer and paper folders the same name to avoid confusion.

Genealogy Software

Eventually, you'll want to buy a genealogy software program and use it for storing the genealogy information you find. Genealogy software has incredibly useful systems for entering and charting genealogy information. Close to forty computer genealogy programs are on the market now. Family Tree-Maker has been the most popular one recently. Among others widely used are Personal Ancestral File, Ancestral Quest, Family Origins, Brother's Keeper for Windows, The Master Genealogist for DOS and Windows, and Generations. New ones continually come on the market.

These systems basically let you do two types of operations: data entry, or entering your genealogy information, and printing out your information. For example, Personal Ancestral File (PAF) is software produced by the Church of Jesus Christ of Latter-day Saints (LDS). It lets you input vital information by names that are linked by family relationship. With names so linked in the database, you can print out pedigrees or family group sheets whenever you want. On the downside, PAF printouts of charts are not too attractive, while Ancestral Quest lets you produce handsome charts.

Documentation Lists

It is vital that you keep a list of documents you've collected concerning each ancestor. Indicate author, title, publishing date, page number, book call number or microfilm number, and name of library or archive where you found the information. List interviews as "Personal recollections of . . ." with details of the date, time and place of meeting, and the health and age of the person you interviewed.

By computerizing your genealogy information, you eliminate the hard work of hand-printing or typing onto blank charts. With the correct software, you can input, store, retrieve, and study information quickly and without searching through boxes and drawers of genealogy charts and file materials. And, you can make your computer quickly create charts tailored to include whatever information you want shown.

Documenting Your Sources of Information

It is vital that you keep a research log. This is a listing of whom you contact, where you look for information, and what you find from each source. Include in it addresses and phone numbers. Also include full names of books or published items from which you take notes, and list where you found those items. This research log helps you find those items or people again, and if you forget what you've examined already, you can check your list to be sure you didn't already look at that source.

"Trust me" genealogy data is not good enough. You need to know where you found your information. Others need to know where it came from, too. Genealogists document their sources right on the pedigree or family group chart. Computer genealogy programs provide places for you to list notes and documentation for any information you enter into your genealogy database.

Step 5: Decide What Gaps You Need to Fill

After doing what you can on your pedigree and family group charts, you'll spot the gaps in your information. You might be missing the day and month of someone's birth, a grandfather's middle name, or the date and place of your great-grandmother's death.

Pick out one or more of these missing facts, and then try to find them. Let these gaps guide your searching online.

Preserving Old Family Records

Collections of family materials deserve to be housed responsibly. You will need some drawers, a file cabinet, shelves, or cupboard space suitable for these items. Your storage place should be safe for records, ideally with the following conditions:

1. Medium temperature between 40 and 68 degrees.
2. No major swings in temperature, such as can happen in garages and unfinished attics.
3. Medium humidity–not too dry, not too humid. Keep records away from steam coming from bathrooms and kitchens, and from humidity produced by air conditioners and washers and dryers.
4. No direct sunlight or fluorescent lights. Light does more damage than either water or fire. Ultraviolet rays from the sun and fluorescent lights cause photographs to fade and paper to yellow and become brittle.
5. Away from water pipes that might leak.
6. Out of contact with floors that could be flooded if water pipes break, a roof leaks, or a sewer line backs up.
7. Not touching basement cement floors from which they will draw moisture.
8. Dirt-free and relatively free of dust.
9. In an area where the air is not stagnant (so that mold doesn't grow).
10. Away from car exhaust, which mixes with humidity to create sulfuric acid.
11. Safe from mice and other rodents, worms, and insects. Books contain the cellulose of paper, as well as proteins or carbohydrates in the form of gelatin sizing, glue, paste, leather, and other organic substances that are attractive to insects and rodents.
12. Safe from children.
13. Safe from spilled drinks or food.
14. For audio tapes, away from magnetic fields caused by magnets, motors, light switches, and TVs.
15. Where they can be rescued relatively easily in case of fire or other natural disaster.
16. In a safety deposit box or fireproof vault if containing extremely valuable items.

Citing Your Sources

In all types of research, it is crucial that you acknowledge where you obtained your information. Here are some valuable reference guides specifically geared at genealogical research.

- *Evidence!: Citation & Analysis for the Family Historian* by Elizabeth Shown Mills. Available at *www.genealogical.com*

- *Family History Documentation Guidelines* by the Silicon Valley PAF Users Group. Available at *www.supafug.org*

- Research Guidelines for the NGS. Available in Appendix A of this book.

Consider Your Source

After scouring your mind, your home, and your living relatives for genealogy information, you're ready to start checking records. It is at this point that you change roles from collector to online researcher of archival and community record databases.

Genealogists search in censuses; birth, marriage, and death records; newspaper obituaries; military records; immigrant records; county tax ledgers; church and cemetery records; wills; and property deeds. In other words, researchers study a huge array of records. It sounds overwhelming, but it's not. There is a logical way in which to narrow your search online. The next chapters will show you where to look and how to do this.

No matter where you look for genealogy details, genealogy research always focuses on location. Where your ancestors once lived is the taking off point for your research. It helps to think about records in terms of their closeness to the person. So, you look close at hand at your own family records, and then you look for local records where the person lived, then state records, and finally federal records. The closer to the person being researched, the better the records.

Genealogists before you have paved the information superhighway for you. Because of the skyrocketing interest in genealogy and family history research, many sites go the extra mile to be helpful, particularly to new researchers. Some Web sites even offer introductory genealogy classes (see chapter 18).

With all this information available, a family historian must develop a discerning mind and continually hone his or her research skills to uncover the facts in the ancestral quest. The National Genealogical Society (NGS) has developed guidelines to facilitate an understanding of how to evaluate the reliability of the source documents and compiled genealogies. The full text of the guidelines are reprinted in appendix A of this book, but right now I'd like to take three essential points from the NGS set of standards and apply them to the context of online research.

The Crucial Original

1. *Seek original records, or reproduced images of them when there is reasonable assurance they have not been altered, as the basis for research conclusions.* Unless a Web site has actual scanned images of original documents you are at least two steps removed from the original. To get closer to the original, you will have to search out original church, court, land, and military records, or view them on microfilm at various libraries and archives.

2. *Use compilations, communications, and published works, whether paper or electronic, primarily for their value as guides to locating the original records.* At this point, most genealogy Web sites and mail lists help you by linking you with other individuals searching the same names and localities, or by providing indexes of census and other source documents. Yes, your communications with other researchers are going to lead you to original records. They may even send you copies of original documents they collected in their research. As far as the online indexes go, don't stop just because you've found a link that lists the wedding date and the names of your great-grandparents. You've got to get a copy of the original record. This not only satisfies your curiosity, but might provide additional information to help you in your ancestral quest. An example is discovering the names of witnesses—relatives or friends whose descendants might be able to tell you more.

3. *State something as a fact only when it is supported by convincing evidence, and identify the evidence when communicating the fact to others.* If you grandmother always told you her father was part Cherokee, don't claim Native American ancestry until you have a document to prove it.

True Identities—Not Forced Lineages

We're in the ancestor hunt to discover our true heritage, not to make a connection to a famous historical figure. Forcing the issue by jumping to unfounded conclusions cannot be in our game plan. As genealogists, we are in the business of locating original documents—which may prove or disprove traditional family stories. Where we are unsure of our findings, we must state so in our notes in our genealogy programs.

To aid in your evaluation of evidence, here's a sample worksheet that lists documents you're likely to find in your ancestral quest. The three columns, reading left to right, indicate the level of reliability for various types of documents.

LEAST RELIABLE	POSSIBLY RELIABLE	VERY RELIABLE
Newspaper birth announcement	Church/baptismal record	Original birth certificate
Old family story	Military pension record	Military service record
Newspaper obituary	Death record (for birth date, birth place)	Death record (for death date, death place)
Marriage record (for birth info)	Marriage record (for parents' info)	Marriage record (date and place)
Family bible (with neat handwriting in single hand)	Family bible entry	Family bible (with different handwriting, ink for each entry)
Church burial record (for death info)		
12-page typed index of "Smiths Who Own Property in Ohio 1850–1869"	Index of grantees/grantors	Bureau of Land Management land records
30-page typed index of tombstone inscriptions written by one local individual	Genealogy society's cemetery indexing project—five teams of two workers	Original sextant's records for local cemetery

Each document you encounter needs to be evaluated in this way. For each document, consider:

- Is it firsthand information? (more reliable) or is it second-hand information (less reliable)?
- How reliable is the witness? A doctor signing a birth certificate is generally considered very reliable. A parish priest who has known the family for generations and makes entries in the parish register may also be considered a reliable source. By contrast, a grieving widow reporting the birthdate of her spouse to the priest might be confused. Under obvious stress, she might also make a mistake when reporting the names of her husband's parents.
- Is there supporting evidence? By gathering every possible document on an ancestor, we may see a trend that leads us to believe something is true. For example, here is a fictitious scenario involving tracking down a birth date:

    Family tradition tells you that a few months after great-great-grandfather Matthew Smith went to fight for the State of Pennsylvania in the "War of the Rebellion," his wife Mary gave birth to your great-grandfather John.

These are the documents you find:

1. A letter between sisters Alice and Maggie, dated May 1861, which states "Cousin Mary had her baby two weeks ago. All are well. We haven't heard a word from Matthew yet and worry for his safety in this terrible war."
2. The 1870 U.S. federal census record on microfilm for the household of Matthew Smith lists Mary as the wife and a son John, age 10 years.
3. The Civil War Pension file of Matthew Smith lists Mary as his wife, and, among his seven children, you find Matthew lists John's birth as April 27, 1861.

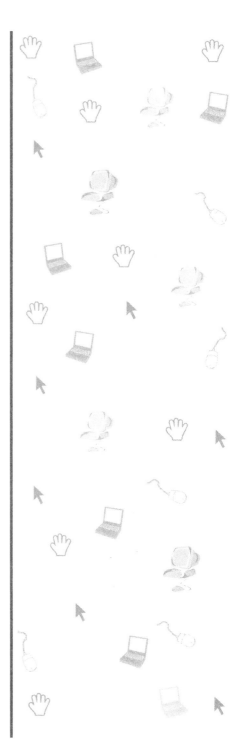

A Quick Analysis

The letter doesn't specify that John was the child, or that "Cousin Mary" is truly Mary, wife of Matthew Smith. In the 19th century United States, "cousin" was a loosely applied term of endearment, not necessarily reflecting a true bloodline cousin connection. At first blush, the birth is thought to have taken place in May 1861, but actually could have occurred two weeks earlier in April, since we have only "May 1861" as the date of the letter.

If I were doing this research, I would not enter the data from the letter into my computer genealogy program. I'd file the copy of the letter in a manila folder under "Matthew Smith Family— Unproved." Eventually all items in an "unproved" file will be proved or disproved as relating to the family.

The second document, the 1870 U.S. federal census, lists a likely Smith household, indicating John's age and relationship to the head of household. But the age of 10 for John seems to be off a year. Was the information perhaps given by a neighbor who may have said, "the boy is about ten"? We may never know.

At this point in my research, I would enter the data into my genealogy program. I'd list John's birth date as "about May 1861" referencing the letter in my possession as the source, noting the conflict in the age of "10 years" between the letter and the census. I'd also list his parents and siblings, referencing the federal census record by date, city, county, state, microfilm number, and census page number. I'd file a photocopy of the census record with the family group sheet for Matthew and Mary Smith. The cousin's letter, which now looks more promising, would be moved to the same place, with a cover sheet detailing my future goals to identify the "cousins" who wrote and received the letter.

By continuing our research, we find, on the microfilm, in the handwriting of Matthew Smith, his official Civil War pension application and a listing of each of his children, their birth dates, and the name and birth date of his wife, Jane.

From this, I would now correct the data in my computer genealogy program by changing John's birth date to April 27, 1861, referencing his father Matthew Smith's official pension application as the source. I'd file the photocopies from the pension file with the Matthew Smith family group sheet for future reference. It will now be easy to photocopy or scan all documents and the family group sheet should a new researcher request source documentation.

Some Errors Are Unavoidable

Sometimes, despite our best efforts at evaluating the reliability of source documents, we'll still fall prey to outright false information, often unknowingly. For instance, my grandmother's birth date was purposefully misstated on her funeral card. When she married the second time, she was a few years older than her spouse—a fact she never divulged. She made my mother promise that she'd never tell, so the birth date on my grandmother's death certificate, funeral card, and obituary is off by several years. (Since my step-grandfather has long since passed away, I guess it doesn't hurt to tell this family secret now.)

If there is a documented fact that would prove harmful to living family members, I believe it's better to omit the info rather than change it to fit the circumstances.

We need to do our best to responsibly report all source documentation, transcribing as accurately as possible. By providing citations of author, title, microfilm, etc., we leave a big trail for future researchers. They may unearth additional documents that will support or refute the lineage assumptions we've made.

It's all just part of the challenge of research, so let's get started!

CHAPTER THREE

Home-Base
Databases

According to Webster, a database is a "large collection of data organized for rapid search and retrieval, as by a computer." The word in fact was coined specifically for the computer, way back in 1962—we're talking huge mainframe computers, predating the invention of the semiconductor, that filled entire rooms!—but its meaning hasn't changed today, even when applied to a desktop.

It is the accessibility of the database, *right there on your desktop,* that has so radically transformed the way we do genealogy. Where once you had to write letters or appear in person at a town's public library or hall of records to do research, or travel—to other states, or to other countries—to visit a cemetery, search out a birth certificate, or other information you needed for your family tree, now much of that research can be done sitting in your pajamas at a keyboard.

In this section, we'll cover databases you can use as a starting point for your ancestor hunt—a home base of sorts. These big-guy mega-sites offer everything, from soup to nuts, but the nice part is that everything is organized into accessible directories. Major subject headings, such as Libraries, Obituaries, Italy, Iceland, etc., are followed by lists of subtopics that link to genealogical sites.

A mega-site is a good place to get acquainted with what's online, plus it can save you a *lot* of time!

The Mega-Sites
Cyndi's List

www.cyndislist.com

Unquestionably, one of the most popular—and thought by many to be the best—genealogy Web sites is Cyndi's List. Founded by Cyndi Howells, an energetic homemaker and mother of a young son in Puyallup, Washington, this site is clearly a labor of love. It is impeccably organized and it never stops growing. Cyndi has collected an amazing number of links to genealogical Web sites, which she has categorized and cross-referenced under 120 subject headings. In June 2000 she had 12,100 links in the works, and probably a lot more subjects to go with them.

Cyndi also lists libraries with genealogy collections, both domestic and from around the world. These are listed in A-Z format. At this point Cyndi still hasn't found one for "Z."—but if you know of one and tell her, she'll be sure to add it.

The 120 subjects in Cyndi's directory range from Acadian, Cajun & Creole to Family Bibles to Ships & Passengers to Wills & Probate to . . . well, you get the idea.

Under the subject Belgium, for example, the following categories are offered, each of which offer multiple links to related Belgian genealogical Web sites:

- General Resource Sites
- History & Culture
- Libraries, Archives & Museums
- Mailing Lists, Newsgroups & Chat Rooms
- Maps, Gazetteers & Geographical Information
- People & Families
- Professional Researchers, Volunteers & Other Research Services
- Publications, Software & Supplies
- Queries, Message Boards & Surname Lists
- Records: Census, Cemeteries, Land, Obituaries, Personal, Taxes and Vital
- Societies & Groups

www.cyndislist.com

RootsWeb

www.rootsweb.com

RootsWeb is about the busiest genealogy site out there. And it was one of the first. In the "About Us" section of the site, Brian Leverich recounts how he and his wife, Karen Isaacson, began this project of "networking" the Internet genealogical community in 1986—before there ever was a World Wide Web.

www.rootsweb.com

The couple's original goal was to gather all the information that appeared on USENET newsgroups, message boards, and mailing lists concerning genealogy and put it in one place. At the time they were both working at the Rand Corporation and were able to use the Rand servers. When the database made the transition to the Web, the new site grew and grew. Today they have their own servers and, in the spirit of the original advertising-free Internet, depend on voluntary contributions to maintain the site.

The RootsWeb site is clearly and concisely laid out on the first two screens, with 14 major headings, which are further broken down into subheads. See the sidebar to get an idea of the kind of databases you can access right off the bat.

There are many other tools and resources on this site. The RootsWeb Surname List (RSL), discussed later in this section, is one of them. This resource lists the results of cross-referencing and categorizing over six-thousand Internet mailing lists dealing with genealogy. (We'll discuss mailing lists later in the book, see chapter 14).

RootsWeb Database Sampler

Major Search Engines

GenSeeker (Web Sites)
Global Surname Search (Message Boards)
Meta Search (Multiple Databases
   and Files)
RootsWeb Surname List/RSL (Surname
   Listings)
Social Security Death Index (Deaths)
Surname Helper (Message Boards,
   Web Sites)
U.S. Town/County Database (Locations)
WorldConnect Project (Family Trees)
USGenWeb Archives Search
Other Search Engines
Mailing Lists

Web Sites—Genealogy Only

Genealogy Sites on Freepages
Genealogical and Historical Societies
International
Miscellaneous
Surnames
U.S. Genealogical & Historical Resources
Requests for Web Space

Hosted Volunteer Genealogy Projects

Cyndi's List
FreeBMD (England and Wales)
Genealogy.org
Immigrant Ships Transcribers Guild
Obituary Daily Times
USGenWeb Project
Census Project
Lineage Project
USGenWeb Archives
Census Project
Map Project
Obituary Project
Pension Project
Tombstone Project
Special Collections Project
WorldGenWeb Project
WorldGenWeb Archives

Helm's Genealogy Tool Box

www.genealogytoolbox.com

Matt and April Helm started this Web site in 1995, and with 70,000 links to genealogical resources they even top Cyndi. You'll need to look at each of the categorized topics so you won't miss anything. Broad categories covered include Adoption, Microfilm, and National Archives.

What the Toolbox has that Cyndi doesn't have is the Genealogy SiteFinder. With this, you can search genealogy sites as you would with a regular search engine, but here the search is genealogy-driven. The hit lists will have full descriptions as well. As icing on the cake, there's a link to GenealogyPortal.com, which features eight more search engines!

The site also offers links to genealogy news stories on the Web, the monthly Journal of Online Genealogy, a bookstore, software reviews, and an easy-to-use place to register your own genealogy Web site and add it to the list.

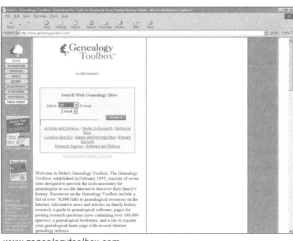

www.genealogytoolbox.com

The Genealogy Home Page

www.genhomepage.com

This is another grand directory of Web sites, with 15 major categories, including Maps, Geography, Deeds, and Photography—all in one category—and Libraries and Genealogy Societies, which are then broken down on the home page into subtopics. The category of "North American Genealogy Resources," for example, offers three screens of links to genealogy-related information pertaining to Canada and the U.S. The servers for these sites, in the words of the may Genealogy Home Page creators, may be "official government services, genealogy society efforts, or maintained by interested individuals."

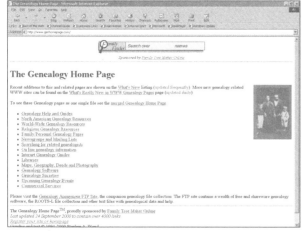

www.genhomepage.com

Mega—With a Price Tag
ANCESTRY

www.ancestry.com

www.ancestry.com

The prominent genealogy firm Ancestry boasts that it adds three new genealogy databases every business day. And guess what—they do. In June of 2000, there were 2,000 databases, holding a total of 500 million records to access. Topping that, Ancestry adds several old maps every week. The site also offers beginners' classes in genealogy, shopping—for various genealogists' supplies and software—and a library of articles and columns on genealogy. So much is happening on Ancestry.com that you might want to subscribe to The Ancestry Daily News to keep up. Although a lot of Ancestry is fee-based, some new databases are available free for the first 10 days after a they have been released. See the sidebar on pages **44** and **45** for a brief sampling of the 2,000 databases you can link to from Ancestry.

Ancestry.com's Data Bonanza

The following represents a random selection of databases available on the huge Ancestry site. This list is simply meant to give you an idea of the range of the 2,000+ databases available.

Abstract of Graves of Revolutionary Patriots
Accomack County, Virginia Births, 1853–1865
Accomack County, Virginia Births, 1866–1873
Adelaide, Ontario Census, 1901
Alabama Land Records
Alexandre Dumas' Trip to California
America's Successful Men
American Biographical Library
American Civil War Research Database Battle
  Summaries
American Civil War Research Database, Officers
American Civil War Research Database,
  Regiments
American Civil War Research Database, Soldiers
American Genealogical-Biographical Index (AGBI)
Anchorage Daily News (Alaska), Obituaries,
  1998–1999
Anderson County, Kansas Marriages, 1857–1894
Baltimore, Maryland Tax Records Index,
  1798–1808
Bangladesh Country Study
Baton Rouge Advocate (Louisiana), Obituaries,
  1990–1999
  Beaver County, Utah Census, 1900
    Beaverhead County, Montana Census, 1910

Belarus Country Study
Belgium Telephone & Address Listings
Belize Country Study
Benjamin D. Wilson's Report on CA Indians,
  1852
Benjamin F. Taylor's Trip to San Francisco, 1870s
Bennington, Vermont Cemetery Inscriptions
Berks County, PA Birth Records, 1876–1906
Berks County, PA Death Rec., 1852–1855 &
  1894–1906
Berks County, PA Estate Records, 1752–1914
Berks County, PA Marriage Records, 1885–1929
Berks County, Pennsylvania Delayed Birth
  Records
Berrien County, Michigan Directory, 1892
Biddulph, Ontario Census, 1901
Biographical Cyclopedia of U.S. Women
Biographical Dict. of Canadian Jewry,
  1897–1909
Biographical Dict. of Canadian Jewry,
  1910–1914
Biographical Directory of the American Congress
Biographies of Notable Americans, 1904
Biography & Genealogy Master Index (BGMI)
Blenheim, Kent County, Ontario Census, 1901

Bolivia Country Study

Boone County, Missouri Obituaries, 1871–1891

Boone County, Missouri Obituaries, 1892–1901

Boone County, Missouri Obituaries, 1902–1913

Boston Births, 1700–1800

Boston Port Arrivals & Imm., 1715–1716,
    1762–1769

California Cemetery Inscription Sources

California Pioneers, 1542–1848

Cambodia Country Study

Cambridge University Alumni, 1261–1900

Caroline Churchill's Travel Letters, 1870–1873

Caroline Churchill's Travel Letters, 1874–1880

Cayuga County, New York Directory, 1867–1868

Chicago Daily Herald, Obituaries, 1998–1999

Chicago Irish Families, 1875–1925

Clarke County, Virginia Births, 1878–1896

Colonial Families in the U.S.

Colonial Families, Southern States

Connecticut Soldiers, Fr. & Indian War,
    1755–1757

Cornell & Princeton University Directories, 1922

Correspondence to the New York Tribune, 1849

Daughters of Utah Pioneers Obituary Scrapbook

David Phillips' Life in California, 1876

Denmark Telephone & Address Listings

Early American Immigrations

Early Germans of New Jersey

Early Quaker Records of Virginia

Early San Francisco Chinese Exclusion List

Early Town Records of the Town of Providence

Encyclopedia of American Quaker Genealogy,
    Vols. 1–6

Essex County, Massachusetts, Probate Records

Faribault, Minnesota Census, 1920

Finding Your German Ancestors

French's Gazetteer of New York

Fresno Bee (California), Obituaries, 1996–1999

Genealogical Dictionary of Maine & New
    Hampshire

Genealogical Dictionary of New England Settlers

Genealogical Library Master Catalog

Georgia Tax Index, 1789–1799

Germany Telephone & Address Listings

Ghana Country Study

Guardian (London, England), Obituaries,
    1992–1999

Guide to Genealogical Research in the National
    Archives

Everton

www.everton.com

Everton, a leading genealogy publisher, offers free on its site a group of databases: surname search, a Vietnam War casualty database, CD-ROM catalog database, Social Security Death Index, and

more. Everton also publishes the subscription-only Genealogy Helper online, which is highly rated by genealogists. The Roots Cellar—where you can list an ancestor you're researching free and a vital record such as a wedding or birth date and see if anyone else has listed the same name—is so popular that the LDS Church has microfiche versions of it in all of their U.S. and Canadian Family History Centers. Of course, the online version is amended more often with the latest additions. It's free for the first three listings, then a fee kicks in. Like Ancestry, the majority of the databases on Everton's site require a membership fee to view them.

www.everton.com

Family Tree Maker and the Genealogy Library

www.familytreemaker.com;
www.genealogylibrary.com

If you enter a name in the search box at the top of the Family Tree Maker home page, you can search 470 million names for links to one of your ancestors—or see what's there about yourself, for that matter. Another free resource is a collection of how-to articles on genealogy. Unfortunately, to access the databases at this site requires ownership of the very excellent Family Tree Maker genealogy management software (discussed in chapter 15).

www.familytreemaker.com; www.genealogylibrary.com

From the Family Tree Maker home page you can click on its Genealogy Library, or you can go there directly at the above

URL. There you can search 2,535 databases of published genealogies and other resources. Many of these are scanned images of the original document; for instance, the 1850 U.S. census and the Dawes Final Rolls (for those researching Cherokees). Three new records are added every business day, they claim—but this precious trove comes at a price, you must subscribe for $79.99 a year.

Without subscribing, a record "lookup" can cost anywhere from $11 up. Genealogy Library explains it this way: "Remember that you are not just paying for a copy of the record, but for the professional researcher's time and skills." They go on to say that if a record cannot be located because it doesn't exist—for instance, the census taker in 1910 seems to have skipped your great-great-uncle Beauregard's house in Macon, Georgia—they won't provide a refund but "will recommend other records as substitutes, if they exist, and other possible avenues of research."

The Genealogy Library also has a Virtual Cemetery, where you can add photos of gravestones or search gravestone archives.

Other Great Jumping-off Points
Genealogy Resources on the Internet

www.rootsweb.com/~jfuller/internet.html

This site is known for its directory of mailing lists (and is covered more thoroughly in the chapter on mailing lists), but it also offers a spectacular directory of genealogy sites. The work of Chris Gaunt and John Fuller, there are currently about 150 subject categories from which to choose, from Archaeology to Yukon Territory sites.

Paying for Ancestors

For those genealogists with the cash to spend and limited time to spend online or offline hunting down records, the opportunity to pay someone to do it for you might well be worth it. A lot of genealogists view this as "cheating," but it's not—you're still doing the research and building your family tree with it.

CHAPTER FOUR

The Vital Vitals

Genealogists collect vital records of birth, marriage, and death from family, government sources (local, state and federal census, military, tax lists), church (christening, marriage, and burial), tombstones, court house (probate, wills, land), newspapers, obituaries, city directories and the like. Any document has the possibility of including other family names and relationships, hopefully leading back to the previous generation. For instance, a christening record lists the parents of the child; marriage records sometimes list parents of the bride and groom. Great on and offline references include:

- Ancestry's Red Book—*www.ancestry.com*
- Everton's HandyBook for Genealogists—*www.everton.com*
- USGenWeb—*www.usgenweb.org*
- Vital Records State Index—*vitalrec.com/index.html*

State Records

Because your goal is to find vital information about a relative, the starting point for your research is with the official vital records—the birth, marriage, and death information recorded in the locality where your relative lived, or where you think he or she lived.

Each state maintains the equivalent of a bureau of vital records. Sometimes it's called "Bureau of Vital Statistics," "Division of Records and Statistics," "Division of Public Health," "Vital Records Division," or something similar. No matter, the state agency has the birth, marriage, and death certificates.

Birth records are confidential in most states, and actual copies are available only to the person whose certificate it is and to that person's descendants. Birth records typically contain the person's name, the date and place of birth of the individual, his or her parents' names (and sometimes their ages, residences, places of birth, and occupations), and the name of the person who delivered the baby.

Death records contain information similar to that found on birth certificates, as well as the residence of the deceased person, cause of death, information about the undertaker, and the doctor's signature. A married woman's death record usually is filed under her married name, not her maiden name.

BUREAU OF VITAL STATISTICS

Amarillo — 1503 Fillmore

CHARLES WALTON SMITH JR

male — yes — May 12 1910

Charles Walton Smith — Wilma Elizabeth Hopkins
Amarillo Texas — Amarillo Texas
white — 24 — white — 23
Iowa — Iowa
Building Contractor — Housewife
Building Contractor — Own home
four — three

STATE OF TEXAS
COUNTY OF BAKER
I HEREBY CERTIFY
CERTIFICATE OF BIRTH of CHARLES WALTON SMITH JR.
8
WITH MY HAND AND SEAL 14 of April , 1949

Until the mid-1800s, divorces were granted by courts and through specific acts of state legislatures. In 1866, the federal government declared that a legislative divorce was illegal. Since then, and in many states well before then, divorce has been a civil action determined in local courts. Divorce records, therefore, are found in court volumes containing normal court cases, in separate records designated just for divorce cases, or in specialized records. Court dockets list the plaintiff and defendant and the date the divorce case started. Divorce records contain the court's judgment. Files in the divorce case include vital facts about the parties to the divorce and about their children. Marriage data is also included. Rights to privacy cause divorce records to be closed for a period of years, so they can be accessed only with the permission of the divorced party. The rules vary from state to state.

Soundex Made Easy

Soundex is a way of indexing the federal census based on the way a name sounds rather than the way it is spelled. Knowing a surname's Soundex code is the essential first step in research.

Sound complicated? Have no fear of Soundex—there are handy sites where you can just pop the surname into the search box and the Soundex code will be generated for you.

- Surname to Soundex Code: *http://resources.rootsweb.com/ cgi-bin/soundexconverter* (or access it from the RootsWeb home page)
- National Archives Soundex Machine: *www.nara.gov/genealogy/ soundex/soundex.html*
- YASC, or Yet Another Soundex Converter: *www.bradandkathy.com/ genealogy/yasc.html*

Most states did not assume legal responsibility for vital records until the turn of the last century. The first to start keeping vital records was Massachusetts in 1841, and the last was New Mexico in 1920. So vital records at the state level exist for people who were born, married, or died during the 20th century, and in a few states for earlier years.

Local Records

Your online search for birth, marriage, and death data before 1900 will take you beyond official state records and into other kinds of records—at the local level. In terms of marriages, local civil governments have been in charge of recording marriage information in marriage registers since the beginnings of the county or town. You can find marriage records from the early 1600s in New England towns, and from the early 1700s in counties in the South.

Prior to the states taking legal responsibility for vital records, a small proportion of the nation's counties and towns registered the local vital information. New England states have more complete vital records from before 1900 because—well, they were there early on. Nearly two-thirds of Massachusetts towns, for example, have published their early vital records. Rhode Island has published vital records annually since 1847.

The Census

Starting in 1790 and every 10 years thereafter, federal government census takers have gone through cities, towns, and countrysides counting and listing residents. These census records now are on microfilm, and most have name indexes. (The 1890 census is an exception: A fire destroyed these records.)

Even though the census officially is a federal government record, it really is a local record that identifies the populace house by house. Many states have name indexes to the federal censuses of their state. A 72-year privacy restriction on access to censuses

This list shows when the states began keeping vital records:

STATE	DEATH	BIRTH	STATE	DEATH	BIRTH
Alabama	1908	1908	Montana	1907	1907
Alaska	1913	1913	Nebraska	1905	1905
Arizona	1909	1909	Nevada	1911	1911
Arkansas	1914	1914	New Hampshire	1905	1905
California	1905	1905	New Jersey	1848	1848
Colorado	1907	1907	New Mexico	1919	1919
Connecticut	1897	1897	New York	1880	1880
Delaware	1881	1881	North Carolina	1913	1913
D.C.	1855	1871	North Dakota	1908	1908
Florida	1899	1899	Ohio	1909	1909
Georgia	1919	1919	Oklahoma	1908	1908
Hawaii	1896	1896	Oregon	1903	1903
Idaho	1911	1911	Pennsylvania	1906	1906
Illinois	1916	1916	Puerto Rico	1931	1931
Indiana	1900	1907	Rhode Island	1852	1852
Iowa	1880	1880	South Carolina	1915	1915
Kansas	1911	1911	South Dakota	1905	1905
Kentucky	1911	1911	Tennessee	1914	1914
Louisiana	1914	1914	Texas	1903	1903
Maine	1892	1892	Utah	1905	1905
Maryland	1898	1898	Vermont	1857	1857
Massachusetts	1841	1841	Virginia	1912	1912
Michigan	1867	1867	Washington	1907	1907
Minnesota	1900	1900	West Virginia	1917	1917
Mississippi	1912	1912	Wisconsin	1907	1907
Missouri	1910	1910	Wyoming	1909	1909

means that the 1920 census is the latest one you can consult. The 1930 census will be open to research in the year 2002.

Copies of the federal censuses are widely available offline, and have finally began to appear online. National Archives branches have microfilm or CD-ROM copies, as do major universities. State historical societies and archives have at least that particular state's complete censuses.

When you come upon your ancestor in a census, you'll uncover a lot of other valuable information, too. You'll find your ancestor's exact address. You'll find how many others were living in the household, and, starting with the 1850 census, the names of those in the household—before that, only heads of household were listed by name. By tracing your relative through several censuses, you'll find out where he or she may have moved to, the occupants of each successive household, and their places of birth. However, census information is only as good as the person who gave the census taker the information, and sometimes guesses or even false information was provided. You may have read reports of disgruntled citizens objecting to some of the questions asked in Census 2000. And, census takers miss people, and so do not count or list everybody.

You need to look for an index to the censuses before you go to the census pages themselves whenever possible. Few of the censuses are well indexed. The indexes are available in books, microfilm, microfiche, or CD-ROM format. You can even find some county indexes to federal censuses, prepared by local genealogists or librarians.

Indexers of the 1880, 1900, 1910, and 1920 censuses used a "Soundex" system, which is a phonetic index. That is, it indexes together those names that sound the same or similar rather than in alphabetical order. Thus, Smith, Smythe, and Schmidt are listed together. Published state indexes show you how to code the consonants in the last names you are looking up, but it's easier to do it on the Web ahead of time. The Soundex code will help you find the microfilm index that contains those names.

That index in turn shows you what microfilm reel of the federal census to view. **Caution:** The 1880 Soundex includes only families with children ages 10 and under.

Federal 10 year censuses are not the only censuses taken in this country. There have been special federal censuses, including the 1840 List of Pensioners, which lists pensioners of the Revolutionary War or other military service, and the 1890 List of Union Veterans, including their widows. American colonies took censuses. U.S. territories seeking statehood administered censuses. Cities and states have conducted their own censuses. Among special state censuses are those conducted prior to 1925 in Illinois, Iowa, Kansas, Massachusetts, Minnesota, Mississippi, New Jersey, New York, and Wisconsin. State censuses can be found by looking in library catalogs under the name of the state and then under the "census records" listings.

When you find a relative in a census, take notes, but also make a photocopy from the microfilm. Be sure you list on the photocopy the name of the census, the location, the microfilm number, and the census book and page number.

Check the Church

Over the centuries, Americans, with their diverse religious backgrounds, have belonged to hundreds of different churches, synagogues, and religious organizations. Religious bodies keep records of their members, of ordinances, and special ceremonies, including baptisms, weddings, and funerals. More often than not, religious records are the only source you'll find for marriage information in early American communities.

Little of this information is computerized, but it's worth doing a search for the church or synagogue to see if it has a Web site. If they do, it's still unlikely they'll have scanned their records and created a database—but you may be able to e-mail and ask for information.

Census Confidential

- Since a congressional mandate in 1790, U.S. censuses have polled different kinds of information.
- Between 1790 and 1850, the 10-year censuses obtained the name of the head of the household and listed others in the household only according to sex and age categories.
- In 1850, the census began to list the names, ages, occupations, and birthplaces of each person and his or her relationship to the head of the household.
- The 1880 census was the first to list the state or country of birth of each person's parents.
- The 1910 census was the first to give the month and year of birth. It also includes each person's age, the number of years the person had been married, his or her immigration year, and citizenship status.

Tombstone Crawling

Cemetery records include tombstones, sextons' lists of burials, and plot ownership and maintenance information. Cemeteries have been created by towns, cities, churches, and even by families on their own farm properties.

Tombstones are excellent sources for birth and death dates, and in some cases for information about military service. The epitaph of your ancestor's tombstone could also offer an insight into the person: Uncle Charlie must have either been a big W.C. Fields fan or pretty wacky himself to have chosen "I'd Rather Be in Philadelphia" for his tombstone. And Aunt Ethel probably loved animals a lot, since she chose St. Francis of Assisi to watch over her.

Although most cemetery records won't be found online, in thousands of counties across the country local volunteers have located public and private cemeteries and hand-copied headstone inscription information, which has then been transcribed and put online.

The awesome USGenWeb Tombstone Project is the place on the Web to post transcriptions from such volunteer projects. Your society can donate its work and post it at *www.rootsweb.com/~cemetery/* or *www.usgenweb.org*, since most genealogy researchers recognize USGenWeb and RootsWeb as top sites to visit. Both sites are fully searchable.

Another place to look for cemetery records is the Virtual Cemetery Project at *www.genealogylibrary.com*, which has a collection of tombstone photos and a fully searchable archive of transcriptions culled from members of the Genealogy.com community. The search is free, and if you become a member, you can add your tombstone photographs to this collection.

If you can't find a cemetery record here, individual cemeteries may have their own Web sites, which you can then e-mail for information about obtaining records. For instance, the huge Roman Catholic Calvary Cemetery in the borough of Queens, New York, where many Irish- and Italian-Americans of the late 19th and 20th centuries are buried, has a site with information on how the cemetery is organized and how to get records, which are not computerized. However, a number of genealogists with ancestors buried there have archived tombstone information on their family Web sites and

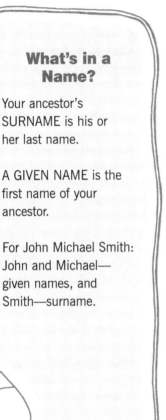

What's in a Name?

Your ancestor's SURNAME is his or her last name.

A GIVEN NAME is the first name of your ancestor.

For John Michael Smith: John and Michael—given names, and Smith—surname.

Census Abbreviations

The following are some of the abbreviations used in census records.
For a more complete list, you may want to check out
http://members.aol.com/FamilyTwig/Abbrev2.htm.

A	Aunt	Gcl	Grandchild
Ad	Adopted	Gf	Grandfather
Ad.Cl	Adopted Child	Gm	Grandmother
Ap	Apprentice	Go	Governess
Asst	Assistant	H.Maid	Housemaid
B	Boy	M	Mother
Bl	Brother-in-Law	Nu	Nurse
Bu	Butler	Ph	Physician
C	Cousin	Prv	Prisoner
Cap	Captain	S	Son
Cha	Chamber Maid	Sa	Sailor
Cl	Child	Se	Servant
D	Daughter	Si	Sister
Dl	Daughter-in-Law	Ten	Tenant
F	Father	U	Uncle
Fa.W	Farm Worker	W	Wife
Fl	Father-in-Law	Wa	Warden

linked them to a "Calvary Cemetery" search. Who knows, you might find a Healy Family Page with your own great-great uncle John—the one who was never heard from again when he left Lahinch in 1908—listed. (R.I.P.!)

Court: Last Resort?

Court records can provide you with birth, marriage, and death details; immigration and citizenship information; names of others in the family; dates and places of residency; and career and religion details. Probate records, dealing with wills and estates and inheritances, contain valuable genealogical information. Citizenship records, too, can tell you a lot about an immigrant ancestor.

America's judicial system includes state courts that handle civil and criminal matters relating to state laws, and federal courts that deal with matters of federal law. Courts have existed to deal with particular areas and jurisdictions, such as county, circuit, district, superior, and supreme courts; and with specific legal matters, such as orphans courts, probate courts, and common pleas courts.

Court records are probably the hardest records to access. They are neither indexed well nor filed together in one book let alone an online database. Court records are in sequential record books related to how the case progressed—from scheduling in docket books, to actual court minutes, to judgments rendered, to case files containing documents relating to the finished case. They contain legal terminology sometimes hard to understand. And, while federal court records before 1950 usually can be located in a National Archives branch, many state and local court records have not been collected into the state archive but remain in the courthouse, where you have to go to research them. Despite their complexities, though, court records are sources to consider, if you've tried everything else.

More Legal: Probate Records and Wills

Probably less than 25 percent of Americans draw up wills, which are legal documents specifying how the person wants his or her estate—belongings and assets—bequeathed to relatives and

Archives for Major U.S. Religious Denominations

Some religious groups have centralized their old records. Archives to check out are listed below. Find more information on contacting them through Web search engines.

Adventists, Washington, D.C.

American Baptists, Rochester, NY

Southern Baptists, Nashville, TN

Brethren in Christ Church, Grantham, PA

Church of Christ, Scientist, Boston, MA

Church of Jesus Christ of Latter-day Saints (Mormons), Salt Lake City, UT

Churches of Christ, Memphis, TN

Congregational, Boston, MA

Disciples of Christ, Nashville, TN

Greek Orthodox, New York, NY

Jewish, Cincinnati, OH; Waltham, MA

Evangelical Lutherans, Chicago, IL

Missouri Synod Lutherans, St. Louis, MO

United Methodists, Madison, NJ

Pentecostal, Tulsa, OK

Presbyterians, Philadelphia, PA; Montreat, NC

Episcopalian, Check local parishes

Reformed Church, New Brunswick, NJ

Roman Catholic, Notre Dame University, South Bend, IN; Catholic University, Washington, D.C.

Quakers (Society of Friends), Swarthmore, PA for Hicksite records; Haverford, PA for Orthodox records

United Church of Christ, Boston, MA; Lancaster, PA

Unitarian and Universalist, Harvard Divinity School, Cambridge, MA

others. When a person who has left a will dies, a probate court carries out the will's instructions. The judge makes the final decision regarding how the estate is to be distributed, taking into account the validity of the will and the legal demands of creditors.

For those ancestors whose estates went through probate, you can find court records of those proceedings. These probate records (alternatively called a probate packet, case file, estate file, or probate estate papers) may contain a copy of the will, the individual's death date, the names and relationships of family members and their current residences, and an inventory of the deceased's property and its value. Records can identify adoption and guardianship details, too.

In many U.S. states, county courthouse records prior to 1900 are found on microfilm through *www.FamilySearch.org*, and viewable at local Family History Centers. The old probate books are loosely indexed in the first 26 pages (one page for each letter of the alphabet). Since there usually aren't many surnames beginning with the letter "Q" or "V" look for spillovers from other index pages.

Be sure to look for probate records in each locality where the person owned property. For example, if James Butler owned land on both side of the Kentucky/Tennessee border when he died, two counties, each in a different state, might have probate files on him.

When records aren't on microfilm, contact the courthouse of record. Find addresses and listings of time periods where records have survived by consulting Ancestry's Red Book at *www.ancestry.com*, Everton's HandyBook at *www.everton.com*, and USGenWeb at *www.usgenweb.org*.

Newspapers: A Goldmine Offline

For many decades, local newspapers have published obituaries and lists of births. Many have published announcements of engagements, weddings, and divorces. If you know the approximate date and place of an event, newspaper notices are a great place to search.

Libraries contain guides, organized by location, to newspapers in the various states. They list what newspapers were published during which period of time, and indicate where surviving copies of those newspapers can be seen. Many states have microfilm collections of their communities' newspapers, and you can see these microfilms at

the state's historical society or in your own library through inter-library loan.

Some researchers obtain information by putting an ad or article in a newspaper in the place where their family had ties, asking for information or for the names of people to contact about the family.

Obituaries

Newspaper obituaries were commonplace during the 20th century, less so in the late 19th century, and rare before that. When you know the death date, or approximate death date, for one of your ancestors, and know where he or she lived at the time, check a local newspaper for an obituary. Obituaries, while not always accurate, sometimes provide the date and place of birth of the deceased, the parents' names, and the names of siblings and other kin and where the deceased lived. Descendants of these relatives (hence your distant cousins) sometimes can be tracked down and asked for information relating to that common ancestor.

The obituaries you'll find online at newspaper sites aren't archived too far back in time—usually they're about as old as the Web site. A better place to look for older records are county Web pages, which are discussed in the next chapter.

A useful Web site is Obituary Daily Times, found at *www.rootsweb.com/~obituary/*

City Directories

Annual city and county directories, which contain alphabetical lists of names and addresses of residents, have been published since the early days of our republic. These are not like telephone books!

City directories provide a wealth of personal information in lists of city residents (head of household) and their occupations and addresses. One researcher was delighted to find that all her German-American ancestors in the New York City directory of 1885 were listed as "piano makers." Directories also give a summary of the city's situation that year (population, description of the place, main economic factors, thumbnail histories of the community, etc.); lists of businesses, churches, and government agencies; advertisements for local businesses; and sometimes maps.

The Domesday Book

When the Normans conquered England in 1066 they set about to compile a land register as a basis of regular taxation. The information was finally put together and published in what was called the Domesday Book of 1086. Copies of the Domesday Book of 1086 can be found in most research libraries. Unfortunately the next edition of the Domesday Book was not published until 1146, however records of taxation or litigation can be helpful in tracing your family's genealogy in Great Britain.

City directories are found in libraries by looking under the city name and under "directories" or "gazetteers." In situations where the cities and towns are tiny, the directories are county directories, with listings for each town and for rural residents, but without street addresses.

For a particular town's directory, contact the local municipal archives, public library, or state historical society. Better yet, major public and university libraries have a massive microfiche collection of city directories dating back from before 1881 called City Directories of the United States. A register accompanies the collection, listing all the cities for which directories are available. The Library of Congress provides the largest collection of city directories.

Immigration and Naturalization

Our immigrant ancestors generated two kinds of records by coming to America: ship arrival passenger lists and naturalization records from seeking citizenship.

Immigration Records

Immigration records for major U.S. ports, Boston, New York, Philadelphia, Baltimore, and New Orleans, have been kept since 1820. Other ports such as Mobile and Galveston began keeping records later in the 1800s. Western ports such as the San Francisco and Seattle ports began keeping records in the last decade of the 1800s.

The immigrations records are microfilmed and available at the National Archives. The information includes: full name of every passenger on ship, including those born or who died on board; age and sex; place of origin and destination.

Ship Passenger Arrival Lists

Between 1820 and 1902, when ships carrying immigrants docked in America their officers were required to turn in passenger lists to U.S. Customs agents. These handwritten lists—usually in beautiful script—in large ledger books contain each immigrant's name, age, sex, occupation, country of origin, and place of intended residence. Often, the amount of money the immigrant was carrying is also listed. Starting in 1883 ships' masters had to turn in a ship manifest of passengers to the U.S. immigration authorities—later the Immigration and Naturalization Service. These lists included the exact birthplace or last residence, marital status, previous U.S. residence, and names of relatives in the home country and the United States for each immigrant.

Immigrants arrived through various ports on the east, west, and south coasts of the United States. Not all passenger lists for all ports have survived, but thousands have. Major port passenger arrival lists have been indexed. New York City was the main arrival port between 1820 and 1920, processing some twenty-four million immigrants. The National Archives has New York passenger arrival lists for the years 1820 to 1957. Passenger arrival lists for Boston cover 1820 to 1943, but for the smaller port of Barnstable, Mass., only 1820–1826 has been indexed. If your ancestor arrived through Barnstable in 1827, you'll have a much harder time tracing the record, if indeed it exists at all.

The National Archives and Records Administration (NARA) Web site (*www.nara.gov/genealogy/immigration*) has indexes to ship passenger lists from the early 1800s through 1959. This is a valuable online resource, as it provides you with a shortcut to finding the microfilm that contains the original ledger entry for your ancestor. You then order the copy of the microfilm—or, if you live close enough to a federal archive or library that has copies of the microfilm (the NARA site tells you where these are), you can go there and make a copy yourself. The LDS Family History Centers also offer this information (see chapter 5).

Naturalization and Citizenship Records

Suppose you can't find your ancestor on ship passenger lists? Then what do you do? You could try to dig up his citizenship record.

Millions of immigrants to the United States filed for or became naturalized citizens. Up until 1952, the immigrant seeking citizenship appeared before a federal or district court judge and declared his

Did They Sail from Hamburg?

Among the main departure ports in Europe for emigrants going to America was Hamburg, Germany. Between 1850 and 1934, Hamburg recorded the names of emigrants leaving from its port. Those departure lists are indexed, and both the lists and indexes can be seen on microfilm in major U.S. libraries.

National Archives Immigration Records

Paper copies of microfilmed immigration records can be ordered by mail using NATF Form 81—you'll need one form for each person or family group that immigrated together.

E-mail your name and mailing address to inquire@nara.gov. Be sure to specify "Form 81" and the number of forms you need. You can also obtain NATF Form 81 by writing to:

National Archives and Records Administration
Attn: NWCTB
700 Pennsylvania Avenue, NW, Washington, DC 20408-0001.

intent to become a citizen. The court required him to file papers of intent, or First Papers. (After 1952, a verbal commitment replaced the filing of intent papers.) The immigrant then had to file Final Papers verifying that he had met the requirements for citizenship. Over the years, requirements for citizenship changed, but basically the person had to prove residency in America for a certain period of time, usually five years, and good moral character. So, the immigrant provided supporting information, such as affidavits and statements by witnesses, which went into his citizenship application file. After 1906, he had to bring to court a certificate of arrival, showing when, where, and how he entered America. He then had to take an oath of allegiance to the United States and sign it. After that, the court issued an order of citizenship and gave the applicant a certificate of his citizenship.

A *naturalization file* contains reliable information about the immigrant's date and place of birth; place of origin; date of arrival in America and sometimes the name of the ship; the Americanization of his name (from an Old Country name to a less foreign-sounding name); and his places of residence in America.

Look for information on whether your ancestor was naturalized, the number of years he lived in the U.S., or his date of naturalization, depending on the census questions asked in the 1900, 1910, or 1920 U.S. Federal Census. When looking for your older ancestor's naturalization records, consider that he could go to any local courthouse before 1906, depending on the dictates of the local government. These were often called Oaths of Allegiance in the colonial time period. Visit State Library Web sites, and the Family History Library Catalog at *www.familysearch.org* for availability of such records.

The Immigration and Naturalization Service in Washington, D.C., has an index and copies of naturalization records for 1906 to 1956. The Service's district offices hold the records for the years after 1956. You can send inquiries to the INS, 425 Eye Street, NW, Washington, D.C. 20536.

Where to View Immigration Records on Microfilm

The following cities have National Archive facilities with genealogical microfilm holdings. Use NARA's online microfilm locator or call before visiting to verify that the facility has the microfilm publications that interest you.

Alaska	Anchorage
California	Laguna Niguel, San Francisco
Colorado	Denver
Georgia	Atlanta
Illinois	Chicago
Massachusetts	Boston, Pittsfield
Missouri	Kansas City
New York	New York City
Pennsylvania	Philadelphia
Texas	Fort Worth
Washington	Seattle

Military Matters

Among the biggest sets of records in the National Archives are those of our country's military units and personnel. America has fought in many wars. Millions of our citizens have served in the armed forces, so chances are good that one or more of your relatives served at some time or another in the military. If they did, there are records.

Families do a pretty good job of passing down the names of relatives who served in the Revolutionary War, the Civil War, or the two World Wars. But even if your family has no tradition of military service, it's still worth checking to see if male ancestors who lived during the war periods did in fact serve. It's possible, too, that an ancestor enlisted in the military during peacetime.

Four kinds of military records contain personal information about the serviceperson.

1. *A service record.* The service record includes a "muster" roll of his or her enlistment; personal details such as physical descriptions, marital status, residence, occupation, and birth information; and the "muster-out" roll and discharge details. For those who served voluntarily during wartime between 1775 and 1903, the federal government created a compiled service record. Also in the service record are miscellaneous records that include payroll information, hospital registers, prison and court martial documents, and promotion facts.

2. *Record of veterans' benefits.* Federal and state governments granted certain veterans pensions or free land as rewards and compensation for their service, or as payments for disabilities caused by war. A veteran's pension file will be found in the National Archives. In the file is his application for a pension and documentation of his disability, if any. Likewise, a veteran's widow's pension file contains useful life and family history details. Indexes to pension records are available for the Revolutionary War, War of 1812, Mexican War, Civil War, Spanish-American War, the Philippines Insurrection, and for various Indian Wars.

Between 1776 and 1855, the federal government awarded bounty lands to those who served. Veterans or their heirs could claim this bounty land by filing an application at a nearby courthouse. Approved applicants received a land warrant, which most veterans either sold or exchanged for money rather than take possession of the land itself. My, how times have changed!

Immigration to Canada

inGeneas—*www.ingeneas.com*.

This good-looking site is a great place for Canada research, though only a small part of it is free: the National Archives of Canada immigration records of 1801–1849, dealing with Great Britain to Canada. For the rest, the inGeneas database contains a variety of immigration records (other than passenger lists) from 1748 to 1906. A shopping cart system is used to pay for each record. The database includes:

- Selected records from the 1901 census of Canada (those which give a year of immigration)
- Various government, estate, immigrant agent, and other emigration/immigration records
- Persons desiring to emigrate to the colonies and requesting government assistance and/or a grant of land
- Settlers' names, including the location of the land they were granted
- Soldiers who had served Britain in British North America and who wished to settle there
- Loyalists coming to Ontario and Quebec from the United States
- Names of sick and dying emigrants admitted to Grosse Isle Hospital
- Names of settlers who swore oaths to the King
- Immigrants who received aid from immigrant societies to proceed inland from Quebec
- Immigrants for whom employment was arranged by the government
- Muster rolls of new settlements
- Census and victualling records for new settlements

What's This Disease?

Having difficulty identifying a disease cited on a death certificate or mentioned in a diary or letter? Names for common and/or fatal diseases often went by another name 75 or more years ago. For example, "Ague" was malarial fever; "Ablepsy" was blindness; and American Plague was yellow fever.

Dan Burrows has helpfully identified a list of maladies, starting with these three, on his Disease Chart at *www.kentuckianagenealogy.org/guide/help/disease.html*.

3. *Draft records.* The government has maintained draft records since 1863 when the government initiated the draft. During World War I, all men eligible for military service had to register for the draft, and those registration cards are available to researchers. The file, called the "World War I Selective Service Draft Registration Cards, 1917–1918," includes cards on about 24 million men. You can see the cards or send an inquiry about a particular serviceman to: Archives Branch, Federal Center, 557 St. Joseph Avenue, East Point, GA 3004.

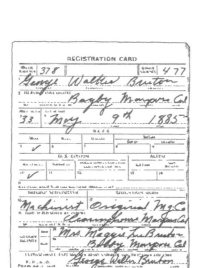
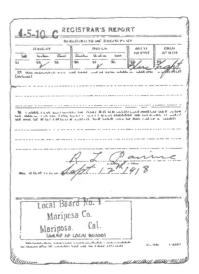

4. *Records of the regular military forces.* The National Archives has 71 reels of microfilm that contain the Registers of Enlistments in the U.S. Army, 1798–1914. These registers contain personal information about each enlistee's birthplace, age, occupation, and physical description.

The National Archives "Select Catalog of Military Service Records" can be seen at *www.nara.gov/genealogy/*. Instructions for ordering records will be found there as well.

The Veterans Administration in Washington, D.C., maintains an index record of all servicemen and women buried in national or federal cemeteries.

CHAPTER FIVE

The Super Indexes: Vitals Online

If you were to pull an 800-page genealogy book off the shelf at the library, where would you turn first? To the index, of course. That is, if there is an index. A lot of old record books are just collections of documents, which you have to thumb through page by page (and bring a lot of Kleenex if you're allergic to mildew or dust!). Yet once again computers have stepped into the breach and eliminated a lot of that heavy lifting and sneezing for you. Every day there are more Web sites devoted to bringing those indexes right to your desktop.

So what's in these indexes? Those vital records of births, deaths, and marriages! We hope. Several indexing databases were discussed in the chapter on vital records. However, when you're dealing with the Web, there's always more to add; there's always overlap; there's always a faster way to do something. Although many of the sites here can be accessed through cross-referencing links on the large database sites such as Cyndi's List, they can also be accessed directly.

FamilySearch

www.familysearch.org

The FamilySearch site is so famous and so dear to the hearts of genealogists that it rightfully claims a spotlight in all that is genealogy online—and offline. FamilySearch is sponsored by the Church of Jesus Christ of Latter-Day Saints, commonly known in genealogy circles as LDS.

For LDS church members, genealogy has enormous religious significance. Identifying ancestors is part of the baptismal process of the church. Any ancestor recorded by a member is baptized by proxy, going back as far in history as one can go and still find records. You don't have to be a member of the church, however, or even know anyone who is, to find an ancestor listed in its database. It is open to everyone. Considering that there are almost 3 billion

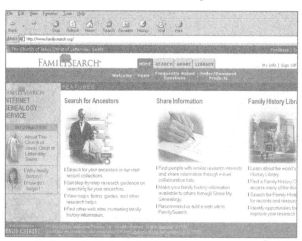

www.familysearch.org

names in it, there's a good chance that someone has included information on a forebear of yours.

The main LDS Family History Library is located in Salt Lake City, Utah, with over 3,500 satellite LDS Family History Centers (FHCs) in North America. Any of these centers can order microfilm from Salt Lake City. The locations of the branches are listed on the site. But the centers aren't open 24-7 like the Web is!

The all-in-one search form in FamilySearch is called "Search for Ancestors," and it searches Ancestral File, International Genealogical Index, Pedigree Resource File, as well as Web sites. Following are descriptions of the indexes:

The International Genealogical Index (IGI)

www.familysearch.org

To use the IGI, click the "search" tab, then enter just a name, and the site will search all available regions, unless you've customized the search for a certain region. You'll then see a list of possible matches. Click on one and the record will come up. The record will show:

- Name of person
- Date of event (birth, christening, or marriage)
- Place of event
- Name of parents or spouse
- Source information (microfilm number for original record or patron entry)

Tips on Using the IGI and Ancestral File

- The Ancestral File is "pedigree based" meaning you may be able to find several additional generations in the database.
- The IGI is "event-based," meaning you'll find no more than two or three people associated with an event:
    Marriage—
    husband and wife
    Christening—
    child, mother, father
- Get to the source by clicking to find "submitter info" whenever possible.
- "Extracted records" are considered more reliable than patron entries, because the work submitted by individual researchers (patrons) is not checked for accuracy.

www.familysearch.org > Ancestor Search

Ancestral File

The Ancestral File could be your true lineage linker, because if you hit gold here, you'll get a printout of your entire family tree! It's unlikely to happen, however—although you might learn something about an ancestor or two. The database is made up of pedigree charts that have been submitted by individuals in GEDCOM form (Genealogical Data Communication). Keep this in mind—you might want to submit your own pedigree chart later on.

To search for your ancestor's name, it's usually best to enter only the first and last name, leaving the parents' and spouse spaces blank. This way you'll get more hits, and you won't lose out on finding something submitted by an unknown distant cousin who knows only your grandfather's name. If your search request were to include his wife, you'd miss the work of that cousin—who perhaps had submitted documentation of seven generations, back to the original immigrant from Poland!

www.ancestry.com

American Genealogical Biographical Index (AGBI)

www.ancestry.com

Noted genealogy author and lecturer George K. Schweitzer recommends the AGBI as a first source for pre-1900 U.S. genealogical research. Up until the Web came along this index was only available in book form at libraries—and not all libraries, at that. It is now online at the Ancestry.com site, in the fee-based data library. If you don't want to pay the Ancestry fee, check your library for a copy of the AGBI.

This gigantic index has vital record entries for individuals going back to the original colonies. It also has Revolutionary War records, pedigree charts, and a 1790 census. In addition to the 13 colonies, it also covers the Midwest.

An unusual feature, and well worth noting, is that the AGBI allows you to search for a woman by her maiden name.

USGenWeb:
Info Highway for Counties and States

www.usgenweb.org

A huge database that has become a Yellow Pages type of reference tool is the USGenWeb project. It is producing a Web page for all of the counties in the United States, state by state. Each of these sites offer a pile of information about each county—lists of other databases; registration spots where you can enter your own research interests and post your particular genealogical questions; lists of holdings in local libraries; addresses and phone numbers for local archives, genealogical societies, and libraries; information on how to find local church, cemetery, court, and land records; and contact persons who are willing to do genealogical research for a fee.

The project's goal, as stated to Web users, is to make genealogy research—arranged by geographical location—available to everyone at no cost.

What you'll find here depends on the experience and creativity of the individual state and county volunteer coordinators. By clicking on "The Project's State Pages" you'll be given the option of a clickable map of the U.S.

I clicked on New York and my computer screen changed to a map of New York State, and the following links:

www.usgenweb.org

- New York State Military Links
    - New York in the Civil War
    - NY Medal of Honor recipients from
        the Civil War
    - World War I Medal of Honor Recipients
- New York Geography
    - County Outline Map of New York
    - Find out in what county a town is located
    - Changed New York Town Names
    - New York State Historical Markers
    - Downward Bound Great Lakes Shipping

- New York GenWeb Project Links
    - New York Family Reunions
    - Cemetery List Project
- New York Research Helps
    - Governors of New York
    - Color Landform Maps of New York
    - Cyndi's NY Genealogy Site
    - Early New York Land Records
    - Gene Stark's Index of Names for All GenWeb Sites
    - Mailing Lists for NY and other NY resources
    - New York Census Lookups
    - New York Genealogical Societies
    - New York Vital Record Information
    - Research Tools—CD Lookups
    - Roots-L New York Resource Page

Obituary Daily Times

www.rootsweb.com
The Obituary Daily Times is a daily index of published obituaries. It is distributed freely, usually once a day by RootsWeb and has approximately fifteen-hundred to two-thousand entries a day. You can search the database anytime with the RootsWeb search engine.

Since I wanted to see what was available for Herkimer County, I clicked on the county in the NY map. I also could have chosen it from a county selection page, which offers information on the date the county was formed, the "parent" county if any, the county seat, and county coordinator. The coordinator for Herkimer County is Martha Magill.

Besides major listings for cemeteries, census, Civil War, and church records, one can also find such county esoterica as profiles of early citizens and family lines, Herkimer County officers of the Eastern Star and the Masons, early 19th-century med school graduate lists, 18th-century land patentees, an 1860s store owner's ledger, profiles of early Russian families, 19th-century lists of schoolchildren, 19th-century recipes and home remedies, a photos section, and other small and medium-sized items contributed by site visitors.

There are over two-hundred items and updates on the Herkimer County site, thanks to an enthusiastic group of typing and HTML-coding volunteers and contributors. If you had family from this area, the old photos, recipes, store ledgers, etc. are the kind of "ephemera" that will add to your family history if you publish it in some form later.

Married in Illinois?

Illinois Statewide Marriage Index 1763–1900
www.sos.state.il.us/depts/archives/marriage.html

Here's a great use of tax dollars—meeting the needs of genealogists by providing access to public vital records!

Beginning in 1985 the Illinois State Genealogical Society worked with the Illinois State Archives to index Illinois marriages prior to 1901. Today more than one million marriages, or two million names, are included in this index. Data entry was done by Archives staff and volunteers working on mainframe terminals at the Illinois State Archives and by volunteers who entered hundreds of thousands of marriages on their home computers.

The sources for this index include original county clerks' marriage records, such as marriage registers and licenses, as well as records from county genealogical societies and private individuals. For each marriage, the index includes the names of the groom and bride, the date of the marriage or issuance of the license, the name of the county in which the marriage was performed, and a citation for the original record.

Social Security Death Index

This database contains vital information for about 50 million deceased persons who had Social Security numbers and whose deaths were reported to the Social Security Administration. Most of the information is from 1962–1988, although some data is from as early as 1937. The file lists the person's name, Social Security number, birth date, state of residence where the Social Security number was issued, month and year of death, and place of residence at the time of death. The index is updated periodically.

Several Web sites offer this database, which was formerly only available on microfiche at LDS Family History Centers. It helps a lot with twentieth century research—how I discovered my maternal grandfather had passed away. He had been estranged from our family for many years.

Other Web sites offering the Social Security Death Index include:

Ancestry.com—*www.ancestry.com*
Everton—*www.everton.com*
RootsWeb—*www.rootsweb.com*
Kindred Konnections—*www.kindredkonnections.com*

www.familysearch.org/sg/SocSec.html

Indexes to the Indexes
GENDEX

www.gendex.com
"Devoted to advancing the progress of family history and genealogy," says the site's creator Gene Stark, and his plain vanilla site, with 12 million names, comes in handy for research on the World Wide Web. It's free, but registering for $10 gets you "hit

credits"—at a rate of 1,000 hit credits per $10 payment. This also gives you access to search filters, letting you do "smarter" searches by having the server show you only the individuals you want to see.

Plug in a surname and GENDEX will present you with a list of sites that contain it. The site has indexed hundreds of databases. The configurable display allows you to modify the default number of individuals you're looking up and number of index tabs displayed in a single screen, thus giving you access to larger amounts data per click.

If you look up the name Flockhart, for example, you'll get 10 entries. I clicked on the most recent, a 1944 Flockhart in California, and was taken to the Barnum family home page and an entry on this ancestor. Connection between Calista Flockhart and P.T. Barnum? Didn't seem like it at first glance!

GENSERV

www.genserv.com

With 20 million entries, almost fifteen-thousand databases, GENSERV is almost double the size of GENDEX. However, here only the first search is free. To get more, you must subscribe, and also submit a GEDCOM file. With a GEDCOM you can get a 2-month free trial membership, or, you subscribe for $12 a year, $6 for seniors. Without doing this, the site is pretty much worthless.

The actor's paradox might apply here: in acting you can't get a job without an agent, but you can't get an agent without a job. In genealogy you can't make a GEDCOM without research, but in this case you can't do free research without a GEDCOM!

Hopscotching the World
World GenWeb

www.worldgenweb.org

Since the Internet is a creation of the U.S., the online genealogy community here had a headstart on everyone else. But the rest of the world is doing its best to catch up, and today foreign genealogy sites multiply on a daily basis.

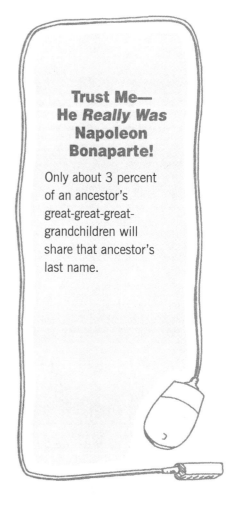

Trust Me— He *Really Was* Napoleon Bonaparte!

Only about 3 percent of an ancestor's great-great-great-grandchildren will share that ancestor's last name.

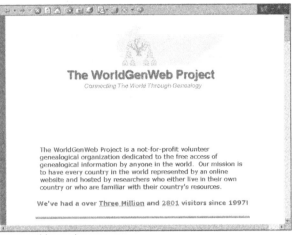

The WorldGenWeb Project

Connecting The World Through Genealogy

The WorldGenWeb Project is a not-for-profit volunteer genealogical organization dedicated to the free access of genealogical information by anyone in the world. Our mission is to have every country in the world represented by an online website and hosted by researchers who either live in their own country or who are familiar with their country's resources.

We've had a over <u>Three Million</u> and <u>2801</u> visitors since 1997!

www.worldgenweb.org

The WorldGenWeb Project is not related to USGenWeb, but it's the international equivalent. You'll probably be surprised by the offerings provided by the country coordinators. In fact, the site is listed as one of Family Tree Magazine's "Top 101 Family History Sites."

WorldGenWeb is divided into 11 world regions. Each region is divided up by countries and each country is divided into individual provinces, states, or counties (terms vary depending on locale) in over 400 Project Web sites. Check the regional home pages to locate the country of your research or you can use the alphabetical index of countries or keyword search.

On May 1, 2000, the WorldGenWeb Advisory Board voted to create a new regional project called the NorthAmericanGenWeb. This project will contain links to USGenWeb, CanadaGenWeb, MexicoGenWeb, and the CentralAmericanGenWeb projects.

British Isles

FreeBMD Project

www.freebmd.rootsweb.com

www.freebmd.rootsweb.com

FreeBMD stands for Free Births, Marriages, and Deaths, and this site provides free access—free, obviously—to the Civil Registration index information for England and Wales. The Civil Registration system for recording births, marriages, and deaths has been in place since 1837 and is one of the most significant single resources for genealogical research in England back to Victorian times.

GENUKI

www.genuki.org.uk

This extensive site covers England, Ireland, Scotland, Wales, the Channel Islands, and the Isle of Man. (GENUKI = GENealogy + U.K. + Ireland) Excellent far-ranging resources include census, cemeteries, church records, military records, and civil registration.

Color in Details:
Abstract versus Transcript

A transcript is a word-for-word version of an original document. An abstract merely lists the high points. However, both can be fraught with errors due to poor handwriting, interpretations of abbreviations, the age of the document, or quality of the microfilm.

In a book or online listing of abstracts of wills you are likely to find: name of deceased, locality, date of will, heirs.

However, a transcript will have details such as:

real property, such as the family homestead;
equipment, such as horses, plows, wagons, buggies;
personal items, such as a watch and chain, furniture, books,
    a linen shirt;
personal comments, such as "my beloved wife"; and/or
unusual notes "my son who went west to Seattle."

Relying on an abstract or index listing for just the name and date of a will is like wearing blinders. You are forced to look in one direction, completely missing the delightful peripheral details. These may lead you to other source documents, such as homestead papers or military service records, thereby giving you a better view of the life and times of your ancestor.

www.genuki.org.uk

The site can be searched by country, and in some cases, by county—probably the best place to look for vital records.

Central and Eastern Europe

FEEFHS—the Federation of East European Family History Societies—may look like the ultimate generic page, but it's home (at *http://feefhs.org*) to over five-hundred-thousand Central and East European surnames, locations, and other unique words in forty-five hundred-plus files. The WebPortal (Web site) index can also refer you to specific FHC microfilm, fiche, or book sources for your surname

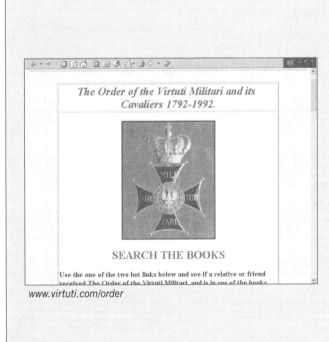

www.virtuti.com/order

A Rare Poland Site

www.virtuti.com/order

The Polish order of the Virtuti Militari was established 200 years ago by King Stanislaw August Poniatowski as the highest military decoration for gallantry the Polish nation bestows. The Virtuti Militari is equivalent to the American Congressional Medal of Honor or the British Victoria Cross.

Prof. Zdzislaw Wesolowski, who created the site, is the former president of the Polish American Congress of Florida. Although this page is advertising the sale of his book, you may search the site for a Polish ancestor's name. If you find him, order a "confirmation" of his military award including a colored photo of it. This is an interesting site, since Polish records seem to be so hard to get.

Digging Up
English Records

In England, parish registers were instituted in 1538 to keep records of baptism, marriage, and burial. Huguenots and Quakers and Jews kept their own records. Information regarding baptism, marriage, and burials of Roman Catholics was kept by the Catholic Record Society.

In 1837 in England and Wales the registration by the government of all births, marriages, and deaths became law. Some records are located online.

- GenWeb Project—*www.rootsweb.com/~engwgw/*

- Guildhall Library Manuscripts Division—*www.ihr.sas.ac.uk/gh/*

- London Metropolitan Archives (formerly known as the Greater London Record Office)—*www.corpoflondon.gov.uk/archives/lma*

- Museum of London—*www.museum-london.org.uk/*

- Public Record Office Home Page (the National Archives)— *www.pro.gov.uk/*

genealogy or location if John Movius, who runs the site, has found them.

Those of us with difficult-to-tackle Eastern European roots are eternally grateful for his efforts. The recently completed Saxony Court Records Project is a master index of 113 Saxony "Amtsgerichts," or provincial courts. Eventually, with the help of volunteer indexers, the name for each court volume will be linked to a page containing all the surnames found in that court volume.

Movius states on the site: "The objective of this indexing is to create new FEEFHS Finding Aids that are based on the surnames contained in each reel of microfilm—a user-friendly way for Saxony record searchers, who—knowing the location of their ancestral home—can then easily find the specific microfilm for the years of court records for that location that contain their surname."

CHAPTER SIX

Name, Please!

Naming Names

Naming patterns vary from country to country and from one time period to the next. In colonial days, most men did not have middle names. As proof, we have two-name patriots like Thomas Jefferson, Patrick Henry, John Hancock, and Paul Revere. By the 1800s it became the custom among some Americans to give their sons and sometimes their daughters the mother's maiden name as a middle name. All the children in one family, in such cases, had the same middle name. From colonial times until the 1800s, it was not uncommon for families to give a son or daughter the same name as a son or daughter who had died.

Two strong currents have influenced American naming trends. One is to name children after famous people. In the early 1800s, for example, many families had sons with first and middle names of such heroes as George Washington, Andrew Jackson, and Francis Marion. In the 20th century, parents have often given their children the first names of stage, radio, movie, and TV stars. A second current is internal to the family—naming the children after a grandparent, uncle, aunt, or other favorite relative.

In biblical times, people had only one name: Adam, Seth, Noah, Abraham, Rebekah, Moses, Isaiah, Daniel, Ruth, Naomi, Amos. Through the medieval period in Europe, people still had but one name. William the Conqueror, when he invaded England from France, had no last name. As evidenced by the title attached to his name, custom grew during the period between 1100 and 1500 to assign a descriptive term to a man. When talking about him, then, or sending someone to see him, people could differentiate him from another man with the same name. "Go see James the smith" or "John the short one" or "Richard living in the oak trees" or "Henry with the beard." In time, such names became James Smith, John Short, Richard Oaks, and Henry Beard.

Enter the Surname

Surnames have definite meanings. Originally they were attached to one of our ancestors to identify him. The identifying word that

European Surnames: Source and Meanings

Name	Origin	Meaning
Aaron	Hebrew	Lofty, exalted one
Barnes	Old English	Owner of barley storehouses
Clinton	Old Norse	Farmstead on a headland
Decker	German	House roofer
Espinosa	Spanish	Thornbush-covered property
Flowers	Old English	Arrow maker
Grant	Old French	Large or great man
Houghton	Old English	Farmstead on a bluff
Irons	English	Strong-willed one
Jesse	English/Hebrew	Wealthy one
Kennedy	Irish, Scottish	Son of the helmeted one
Lang, Lange	Various European	Very large man
Monroe	Scottish	Lives by a red swamp
Noyes	French	Owner of nut trees
Owens	Old Welch	Well-born one
Presley	Old English	Priest's meadow
Quinn	Old Gaelic	Descendant of intelligent man
Ryan	Gaelic	Descendant of the young ruler
Seymour	Old Gaelic	Victorious and famous one
Talbot	Old French	Pillager
Underwood	English	At the foot of the forest
Valenzuela	Spanish	Young, valiant one
Wasserman	German	Water carrier
Xavier	Spanish	Owner of a new house
Yates	English	Home at the town's gates
Zuniga	Spanish	Man who frowned constantly

became the surname referred to either a physical characteristic of the man, his relationship to another person, his employment, where he lived, or some accomplishment for which he was known. The prefix "Mac" means "son of." The addition of "son" to the end of a name means "son of," so Johnson means son of John.

From one generation to the next, the spelling of surnames has varied, particularly during the era of verbal rather than written information. Names were spelled phonetically, according to how someone pronounced them. Thus, Smith was recorded alternatively as Smith, Smyth, Smythe, and Smits, and a name like Pearce was spelled variously as Perce, Peirs, Pierce, Peirce, Peirse, or Pearse.

Names sometimes became transformed merely through pronunciation. Those beginning with a vowel or with h or wh could end up starting with another vowel instead. Aiken could become Eakin. Harbach might change into Arbach. Whitmore could end up as Whetmore or Wetmore.

Very often, immigrants with an old country surname anglicized it after they arrived in America. German names like Braun and Schwartz became translated into English as Brown and Black. The Italian surname Roberto became Roberts.

Scandinavian Patronymics

A Swede named Christian had a son he named Peter. Peter was known as Peter Son-of-Christian, or Peter Christian's Son, or Peter Christianson. When Peter had a son he named Nels, Nels was known as Nels Son-of-Peter, or Nels Peterson. Then, when Nels had a son, he named him Frederick, and Frederick was known as Frederick Son-of-Nels, or Frederick Nelson. For girls the name ended in "dotter" instead of "son," for example, Petersdotter or Nelsdotter.

This practice, whereby the surname of the child is derived from the given name of the father, is called patronymics (patro meaning "father"). Until late in the 19th century, the patronymic custom for naming children prevailed throughout the rural and common classes in Denmark, Norway, and Sweden. In the higher social classes, fixed surnames emerged much earlier.

Weird Spelling and Strange Handwriting

Reading old records is sometimes difficult because of poor spelling, lack of punctuation, words no longer in use, and unusual forms of handwriting.

America lacked a widely available book of words until 1828, when Noah Webster published his first popular dictionary. But it took two generations before standardized spelling became the thing to do. The norm until then was for people, educated or not, to spell phonetically. They might even spell the same word five different ways in the same letter, such as wagon, waggon, wagun, wagin, or waggen. Also, many wrote without using punctuation—at best they would leave a space to indicate a new sentence or what we now call a paragraph.

When trying to read old handwriting in old documents, use a magnifying glass so that you can closely inspect the lines and loops. When a letter in a word is hard to decipher, look for other words in the document containing that same letter. This can help you determine what the letter is. When you find a strange word, pronounce it out loud. That way, if it was spelled phonetically, you can understand what the word is.

One main handwriting problem is the double s. Prior to the 1870s, writers would make the second s normal but the first s to look like a huge, swirling f or p. As with present handwriting, the letters a and u in old handwriting can be hard to differentiate, as well as the letters m, n, or r. The letters o and e are often confused with each other. The old handwritten capital L often resembles our handwritten capital T or S; the capital I resembles a J; and the capital T and F look alike.

The Word Game

The meanings of words change over time. Some words used in the "old days" are no longer in use. If you find words not in our modern vocabulary, you can look them up in old dictionaries, which major libraries can provide.

A more challenging problem than extinct words, however, are words in use today that had radically different meanings in former

years. Particularly misleading are terms dealing with family relationships. Today's terms like "in-law" and "cousin" or "stepchild" have specific and clear meanings. Before the 1800s, they did not carry the same meanings. Take the word *cousin*, for example. In those days it meant anyone who was not a brother, sister, son, or daughter. A woman's nieces and nephews, and even her grandchildren, were considered to be her cousins. In his will, a man might term his wife's children by a former marriage—his stepchildren—as his "son-in-law" or "daughter-in-law"! And, the actual son-in-law or daughter-in-law according to our meanings were called "son" or "daughter." The word *brother* could mean a brother, brother-in-law, stepbrother, or fellow member of the church. "Mother" and "father" referred not only to parents but also to the mother-in-law and father-in-law.

Junior and Senior after a person's name did not necessarily mean son and father. The terms instead applied to two men of the same name, the older one being senior and the younger one junior. The terms "Mrs." and "Mistress" had meanings different than ours. The title "Mrs." referred to a woman of high social standing, not to marital status. "Mr.," in turn, is an abbreviation for "Mister," which refers to a gentleman of high social class.

From Coats of Arms to Family Web Sites

Many Americans are delighted to find objects containing their family name and its coat of arms. Shops in malls and online cater to interest in obtaining objects bearing the coat of arms of a family line. Commonly, the terms "coat of arms," "family shield," and "family crest" are used interchangeably—revealing a total lack of understanding of heraldic realities. These display items are in fact fluff, out of touch with legitimate hereditary rights to heraldic symbols. Nevertheless, they are fun to have and allow us to show pride in family heritage.

Medieval Surname "Sites"

To make sense of medieval coats of arms, imagine a medieval warrior or knight, dressed in armor, going forth to battle. How can this guy be recognized in an army of knights likewise dressed in armor? As early as 1150 he incorporated four elements in his battle gear in order to identify himself:

1. A coat that wrapped around the armor, called his "coat of arms," to protect the armor from cold, heat, and rain, decorated with a design uniquely his.
2. A shield, used to block sword thrusts, arrows, and spears, painted the same design as on the coat.
3. A unique crest atop his helmet. This was a figure—like a leopard, eagle, or horse—that crest gave a top-side identity to the knight during a crowded hand-combat situation when shields were engaged in battle and not visible.
4. A rope-like wreath (torse) of silk, with one to three colors twisted in it, that attached to the top of the helmet.

The total "armory" design became incorporated into the knight's seal, which served as his signature. The knight's armor, helmet, torse, coat, and seal passed to his firstborn son, but not to every son. Other sons used the design with slight alterations, so that each could be identified individually in battle and not be confused with the firstborn son.

With the advent of firearms, the face mask disappeared, and so did the need for quick identification by simple symbols. As a result, designs increased in detail and complexity since their purpose was now show rather than identification. Also, designs began to incorporate words, which were not used earlier (when even the nobility was illiterate).

Based on the knight's fighting regalia, then, a drawing of the family's "armory" incorporates the shield, the helmet, and a crest or crown. The insignia or design painted on a shield is called the armament. A rendering of all of the elements of a complete coat of arms—crest, crown, mantling, shield, and motto—is called an "achievement."

Authentic Coat of Arms

Those who hope to authenticate that they are entitled by birth to use a recognized and registered coat of arms must apply to the College of Arms. They must prove through documented pedigree charts their direct descent through male lines from the original bearer of those arms. Then, if declared eligible, they must pay a hefty fee for the right to display the decoration legitimately as their own. (Daughters had some inheritance rights in cases where there was no son, but rules governing female use of heraldry symbols is a complex matter that you can study in official heraldry handbooks.)

Tartans and Scottish Surnames

Tartans are claimed by Scottish clans to give distinguishing identity to principal portions of their costume. By the 1700s, each clan had adopted its own distinctive design pattern in its dress, including its kilts. The tartan for the Campbell clan, for example, features a green background with black and blue half-inch crossings and a yellow overcheck. The MacGregors' tartan has a red background with wide and narrow crossings of green and a white overcheck edged in black.

To help suppress Scottish Highlanders after their rebellion in 1745, the English parliament passed acts to disarm the Scots and to prohibit the use of their distinctive tartan-based Highland dress. The ban was repealed a generation later, and since then the clan tartan has become popular again in Scottish fashion.

If you discover a tartan design attached to your Scottish name you might want to use it as wallpaper for your family Web site.

When you come across a coat of arms assigned to one of your family names, you may be tempted to claim it as your own family's coat of arms. Technically, of course, that is not true, unless you are the authenticated legal successor in the long line of firstborn sons. To be correct, the best you can say is that it is the coat of arms of someone with your surname.

Surname-Specific Web Sites

Just as a coat of arms was designed long ago to identify a family, your family tree and other significant material from your genealogical research can be your symbol of identification today on the World Wide Web. In a similar (though far more peaceful!) way that a shield design identified a friend or foe in battle, your Web page, when it's linked to the other same or similar surname sites, can help those who share your surname find you, and perhaps add to your knowledge of family history.

Online Surname Helpers

With the vagaries of spelling changes over the centuries, immigration errors, "dit" names for French Canadians, etc., or perhaps for completely unexpected reasons (your great-great-great grandfather changed his name to MacGillicuddy just because he felt like it), your surname has likely not always been what it is now. For those who are having trouble locating records because of variations on the family name, the Web offers some nifty problem solvers.

RootsWeb Surname Helper

www.surhelp.rootsweb.com/srchall.html

The RootsWeb programmers added the Surname Helper search option to help you search through genealogy Web pages, mailing lists, and other resources that might include a mention of your ancestor specifically, or his surname generally. In the Surname Helper you can set the parameters of the search to include:

- Surname and alternate spellings of surname.
- Sites to search, such as all of RootsWeb, only USGenWeb or WorldGenWeb, only Personal Genealogy pages, or only surname-specific pages.

- All message boards or surname-specific pages or only those created to include a bible record, biography, birth record, cemetery record, census, church record, court record, death record, city directory, first families, gazetteer, genealogy, history, land record, marriage record, map, migration record, military record, naturalization or citizenship record, newspaper, obituary, pension record, query, surname registration, tax list, vital record index, will, or related indexes.
- Only names appearing after a certain date.

To get a range in the surname use one or both of the following wildcard characters:

_ : any one character
LINDS_Y will find LINDSEY or LINDSAY.
DAVI_SON will find DAVIDSON or DAVISSON, but not DAVISON.
% : any number of characters.
%DONALD will find DONALD, O'DONALD, or MACDONALD.
ST%ART will find STUART or STEWART or START.

Other surname-specific sites offered at RootsWeb include:

- RootsWeb's Notable Kin—
  www.rootsweb.com/~rwguide/notable/elvis.htm
- RootsWeb's Royal and Noble Lineages—
  www.rootsweb.com/~rwguide/royal/
- RootsWeb's Surname Search (most common names)—
  www.resources.rootsweb.com/surnames/
- RootsWeb's WorldConnect—
  www.worldconnect.genealogy.rootsweb.com/

Surname Web

www.surnameweb.com/
The folks behind Surname are busy, as you'll be able to tell when you see the very busy main page. I go here for the PAF

surhelp.rootsweb.com/srchall.html

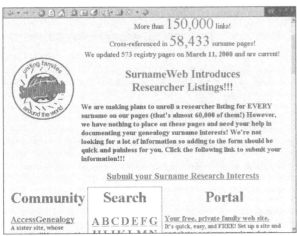

More than 150,000 links!

Cross-referenced in 58,433 surname pages!

We updated 573 registry pages on March 11, 2000 and are current!

**SurnameWeb Introduces
Researcher Listings!!!**

We are making plans to unroll a researcher listing for EVERY surname on our pages (that's almost 60,000 of them!) However, we have nothing to place on these pages and need your help in documenting your genealogy surname interests! We're not looking for a lot of information so adding to the form should be quick and painless for you. Click the following link to submit your information!!!

Submit your Surname Research Interests

Community	Search	Portal
AccessGenealogy	A B C D E F G	Your free, private family web site.
A sister site, whose		It's quick, easy, and FREE! Set up a site and

www.surnameweb.com/

(Personal Ancestral File) tech support. But that's only a tiny part of the site.

The Surname Resource Center (SRC) is a page where all the information available on a surname can be centrally located. SurnameWeb encourages you to build a home page for your major surnames, "where you can gather all your cousins together." Then SurnameWeb links the SRCs to others on the Web; there are over twenty-one hundred so far. See if your surname is already included.

SurnameWeb's Genealogy Search Center has access to two billion names. In addition, SurnameWeb offers some unique opportunities for your surname-specific home page.

- The Surname Ring Center—A ring is a collection of Web sites that have banded together to form their sites into a linked "circle"—or ring. A ring's purpose is to allow more visitors to reach the sites quickly and easily. Information is here on how to join the surname ring, how to join surname-specific rings, and how to set up a surname-specific ring of your own.
- The Genealogy Resource Center—Lists other genealogy Web pages to which to submit your surnames and to search for your surnames.
- The Surname Web Home Page Construction Kit—A help section for Webmasters of genealogy surname home pages. Shows how to build a page, step by step, for free!
- Genealogy Rings—A variety of genealogy rings to surf, such as the Benelux countries and UK Genealogy Web rings. To join a ring, submit information about your site.

Surname Discussion Forum

www.genexchange.org

This GenExchange message board was set up to discuss surnames of interest, and connect with others researching similar surname lineages. You can post queries, receive automatic notification of responses, and browse or search through recent and past entries. To define your own default settings, include the number of days' posts you want to see each time you visit.

CHAPTER SEVEN

Digging Deeper for Names: Ethnic Lineage

Decades of genealogy research by America's European-rooted, white population have established the basics of how to track down ancestors. But to move beyond the western European, Christian, mainstream, bloodline family is to encounter different kinds of genealogy problems requiring special, tailored approaches.

African-Americans, for example, face unique and difficult challenges in tracing their family tree. Slavery created naming and record-keeping circumstances that make it impossible in too many cases to find out who a particular slave's parents were. Jewish people have unique cultural and political/geographic backgrounds that require specialized kinds of research. For families newly arrived in America (such as the large numbers of Hispanics), their genealogy efforts must concentrate on homeland records more than American sources.

For many of these special situations, genealogists online and offline are still in the pioneering stages of finding sources and figuring out research directions. Nevertheless, good Web resources are available. In this chapter we'll address these specialized ethnic concerns.

African-American "Roots"

During the late 1960s, in reaction to student protests and pressures universities across America began to offer Black History and Black Studies classes. Research into black history immediately became a vital part of the historian's work. Serious studies soon appeared in historical journals and books, providing new information and identifying new records and source materials about African-Americans in U.S. history: slavery, the abolition movement, the Underground Railroad, the Civil War, Reconstruction, the Freedman's Bureau, black cowboys and soldiers on the American frontier, black migrations north, black music and literature, black soldiers in America's wars, and black men and women who made major contributions to the nation's development.

Alex Haley's book and TV series *Roots* appeared during this information explosion in black history. *Roots* not only sparked

much genealogy research by African-Americans, it excited the nation too. Since then, our understanding of how to pursue black genealogy research has passed through an infancy stage and is now nearing maturity.

First: Basic Genealogy

Even when ethnic backgrounds are involved, the genealogy quest begins in the same way for everyone.

- Write down what you already know, using pedigree and family group charts.
- Draw information from your home records.
- Ask relatives for information and tape-record interviews with them.
- Create a notetaking and file system.
- Decide what missing details you want to find.

Then you look for vital records, do census research, check for wills, seek church records, check newspaper and city directories, and pursue many of the same research approaches outlined earlier.

Unique to African-Americans

In addition to checking the usual genealogy sources, African-American genealogy research entails special knowledge of black history. For example, in terms of the federal censuses, blacks appear by name starting with the 1870 census. Censuses from 1870 to the present have listed the race of the person being enumerated. The censuses for 1790, 1800, and 1810 counted only free persons, not slaves. The 1820 census lists slaves by category but not by name. Both the 1850 and 1860 censuses include slave schedules that list slaves by sex and age, but not by name. To research census databases for black ancestors, use your families' surnames and look for slave owners with that same name or one spelled somewhat like it (Wight, White, Waite). By checking the age and sex of the owners' slaves, perhaps you can find circumstantial evidence that your ancestor was in that group.

Afro-American Historical and Genealogical Society

There is a national organization created to assist and further African-American genealogy. You can join it and/or receive help from its national center and affiliated state chapters by contacting:

Afro-American Historical
 and Genealogical Society
1700 Shepherd Street, N.W.
Washington, D.C. 20011
(202) 234-5350
www.rootsweb.com/~mdaahgs/

The AfriGeneas site (discussed below) has a slogan: "Helping the African-American climb the 1870 Brick Wall." The site is in the process of gathering as much pre-1870 "Free Person of Color" census data as possible.

Blacks were being included in vital records compiled by the states by the turn of the 20th century. However, through the first quarter of this century, midwives rather than doctors delivered many African-American children, so no birth certificates were issued. For birth records, then, you must look for records such as family Bibles and church records.

African-Americans who served in the U.S. military and in state militias can be found in military records, including military pension records. Slaves fought in the Revolutionary War and in the War of 1812. Many were granted their freedom in return for their service. Blacks also fought in the Civil War. The North had several all-black units. Since then, African-Americans have served their country in all of America's major wars. So, military records are a valuable source to be searched.

Slavery and Genealogy

Slavery impacts severely on our ability to trace African-American family connections. Slaves were given first names in place of their African names, and their surnames, if any, were those of the white family who owned them. Also, slave codes forbade slaves from learning to read or write, so their version of a life story or journal was oral, passed from one generation to the next by tellings and retellings from memory.

Because slaves were property, transactions involving them produced property records. Bills of sale were recorded. The buyer received a copy, and a copy was filed in the county's deed books. Tax collectors assessed the individual taxable value of residents' personal and real property, including the value of their slaves.

Plantations, being farm businesses, also produced business records. Those that survive include financial ledgers with entries regarding slaves bought and sold, and who died. (Check for plantation records at historical societies—see chapter 12—in the states where your relative was a slave.)

Runaway slaves caused owners to post notices and obtain warrants for arrests, naming the slaves being sought. Some of those documents can be used to trace ancestors. Freed slaves, or *manumitted* slaves, had to be legally certified as such in order to prove they were freedmen. This was a property transaction, so the manumission record was recorded in the county deed book. Manumission records are not indexed online, although examples appear on Web sites, and are being added by African-American genealogists as they find them. Two archives are the main sources of manumission records: the Pennsylvania Abolition Society in Philadelphia (in the public library) and the Schomburg Center for Research in Black Culture in New York City.

Wills can be excellent sources for finding names and ages of slaves. In their wills, slaveholders often mentioned slaves by name and indicated to which white relative or associate they were leaving the slaves, or that the slaves were to be sold. If a slaveholder died without a will, or intestate, probate courts probably handled the estate. If so, the court had to make an appraisal of the estate, including the slaves by name and their market value. This appraisal, or return, was filed with the court records, so look for the returns as well as the probate records themselves.

Some slaveholders were religious and cared about the salvation of human souls. They therefore allowed ministers to perform baptisms, marriages, and other church ordinances for their slaves, and some records of these religious rites name the slaves who received them. Blacks who attended church services did so at a church fairly close to their home. Some white churches kept records of their slave members.

Post-Slavery Records

Before, during, and after the Civil War, black churches sprang up in order to serve free blacks, in both the North and South. The African Methodist Episcopal Church became the most popular. You can contact its church headquarters in Williamstown, MA, to find out how to access its records. Two other churches to contact are the National Baptist Convention, USA, in St. Petersburg, FL, and the Christian Methodist Episcopal Church in Memphis, TN.

1861

Civil War

After the Civil War, former slaves had to find ways to earn a living. Many became sharecroppers; that is, they farmed on someone else's land, paying in return a share of their produce to the landowner. Some of these share-cropping account books survive. To find them you must look in local records and in the small collection in the National Archives.

At the end of the Civil War, the federal government established the Freedman's Bureau to assist former slaves, or freedmen. This agency set up offices in the southern states and the District of Columbia. These offices established schools; provided food, clothing, and medical help; assisted former slaves to get married; helped black war veterans to apply for pensions; and set up employment programs. Freedman Bureau records are a major collection now housed in the National Archives.

In 1865 the federal government established a banking system for freedmen throughout the South, which lasted a decade. The Freedmen's Saving and Trust Company ledgers, which detail deposits and withdrawals, are in various national, state, and local libraries.

African Research

For more than two centuries the slave trade between West Africa and North America was big business. Slave traders, some of them black, bought or captured blacks in Africa and shipped them like prisoners across the Atlantic to America's East Coast and the West Indies. The enslaved men, women, and children were from many different African nations and tribes.

To trace an ancestry back through slavery to people and villages in Africa is possible only for a fortunate few. Some succeed, like Alex Haley claims he did in *Roots*, because of oral stories that include African names, words, and traditions. Others manage to track the genealogy back to the bill of sale of their African immigrant ancestor in America.

Another source that might prove fruitful is the logbook of slave ships. Identify the closest port of entry to the earliest location you have for one of your ancestors. Search for ship logs and records for that port in state archives and ship museums as well as online.

Top African-American Sites

AfriGeneas

www.afrigeneas.com

This site is considered one of the 101 best Web sites by Family Tree Magazine, and it's easy to see why! It includes a searchable surname database, news archives and links, photo album, poetry, listing of family reunions and the excellent Slave Data Collection. This ever-growing database is designed to assist descendants of both slaves and slaveholders and other researchers to share information they find with any slave reference in records. These range from birth, marriage, death, plantation, tax, and court records to advertisements, inventories, manumissions, and Run-A-Ways.

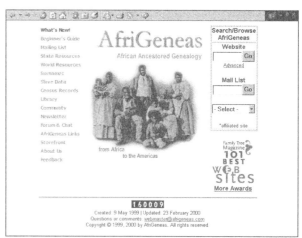

www.afrigeneas.com

So much is here all the time that I recommend joining the AfriGeneas mailing lists. Many of the powers that be behind this Web site lead the African-American chats in the Genealogy Forum on AOL, keyword: roots or gf.

Christine's Genealogy Web site

www.ccharity.com

Another worthy member of the 101 top Web sites. The surname search engine is Ancestry.com's; thus, there's a huge database. Subscribe to her free e-mail list to keep up with the latest African-American research advice. Recent offerings at the site:

www.ccharity.com

- Papers Relating to the Return of the Kickapoo and the Seminole (Negro) Indians from Mexico to the United States, 1870–1885
- Records of the Board of Commissioners for the Emancipation of Slaves in the District of Columbia, 1862–1863 "A partial list of the record of petitions filed under the Act of April 16, 1862, dated April 29–July 15, 1862 showing the date the petition was filed, the number of

A Complex Heritage

"Many genealogists estimate that 90 percent of African-Americans have white ancestors in their family tree. That may not surprise you. But did you also know that 80 percent of you are just as likely to have a Native American ancestor in your family tree?"

—Donna Beasley,
*Family Pride: The Complete
Guide to Tracing
African-American Genealogy*
(1997).

the petition, name of petitioner, names of slaves, and value of slaves as claimed in the petition."

- Roll of Emigrants that have been sent to the colony of Liberia, Western Africa, by the American Colonization Society and its auxiliaries
- Statements, depositions, and other records submitted by Gov. William W. Holden relating to crimes of the Ku Klux Klan against citizens of North Carolina, 1869–1871
- The Lynching of Anthony Crawford. Doria Johnson, the great-great granddaughter of Anthony Crawford recounts his lynching and the effect it had on the lives of his descendants

More African-American Sites

- Cyndi's List—*www.cyndislist.com/african.htm*
- African-American Resource Center— *www.genealogyforum.com/gfaol/resource/AfricanAm/index.htm* Although this is the Web site of AOL's Genealogy Forum, you don't need AOL for most of the links to work. Find Family Research, Understanding Our History, Timeline of Historical Events, Biographies of Ancestral Heroes, Reunion Announcements, and many links to other sites. "AOL-only" links connect you to the African-American message boards and weekly live chats with experienced African-American genealogy hosts.
- Guide to Tracing Your African-American Civil War Ancestor— *www.coax.net/people/lwf/cwguide.htm*. From the book of the same name by Jeanette Braxton-Secret:

> "Approximately 166 Black regiments (145 infantry, 7 cavalry, 12 heavy artillery, 1 light artillery and 1 engineer), and approximately 180,000 freedmen and former slaves were recruited and organized into the U.S. Colored Troops between June 30, 1863 to December 31, 1867."

- Lest We Forget—The Untold History of America—*www.coax.net/people/lwf/default.htm* offers the history, culture, preservation efforts, and current events of African-Americans, and other ethnic and non-ethnic groups and individuals, focusing on their contributions to the growth and development of the U.S.
- The Walk to Canada—*www.ugrr.org/walk.htm*. Anthony Cohen, creator of the site, traces one of the possible routes of the underground railroad from Montgomery County, Maryland, to Ontario, Canada."
- Underground Railroad: Special Resource Study (National Park Service)—*www.nps.gov/undergroundrr/contents.htm*. A study of the loose network of aid and assistance to fugitives from bondage.
- African-American Odyssey—*http://memory.loc.gov/ammem/aaohtml/aohome.html*. A thoughtful approach to the description of African American life in the U.S.

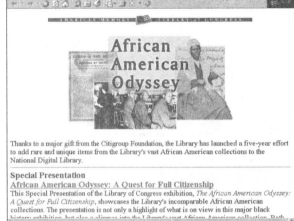

memory.loc.gov/ammem/aaohtml/aohome.html

Jewish Genealogy

Jewish families in America, like those with European or African backgrounds, are composed of both those who have been in this country for many generations and those who have arrived recently.

To find genealogies for those who have been here a long time, you can follow the basic genealogy steps. For more recent arrivals, you'll need to research records in the countries your people emigrated from or find copies of such records that are here in America.

It helps to be conversant with Jewish customs and the Hebrew and Yiddish languages to conduct Jewish genealogy research. Several features of the Jewish culture illustrate the complexities the researcher encounters, such as religious rites and practices, synagogue customs, and the Yiddish language. Old *Mohel books* contain records of circumcisions. Some families save a *ketubah*, or marriage document, and pass it on to the next generation. Tying in to a rabbinical family might connect you to genealogies reaching back centuries.

www.avotaynu.com

Top Jewish Sites

Avotaynu

www.avotaynu.com

New as well as experienced researchers must consult the site of the highly regarded Jewish genealogical quarterly, Avotaynu, which was first published in 1985. It deals with Jewish genealogy not just in the United States but throughout the world.

The online newsletter version, *Nu? What's New,* is published bi-weekly and ably edited by genealogist Gary Mokotoff. The Consolidated Jewish Surname Index contains more than two hundred and thirty thousand Jewish surnames from 28 databases—more than one million entries."

The Avotaynu site also includes a linkable list of some fifty sites that are "worth visiting."

JewishGen

www.jewishgen.org

One of the most popular sites for Jewish genealogy. Its mailing list has 3,000 subscribers and posts more than fifty messages a day.

Components of the JewishGen site include a discussion group, Family Finder (a database of over onehundred and eighty thousand surnames and towns), Shtetl Links for over two hundred communities, and databases such as the Shtetl Seeker and Family Tree of the Jewish people, which contains data on over one million people.

The International Jewish Cemetery Project (*www.jewishgen.org/cemetery*) is an attempt to find the names of Jews interred in cemeteries around the world. So far over four hun-

www.jewishgen.org

A Manumission Record

Affidavit of Freedom, Joseph Ambush
Filed 8th August, 1857
District of Columbia
Washington County

On this 8th day of August 1857 personally appeared Augustus E.
Perry before me the subscriber a Justice of the Peace in and for the
said County, and makes oath on the Holy Evangely of Almighty
God that he is well acquainted with a negro man named Joseph
Ambush about twenty one years of age, and knows him to be free
and verily believes he was born free in the city of Washington D. C.

H. Naylor, J. P.
Found on Christine's Genealogy Web site.

dred thousand names of individuals from over eight hundred and seventy five cemeteries have been indexed. JewishGen invites submissions to this database.

The International Association of Jewish Genealogical Societies (*www.jewishgen.org/ajgs*) is the umbrella group for the more than seventy-five Jewish genealogical societies. At its Web site, look up the nearest society, where you'll have access to books and databases of use in further research.

More Jewish Sites

- The Balch Institute for Ethnic Studies—
  www.libertynet.org/~balch/
    Homepage of the Philadelphia Jewish Archives Center.
- Beth Hatefutsoth Museum of the Jewish People—
  www.bh.org.il/
    See the Beth Hatefutsoth Family Names Database and the advice to researchers.
- US Holocaust Memorial Museum—*www.ushmm.org/*
    Be sure to see the listing of academic publications as well as the registry of Jewish Holocaust Survivors.

Native American Research

It is possible in many cases to trace Native American (NA) genealogy back several generations. A number of records contain useful information. However, as with any ethnic group, you'll face unique problems.

You must know the tribal affiliation and learn about the historical background and customs of that tribe. You need to consult histories of the various tribes to know when they lived where. Then, you must find out about naming customs among the various tribes. Kinship systems of the various tribes must also be understood. Federal records divide Native Americans into two categories—those who participated in government programs and supervision and those who did not.

The basic genealogy sources about Indians through 1830 are church and land records. The federal government became vigorous in transferring Indians to reservations between 1850 and 1887. Census records are sometimes helpful for the Reservation Period. Reservations meant government paperwork—school documents, censuses, and annuity rolls—involving Indians by name. The period between 1887 and about 1930 was what is termed the Allotment Period, when land was allotted to individual Indians. Government land grants to individual Indians generated allotment and family registers. Government files also contain vital facts, health records, court claims, and wills from this time.

The National Archives has many records relating to Native Americans who kept their tribal status. Most of the records, arranged by tribe, are dated 1830–1940. These records include:

- Lists of Cherokee, Chicksaw, Choctaw, and Creek Indians and others who moved west during the 1830–1846 period. Each entry on the list usually contains the name of the head of the family, the number of persons in the family by age and sex, a description of property owned before removal, and dates of departures from the East and arrival in the West.
- Annuity payrolls, 1841–1940. These show for each person in a family the Indian or English name (or both names), age, sex, and relationship to the head of the family or sometimes to another enrolled Native American. Payrolls can contain supplementary information, such as names of persons who died or were born during the year.
- The Eastern Cherokee claim files, 1901–1910. These usually contain the applicant's name, residence, date and place of birth, name and age of spouse, names of father and mother and children, and other genealogical information.

After the Indian Reorganization Act of 1934, several individual tribes began to keep their own records.

For Native Americans not linked to reservations, oral information from living relatives is your best source.

Jewish Historical and Genealogical Societies

Dozens of Jewish historical societies exist in the United States. They include the Southern California Jewish Historical Society in Los Angeles, the Chicago Jewish Archives, the Jewish Historical Society of New York in New York City, and the National Museum of American Jewish History in Philadelphia.

Similarly, there are Jewish genealogical societies throughout the country. Sampling:

- Jewish Genealogical Society of Los Angeles (Sherman Oaks, CA)
- San Francisco Bay Area Jewish Genealogical Society (San Mateo, CA)
- Jewish Genealogical Society (New York City)
- Jewish Genealogical Society of Philadelphia
- Jewish Genealogy Society of St. Louis.

At times various religious groups have worked among the Native American tribes. Records of the Quakers, Moravians, Presbyterians, Baptists, Catholics, and the LDS Church (Mormons) can contain useful information filed by their mission agencies and missionaries.

Several universities also have record collections relating to Native American tribes. A number of oral history projects in various states have tape-recorded Native American interviewees, supported by the Doris Duke Oral History Project.

Researchers need to search the basic Internet sites for genealogy to see updated information as well. They should also study Paula K. Byers' edition of the Native American Genealogical Sourcebook (Detroit, MI: Gale Research, 1995).

Top Native American Sites
Native American Genealogy: Osiyo
http://hometown.aol.com/bbbenge/front.html

This site has won no less than six awards for outstanding work, including Britannica.com's Guide Award. You'll find a plethora of links to other Indian pages and articles such as "So Your Grandmother Was a Cherokee Princess." An excerpt: "More and more frequently, more and more people are discovering their Cherokee ancestry. The reasons are varied. Many times, elders have not passed this information along, and it is only as they are passing to the next world do they talk about their parents and grandparents—their roots. In the early part of this century, there were many economical reasons for leaving your Native ancestry unclaimed."

www.geocities.com/Heartland/Cabin/5804/

Runs With Ponies' Search for Our Elders
www.geocities.com/Heartland/Cabin/5804/

Karen Price-Pfister takes on her Creek Indian name to share insights and information gleaned from searching her own NA roots. There are pages on the use of various special census rolls—the Dawes Rolls, Guion Miller Rolls, Siler Rolls, and Territorial District Rolls (includes all Tribal Nations, not just the Five Civilized Tribes).

Another page, "Degree of Blood," details the history of the government's laws defining Indians, and how Indians dealt with them.

GenealogyForum—Native American Resource Center

www.genealogyforum.com/gfaol/resource/NA/index.htm

This is an AOL site, but you don't have to be a subscriber for most of the links to work. Offerings include: Internet Center for Native American Genealogy, Native American Lecture Library (created from online chats), five Steps to Native American Genealogy, Native American History, Time For Sharing—The Native American Newsletter, and the Native American Tribal Directory. The site also provides a link to AOL's African Native Genealogy Homepage, for those researching Native American/African-American genealogy.

More Native American Sites

- Cherokee By Blood—*www.tngenweb.org/cherokee_by_blood/* Jerry Jordan's work here is well-designed to help you in your search for Native American roots.
- Black Hawk and Descendants— *www.augustana.edu/library/index.html*

I stumbled across this interesting collection on the Web site of the Augustana College Library in Rock Island, Illinois.

Photo-journalist John Hauberg researched the traditions and daily life of the Sauk Indians, the trails they followed, and the homeland from which they unwillingly departed. Biographies of Black Hawk and descendants are included.

- First Nation's History—*www.dickshovel.com/Compacts.html* Here you'll find brief historical descriptions of 50 Native American groups, from Abenaki to Winnebago.
- USGenWeb Maps Library of Indian Cession Lands— *www.rootsweb.com/~usgenweb/maps/cessions* Contains all 67 maps from the 1899 paper, "Indian Land Cessions in the United States."

Hispanic Research

For Hispanic Americans, the basic steps of genealogy research apply, and in this case knowledge of Spanish may be essential for very old records. Remember, Hispanics have been in this country since the mid-16th century. They brought the Catholic Church with them, so Catholic Church records are a fundamental source of information for Hispanic genealogy.

For Web sites, the amazing Cyndi has a master list of them at *www.cyndislist.com/hispanic.htm*.

Genealogy Forum Hispanic Resources *http://members.aol.com/mrosado007/hgn.htm* is an AOL site, but you don't have to be connected to AOL for most of the links to work. Check out Cuba resources, Puerto Rico resources, Hispanic Genealogy Sites, and look for the link to Mike Rosado's AOL Hispanic Genealogy Group Web page.

If you'd like to search the Family Tree Maker site for Hispanic references, use the search engine *www.familytreemaker.com/allsearch.html#site*. On the day I visited, I got 109 hits for "Hispanic" including articles on Mexico, Spain, Cuba, Puerto Rico, colonial Latin America, bibliography of suggested books, contents of related genealogy CD-ROMs, and numerous Web pages by individuals tracing Hispanic roots.

Additional Asian American Sites

Chinese Culture Center
www.c-c-c.org/roots/roots.html

Chinese Surnames
www.geocities.com/Tokyo/3919

Japanese Genealogical Resources
http://distantcousin.com/Links/Ethnic/Japan.html

Asian American Research

The U.S. has a sorry history of immigration laws that maintained quotas for Asian entries; these were especially applied to the Chinese. Still, there is a growing interest among all Asian Americans in tracing their ancestry through the standard genealogy steps and then back to the homelands. More and more Web sites are opening to help.

Once again, Cyndi gives us a starting point for Asian American research with her List of Genealogy Sites, this time for Asia & The Pacific at *www.cyndislist.com/asia.htm*. Fifty Asian countries are listed. A section on Angel Island at California's "Immigration Station" is brilliant.

Another site to check is AsiaGenWeb (*www.rootsweb.com/~asiagw*) with its many pages for Asian countries. Also, from PBS you can check out Ancestors in America (*www.cetel.org*). Here you can view clips and historical documents from the acclaimed PBS series. It also provides links to other resources.

CHAPTER EIGHT

Buried Names: Adoptions

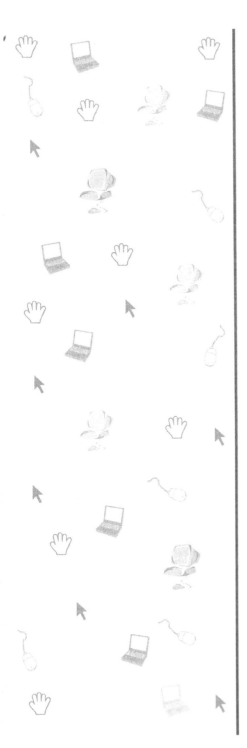

Adoptions make genealogy research difficult, even though legal adoptions generate a good amount of records and documentation. Court records for adoptions include such legal documents as consents to adopt, consents for adoption, and decrees of adoption. But adoption records are sealed by court order and inaccessible to the public.

Adoptees who are legally blocked from knowing the identity of their birth parents face two choices, one easy and one hard. Many accept their adoptive parents as their only parents. Law makes the adoptee belong to this new family—it grafts them onto the family tree. So, they take their adoptive parents' family lines and research genealogy along those. But others pursue an abiding curiosity about their biological parents and the generations before them. It is not uncommon, however, for adoptees to seek and collect the genealogy of both their adoptive parents and their birth parents.

The Case for Secrecy

Women, usually single mothers, give up their children for adoption for many reasons. Courts and child welfare agencies have a legal say in how adoptions are arranged and carried out. The well-being of the mother giving up the child and the well-being of the child who becomes adopted are both best preserved when the adoptive parents can become the child's full parents in reality. Many adopted children never discover they were adopted. The state, the courts, and the adoption system must guarantee to the mother giving up the child and to the parents adopting the child that the birth mother's identity can be kept secret. Therefore, children who learn they are adopted face sturdy legal blockades when trying to find out who their birth parents are or were.

In most cases the birth parent or adopted child can be found, and most searchers ultimately get closure. But the search often is very difficult, and it sometimes uncovers death, prison, or other problem situations. When something intended to be kept unknown becomes known, great risks emerge—both to psychological well-being and to family relationships. Not everyone welcomes a reunion. Some birth parents absolutely do not want to be found. Some biological parents never tell their subsequent spouses or children that they have another child out there somewhere. A generation ago, most adoptions were entered into with the understanding that everyone's privacy would be protected. Fears of rejection haunt both the parent who seeks the child she gave up and the child seeking his or her biological parent.

A Changing Legal Landscape

Today, passionate debate and public interest swirl around the legal right of the adopted child to know who the birth parents were. Increasingly, states are opening adoption records by passing laws that say an adoptee has the right to a copy of the original birth certificate listing the biological parents' names. Those with medical problems linked to their heredity are gaining sympathy from the courts and becoming exceptions to the guaranteed secrecy. If you fit that category, you should talk with an attorney who can explore with you your state's laws regarding an adoptee's right to be provided with needed hereditary and health-related information about his or her birth parents.

At least four states—Oregon, Tennessee, Alaska, and Delaware—have various provisions allowing adoptees access to their birth certificates. Kansas has never had a prohibition against access.

Many states provide an adoption registry, operated through the department handling their vital records. For a fee, they will feed search registrations into their database. If both a birth parent and an adoptee register for information, the department will help arrange a contact.

The International Soundex Reunion Registry (ISSR) accepts registrations from parent and child reunion-seekers. The registry is committed to keeping the identities of the birth parents and the adopted child undisclosed unless all parties are agreeable to the reunion. Children must be of legal age in order to register. If both parties are registered and want to find each other, a match is made.

Contact Information

International Soundex Reunion
   Registry
P.O. Box 2312
Carson City, NV 89702
775/882-7755
www.plumsite.com/isrr

Long-Ago Adoptions: Your Ancestor?

But what about adoptions back a few generations? Genealogy research often hits a dead-end when the adoptee involved is long deceased. How to find his or her birth parents becomes a big-league research challenge.

In times past, but less so today, society was cruel to unmarried women who gave birth and also to the child involved. The child was considered illegitimate, which carried a strong negative social and legal stigma. To avoid public humiliation, mothers facing such births, and often their family members, tried to take care of "the problem" as quietly and secretly as possible. One common solution was for the expectant mother to leave town for an extended visit somewhere, deliver the baby, give it up for adoption, and return home without her community and even close family knowing she had given birth.

If genealogy answers about parenthood are to be found for long-ago adoptees, they will come from pursuing clues regarding date and place of birth or of adoption. You must search for birth records for that time period to find out which mothers delivered around the birth date of the adoptee. Church baptism or christening records might be helpful.

Also, you can make educated guesses about the adoptive parents' distant relatives—often a family arranged for a distant relative to adopt the child, especially if that family was having trouble bearing children of their own. Sometimes the adopted child's name includes a name linked to the birth parents.

In some families, one of the older relatives might remember hearing some family rumors about where the adopted child came from. So, those older relatives should be asked. Old letters and life sketches relating to the place and the time period of the adoption also might contain useful information or hints regarding the parentage question.

When collecting genealogy "down" the family to the present—tracking the children, grandchildren, and other descendants of an ancestor—any child adopted into the family should be treated like a birth child. His or her descendants ought to be treated as bloodline family.

A Success Story

I came to understand the difficulties adoptees have searching for their bloodline roots from helping a friend do it. She learned that her birth mother had died three years before we could trace her. Happily the story didn't end there. The widower was willing to share photos and information about his wife. In her later years she had told him of the birth and adoption of a baby girl prior to their marriage. He was not the father. Hers was a typical WWII story—boy meets girl, he goes off to war and is killed, and she finds herself pregnant and alone.

Although my friend does not know anything about her biological father, she is much at peace having found so much information on her biological mother. Her mother never had any other children, so it was doubly wonderful that her husband was so generous with his caring attention to her daughter's need to know.

Not all reunions work out so smoothly. It can be a very stressful situation, so you need to give yourself and your birth child or birth parent lots of space and time to adjust.

Orphan Trains

www.pbs.org/wgbh/amex/orphan

PBS deals with the phenomenon of "orphan trains" that were devised as a method to find homes for homeless children from the streets of New York. Typically as the train came to a stop, the guardian matron would line up the children for the locals to pick and choose from. Then the train would travel to the next stop, repeating the process. These "adoptions" were not usually formalized, so tracing ancestries has proved difficult.

Important Adoption Web Sites

The Web has become a new medium where adoptees and birth parents can look for each other. Here are general adoption Web sites that provide current information and guidance. You can also search for adoption sites using a particular country's name.

Adoptee Birthfamily Connections
www.birthfamily.com

Adoption Channel Home Page
www.peoplesite.com/indexstart.html

Adoption.com
www.adoption.com/

Adoption Information, Laws and Reforms
www.webcom.com/kmc/

Adoption Search
www.adoptionsearch.com/

Adoption Search and Reunion
www.nmia.com/~rema2/index.html

Bastard Nation
www.bastards.org/

Becky West's Adoption Page
www.geocities.com/Heartland/Prairie/8066/ adoption.htm

BirthQuest
www.birthquest.org/

Cyndi's List
www.cyndislist.com/adoption.htm

Forget Me Not Family Society
www.portal.ca/~adoption/

Lost and Missing Relatives
www.cyberpages.com/lostprsn.htm

World Wide Registry
www.phoenix.net/~aquarian/davids/birth.html

Yahoo!...Adoption
http://dir.yahoo.com/Society_and_Culture/ Families/Parenting/Adoption/

Yourfamily.com
Long Lost Family Bulletin Board
www.yourfamily.com/lost_family.shtml

CHAPTER NINE

Putting the History into Family History

Ancestral Color

The times in which the ancestor you are researching lived were different than life today. People back then did almost everything differently than we do now. The cliché that "the past is a foreign country" is more true than false. To tell the story of your relative accurately, you need to become familiar with what life was like back then. What was the town like when he or she lived there? The schools? The transportation?

It is possible to pile up facts for a family history yet not draw understanding from them. To get a sense of past people and events, you've got to put the "flesh on the bones" of your ancestors. They aren't just names on a pedigree chart. During their lifetime, they experienced the challenges of the economic, social, political, and cultural situations in which they lived. You've got to get that in there, but how? We might give up at this point, since most of us weren't blessed with our fully-documented family Bible, well-labeled oil portraits going back 12 generations, and numerous diaries compiled over the adult lifetime of each ancestor.

One way genealogists augment their family history is to include surviving firsthand accounts of the time period and locality where their ancestors once lived. This might take the form of:

- Newspaper advertisements for such items as clothing, kitchen utensils, and farm implements
- Diary transcripts from someone in the same military unit as your ancestor
- Photos from the Matthew Brady Civil War Collection at the Library of Congress
- Military unit histories
- County histories
- Diaries of doctors from your ancestor's area
- City directories (the kind they had before telephones)

There are of course a gazillion sites dealing with history on the Web, a daunting prospect, searchwise. To narrow that search, what follows are some truly outstanding history sites. These will perhaps guide you to just the right document or, if not, provide the links or inspiration to fine-tune your research.

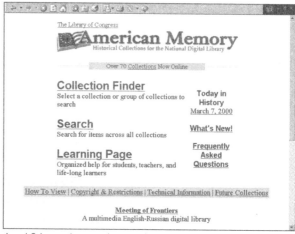

lcweb2.loc.gov/ammem/ammemhome.html

Americana in General
American Memory

http://lcweb2.loc.gov/ammem/ammemhome.html

Here at this Library of Congress site you find searchable collections of manuscripts, printed texts, sheet music, maps, motion pictures, photos and prints, sound recordings, and other document databases. Note that the Library of Congress has a "This Day in History" option, highlighting events that took place in American history on the same date as the current one. See also the Life History Manuscripts from the Folklore Project, WPA Federal Writers' Project 1936, located on another page at this same site: *http://lcweb2.loc.gov/ammem/wpaintro/wpahome.html*.

Here is a sampling of the approximately 75 American Memory collections at the Library of Congress Web site:

- African-American Sheet Music, 1850–1920: Selected from the Collections of Brown University
- Architecture and Interior Design for 20th Century America: Photographs 1935–1955
- By Popular Demand: Jackie Robinson and Other Baseball Highlights, 1860s–1960s
- Buckaroos in Paradise: Ranching Culture in Northern Nevada, 1945–1982
- Civil War Maps
- Selected Civil War Photographs
- Prosperity and Thrift: The Coolidge Era and the Consumer Economy, 1921–1929
- The Northern Great Plains, 1880–1920: Photographs
- An American Time Capsule: Three Centuries of Broadsides and Other Printed Ephemera
- Railroad Maps, 1828–1900

- American Leaders Speak: Recordings from World War I and the 1920 Election
- Historic American Sheet Music, 1850–1920
- Small-Town America: Stereoscopic Views from the Robert Dennis Collection, 1850–1920
- Voices from the Dust Bowl: the Charles L. Todd and Robert Sonkin Migrant Worker Collection, 1940–1941
- Inside an American Factory: Films of the Westinghouse Works, 1904

The History Channel

www.historychannel.com

Of particular note is "This Day in History" broken down into special categories: This Day in Wall Street History, This Day in Civil War History, and days in Automotive, Crime, Literary, and Technology history. For example, This Day in Technology reported for March 7:

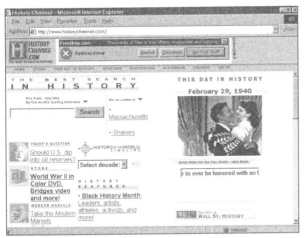

www.historychannel.com

In 1876 the telephone was patented. Twenty-nine-year-old Alexander Graham Bell received a patent for the telephone, which he invented as a result of his work with the deaf. Three days after receiving the patent, issued for "improvements to the telegraph," Bell made the first successful telephone call, to another floor in his house. The following fall, he completed the first call over outdoor wires, from Boston to Cambridge, Massachusetts.

In 1792 John Herschel is born. He was a mathematician and astronomer, studied at Cambridge with Charles Babbage, the pioneer of the electronic computer. Babbage and Herschel realized that England lagged behind other modern nations in the realm of mathematics.

The first successful transatlantic radio telephone conversation took place between London and New York on March 7, 1926.

The Immigration Experience

Ellis Island looms large in the history of U.S. immigration. Between 1892 and 1954 more than twelve million immigrants arrived on this island in New York harbor and were processed through its facilities as the first step in their new lives in America. This experience was often not a pleasant one, especially following a brutal voyage in steerage class, which was the lot of the overwhelming majority of immigrants. Despite the cheery depiction of Leonardo DiCaprio's quarters in steerage in the movie *Titanic*, steerage was more often than not overcrowded and unsanitary. Quarantine for disease upon arrival was not uncommon. Thus the story of immigration ports and documents and photographs dealing with the immigrant's experience are of much value to a family history.

Ellis Island Home Page

www.ellisisland.org

Here you can take the online tour of the museum, add your ancestor's name to the Wall of Honor, and find more of the immigrant experience.

Riverside Keystone-Mast Photo Collection

http://cmp1.ucr.edu/exhibitions/immigration_id.html

This small but powerful collection from the California Museum of Photography is called *New York, NY, Ellis Island—Immigration: 1900–1920.* Here you'll find photos of the ships that carried immigrants during the peak years of immigration, and photos of immigrants being processed, including one showing where physicians examine their eyes.

www.ellisisland.org

More than likely photos in collections like these won't show your ancestor, but if you save the picture as a jpeg file you can include it in your personal family history as an example of what immigrants faced during this time period. If you wish to use the photo in a printed genealogy or on a Web page, you'll have to ask for permission to reprint it in your publication.

Do You Know What *Diptheria* Means

To use words without understanding them is to parade semi-empty facts. That applies to present vocabulary as well as to past usages different from today's. For instance, if your relative suffered from diphtheria, you can say that, but you and the reader both may end up not knowing what that means. What is diphtheria? What does it do to the victim? How does it spread? How long does it last? How was it treated? Simple online research will help you inform the reader what it meant for your relative to have diphtheria at that time.

For more about the immigrant experience, see the National Archives—*www.nara.gov/genealogy/immigration/immigrat.html*—for immigration records and histories of immigration.

Local Color
GenExchange Histories

www.genexchange.org/us.cfm

GenExchange has added an impressive collection of biographical and historical entries, taken principally from out-of-print late 19th- and early 20th-century county histories. This URL takes you to the United States page. There I clicked West Virginia, selected the topic Bios & Historical Accounts and found screens of documents such as those listed below. These stories of a lovers' leap, a mine explosion, and an early Indian massacre are just the sort of thing you're looking for to flesh out a family history.

- Charleston Becomes a Town
- Church Development—Baptist
- Clarksburg [sic], the Establishment of
- Early History of Boone County
- Early History of Cabell County
- Early History of Calhoun County
- History of Lovers Leap, Fayette County
- History of the Immaculate Conception Catholic Church and Clarksburg Indians
- Kanawha County's First Prison
- Massacre of the Wheelers
- Mine Explosion Takes Toll of Eleven Lives

Plimoth Plantation

www.plimoth.org

Here's an instance of spelling the name the old-fashioned way. Plimoth, known generally to history as Plymouth, has its own Web site. It offers a virtual tour with photos of the town and the costumed

Maps on Your Site

Use computer software that generates maps, or enlist the help of an artist in the family, to create a map to show the family's historic sites on your site. This can be a map of the United States, Europe or another continent, or the world. Mount short explanations of each site by its name. Such maps give relatives a sense of the family in the larger perspective of nation and world.

For the United States, you can use the generic "fill-in the blank" map provided in the U.S. Research Outline produced by the LDS Family History Library. Place tiny colored markers for each of the towns where your ancestors once lived and play connect the dots as they move from one state to the next, generation by generation. You'll find the blank map at www.familysearch.org/sg/MUSA.html.

You'd want to make a separate map for each of your major sur-names and file these in the front of your research notebook for each family group. In this manner you can not only illustrate an individual family's migration pattern but also look at archives, libraries, and courthouses along the path for additional records documenting your ancestors' lives.

guides you'd meet if you went there in person. Be sure to check the site for the schedule of events. The page also provides a library of online bibliographies and articles to help you understand more about ancestors who lived nearly four hundred years ago. For those with New England ancestry, this is a great site.

Military History

Practically everyone has had relatives or ancestors who served time in the military, and the military has kept records throughout modern history, which means there is a wealth of material available. Drawings, photographs, citations, soldiers' diaries and journals, battle plans, etc., can add vital color to the story of your ancestor. Here are some guidelines for organizing your research.

1. Find sources citing your ancestors by name.
2. Search the histories of the military units in which they served.
3. Deduce which battles your ancestors may have participated in by comparing your ancestor's service dates with the unit's history.
4. Obtain copies of individual or military unit photos.
5. Develop maps detailing the whereabouts of your ancestor during the military conflict.
6. Locate diary entries from eyewitnesses who were there at the same time as your ancestor.

U.S. Army Military Institute

www.army.mil/usamhi

Documents pertaining to virtually the entire history of warfare are housed in this library facility, and a lot of material is online.

A collection-in-progress of digitized documents give an example of the many and varied types of documents available from the U.S. Army Military History Institute. For example, you can now find a Christmas Menu for the 533d Combat Support Group in Vietnam 1969.

Other databases to explore are:

- Unit photos—*www.carlisle.army.mil/usamhi/PhotoDB.html*
- Unit History Bibliographies—
  www.carlisle.army.mil/usamhi/UnitHistories.html
- American Civil War Unit History Bibliographies—
  www.carlisle.army.mil/usamhi/ACWUnits.html
- Civil War Biographical Bibliographies—
  www.carlisle.army.mil/usamhi/ACWBiogs.html

The Vietnam War

The Vietnam War is known as the first television war, but it's also the first "cyberspace war." The Web abounds with Vietnam War-related sites, many created by veterans or their relatives.

The Virtual Wall at *www.thevirtualwall.org*, sponsored by the Vietnam Veterans Memorial Fund, is an astonishing cyber-replica of the Vietnam Memorial in Washington, DC. All 140 panels of the actual wall can be viewed—58,220 names—and when you click on a name a pop-up screen appears with name, birth date, rank, and date of death, along with links to other material available on other sites. If you lost someone whose name is on the Wall, a link—say a text file you set up on your Web site with questions—could perhaps connect you to still living members of your relative's unit and information you might never have had otherwise.

Other Wars

- Historic Valley Forge—
  www.ushistory.org/valleyforge/index.html
  Among the offerings, the story of Valley Forge, a timeline, weather reports for Valley Forge 1775–1782, Franklin's contributions to the American Revolution
- Civil War Home Page—*www.public.usit.net/mruddy/index.html*

U.S. Army Military History Institute

Historical Reference Branch
22 Ashburn Drive
Carlisle Barracks
Carlisle, PA 17013-5008

U.S. Army military history has much to offer researchers, and if you can't find it online it might be worth a trip to this excellent library facility. You can review the online card catalog before you go to see if the material you're seeking is available.

History Dating Game: Calendar Changes

In 1582, Pope Gregory XIII ordered that 10 days be dropped from Western society's calendar. His decree also changed the beginning of the new year from March 25 to January 1. The new system, still known as the Gregorian calendar, brought the old Julian calendar into synchronization with the sun, so that the equinox occurred on March 21.

However, some colonial American records contain double dates—the date written correctly for both calendars. For the January to March period, the years differed by one because New Year's was January 1 on the new calendar but not until March 25 on the other. Thus, in colonial records February 3 might be written as 1680/81—it being 1680 by the English calendar but 1681 by the Gregorian calendar. A person might write a letter dated March 23, 1664, and another one five days later was dated March 28, 1665.

You can also become confused when using records in which the month is written not by name but by number. On the new calendar April was the fourth month, but on the old calendar it was the second month. So, when you read a record dated something like "the 10th daye in the third month," you must determine if that means March 10 or June 10! Usually the day was given first and then the month, but not always, which exacerbates the confusion sometimes.

When England adopted the new Gregorian calendar in 1752, it had to drop 11 days from the calendar. Thus, the day after September 2 that year was September 14!

George Washington was born on February 11, 1732, but when the English changed the calendar two decades later, he adjusted his birthday to the new system and redated it as February 22. Rather than get into the business of doing what Washington did and adjusting all old dates to fit the new calendar, genealogists use the original date with "(O.S.)," initials standing for Old Style, after it.

More on Calendars

- The British Switch to the Gregorian Calendar— *http://www.crowl.org/Lawrence/time/britgreg.html*
- Genesis of the Gregorian Calendar— *www.sdsu.edu/doc/texi/gcal_5.html*
- Gregorian Calendar— *www.veda.is/~adam/calendar.html*
- Gregorian Calendar and Leap Years— *www.as.wvu.edu/~jel/skywatch/skw9602a.htm*
- Quaker Calendar— *www.quaker.org.uk/gcal.html*
- Trans Image: Calendar and Leap Years— *www.transimage.com/Cal/CalOther.html*

CHAPTER TEN

Where Did They Live?: Maps

Beginning genealogists soon wish they'd paid more attention in their high school geography classes. Which state did great-great-aunt Matilda mean when she said in her diary they were moving "just west of Ohio"? And what about those ancestors who settled in states that weren't states yet? Or lived in counties that changed from one year to the next?

Not knowing exactly where an ancestor lived certainly complicates finding records. This is why old maps can be valuable leads in tracking them down. Aside from that, a map gives you a sense of the period in history in which your ancestors lived, the roads or trails they followed to get there, even how far apart your relatives lived from each other.

The old maps show migration trails, old county and country boundaries, and lists the towns as they used to be called. By including them in your genealogical research, you get a better view of how far your ancestor had to go by horse drawn wagon to "get to town." There is still a place in our lives for current maps, since they'll help us get from point A to point B when planning a family genealogy vacation or research trip.

Maps We Need

Three types of maps in particular are valuable to genealogists. One type of map shows the evolution of county boundaries over time. One older county could become two, and then four, counties as settlements thickened. So, a person might not have moved but ended up living in four different counties. All four counties need to be checked when looking for records about that person. Libraries have guides to America's counties and their changing boundaries.

The second type of map that is helpful to researchers is a period map, which shows the place decades or centuries ago when your ancestors lived there. Also of great value to genealogists are land ownership maps, produced by local governments and by commercial companies.

Tracking Counties

It's not usual to recommend books in an online guide to genealogy, but a book on county maps by Bill Dollarhide, an experienced genealogical researcher and lecturer, available from his publisher on the Web is invaluable. This is the *Map Guide to the U.S. Federal Censuses, 1790–1920*, text by William Thorndale. The book is available at *www.genealogybookshop.com*.

The publisher states: "On each of the nearly four hundred maps the old county lines are superimposed over the modern ones to highlight the boundary changes at 10-year intervals. Also included are (1) a history of census growth; (2) the technical facts about each census; (3) a discussion of census accuracy; (4) an essay on available sources for each state's old county lines; and (5) a statement with each map indicating which county census lines exist and which are lost."

The U.S. Digital Map Library

www.rootsweb.com/~usgenweb/maps/

The United States Digital Map Library is a project of USGenWeb Archives. Their goal is to make useful, readable, high quality maps available to genealogists. Here you'll find both archival maps and newly made maps based on scholarly research.

On this map page, find links to:

- State and county maps
- United States maps
- Indian land cessions to the U.S. treaty maps

A Texas Bonus

One of my genealogy chat members, Ken Short, working with the US GenWeb project described above, has put a few old and special interest maps of Texas on his site. He is currently working on a collection of maps of all 254 Texas counties.

Help from the U.S. Geological Society

For more information on the use of maps in genealogy, see:

Fact Sheet 140-99 (August 1999) from the U.S. Geological Survey at *http://mapping.usgs.gov/mac/isb/pubs/factsheets/fs14099.html*.

To see the maps Ken has uploaded for Texas, check out *www.rootsweb.com/~usgenweb/maps/texas*. In addition to the maps Ken has provided links to such Texas lore as:

- Texas State Library and Archives Commission (TSLAC) collection of online maps (downloadable).
- Texas 1820–1836 Map, from the *Atlas of American History* (1943). Drawn under the supervision of Carlos E. Castañeda, published by Charles Scribner's Sons.
- Fredonia 1826–1827 and Texas Revolt 1835–1836, drawings of campaign routes.
- West Central States and States of the Plains, Southern Division
- Big Bend Area of Texas circa 1920, prior to establishment of Big Bend National Park
- Big Bend National Park
- Spain in Texas: Spanish Expansion into Texas.

Historic U.S.
Boundaries of the Contiguous United States

www.ac.wwu.edu/~stephan/48states.html

This is an animated map of the North American continent. It redraws state boundaries to indicate each time period selected. This is one of the best graphic depictions of westward settlement patterns, and is most certainly an excellent use of Internet design capabilities.

Early American Roads and Trails

http://members.aol.com/RoadTrails/roadtrai.html

Beverly Whitaker, CGRS, describes 16 of the major early roads:

The Boston Post Road	The Natchez Trace
Braddock's Road	The National Road
The California Trail	The Oregon Trail
The Fall Line Road	The Pennsylvania Road
The Great Wagon Road	The Santa Fe Trail
The King's Highway	The Upper Road
The Mohawk (Iroquois) Trail	The Wilderness Road
The Mormon Trail	Zane's Trace

He Never Moved!

A man stated on the 1850 federal census that he was born in Virginia. His grandson later stated that his grandfather was born in Kentucky. Both were right, to some degree.

At the time Paul Froman was born, Virginia extended to the Mississippi River. Yet, as the country developed, the county boundaries changed to accommodate the burgeoning population. The history of Lincoln County shows that it changed county designations 13 times.

In genealogy, you list the exact locality at the time an event occurred. So for Paul Froman, who was born on the family farm, never moved, and died there, you might have a total of five or six different courthouses that recorded important events. It might be that you would consult Kings County, Virginia, for the birth record and Lincoln County, Kentucky, for the death.

Lewis and Clark Expedition

www.pbs.org/lewisandclark/

Follow an expedition timeline and maps and read what expert historians have to say about Lewis, Clark, and the rest of the Corps of Discovery as they attempt to find a water passage between the Mississippi River and the Pacific Ocean, at the behest of President Thomas Jefferson. The maps will show you what the country looked like then.

Ancestry Map Center

www.ancestry.com

Ancestry.com's huge collection grows by two or three maps each business day. That's a lot of maps at this point! If you subscribe to the "Ancestry Daily News" you'll receive announcements of the new maps of the day.

I clicked on the down arrow next to U.S. State and County Maps and selected Georgia. The map I found could be used quite nicely to pinpoint where my ancestors lived in the 1732–1755 time period.

1895 U.S. Atlas

www.livgenmi.com/1895.htm

Here find an incredible collection of scanned images from an out-of-print atlas, thanks to volunteer Pam Reitsch.

Land Ownership and Maps

Since the first decade that Europeans came to the United States, settlers have claimed ownership of land and have bought and sold it. Land transactions involved scads of paperwork—deeds of ownership, a government record of sales and purchases, and maps and written descriptions of the land. Land records, then, can provide names of people and show when they lived and exactly where they owned property, and they can provide maps.

Much of the present United States started out as federal land, which the government sold to landowners. Therefore, the National Archives branches have federal lands records showing transactions wherein private individuals obtained public lands, putting those lands forever in the private domain. The Web also has a growing number of databases, described below.

Several types of federal land grants produced the transfers of public-domain lands to private ownership. The best-known grant is the *homestead*, which, after 1862, private persons obtained at minimal cost by living on a parcel of land for five years and making improvements on it. The federal government granted lands to states, to railroads, and to military veterans ("bounty" lands). The government opened a case file on each person who obtained land, filing therein applications, affidavits, and correspondence relating to the transaction.

Property Titles

Records of property transactions go back to the settlement of every state in the union. County recorders, and their earlier equivalents, kept property deed books that list changes of ownership. When someone buys a house, they must have a title search done in order to show that the seller has full ownership of the property. Title searches are recorded in the county's deed books. Many country land records can also be seen on microfilm at your local Family History Center.

Property must be described by exact location and size in deeds or in sales transactions. In the early South, property descriptions often read something like "Beginning with the oak tree and continuing west for six rods, then at the creek continuing northeast for two rods, then northwest for sixty rods . . ." Today's property descriptions are in feet, but the early surveyors used measuring terms not familiar to the general public. They measured property boundaries in units relative to their measuring chains:

link = .92 inches
rod = 25 links, or 16.5 feet or 198 inches
chain = 4 rods
mile = 80 chains

Deeds that use these old measurements usually mention the names of surrounding landowners to clarify the boundaries. Most of America's land is surveyed into "townships." Townships are six miles square, thereby containing 36 square miles. Each square mile is a "section" of land and has a number between one and 36. Here is how the sections in a township are numbered:

Township
R2W T4N

6	5	4	3	2	1
7	8	9	10	11	12
18	17	16	15	14	13
19	20	21	22	23	24
30	29	28	27	26	25
31	32	33	34	35	36

T4N

R2W

Ancient Maps

www.iag.net/~jsiebold/carto.html

Can you track an ancestor back to ancient Italy? Or would you just like to know what Naples looked like three millennia ago?

Here you'll find ancient maps—90 images, 6,000 B.C. to 400 A.D.; early medieval maps—175 images, 400–1300; late medieval maps—200 images, 1300–1500; Renaissance maps—800 images, 1500–1870 and links to other great map collections on the Web.

Every township is identified by a north-south "township" number and an east-west "range" number. A township might be in Range Number 2 West, from a surveyor's main meridian, and Township Number 4 North, from another main meridian. So, the township's location is described as R2W and T4N. (In much of the East and Midwest, these townships not only are named by their R and T numbers but are given actual names, like Walker Township or Fremont Township.) Let's say your relative bought land in Section 27 in the above township grid. His property would be described in the property title as "Sec. 27, R2W, T4N."

Because most people did not want to buy or own an entire square-mile section, land dealers liked to work in terms of quarter-sections. So, Section 27 has a northwest, northeast, southeast, and southwest quarter. Let's say your relative owned only the southwest quarter of Section 27:

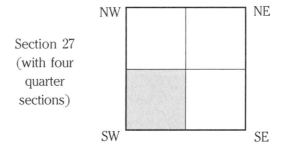

Section 27
(with four
quarter
sections)

Officially, his land, shaded in SW, was "the SW 1/4 of Sec. 27, R2W, T4N."

Land records may also reveal other valuable genealogical facts, such as where your ancestor lived before he arrived to own the land. Or they can show the name of his neighbor landowners (if

you can't dig up enough on your own ancestor, you could try to find descendants of his neighbors, who may be ahead of you in research!). If upon death the land was to be deeded to children who had left the area, their new addresses will be shown.

Land on the Web

More and more land records are finding their way online. One of the most ambitious is that of the Bureau of Land Management at *www.glorecords.blm.gov.* Twelve states are included, over two million records. The site is searchable by state, using names or land descriptions. You can then view a scanned image of the original document.

Since new material is coming online all the time, it's a good idea to use a search engine to search for "state name AND land records" to see if you can find an archive. Maryland State Archives, not currently in the BLM database, has a complete set of county land records on microfilm at this writing, but who knows, it pays to check to see if it's online, or if you can order records. See *www.mdarchives.state.md.us/msa/homepage/html/homepage.html.*

Railroads and Fire Sources

Yes, these are two separate categories of maps, one likely, the other not so likely—except when you think about it, and go yeah, right!

Railroads, of course, enabled the expansion of the U.S. with the ability to move goods and the population westward. When new track was laid for railroads, towns sprang up beside them and brought new settlers.

The American Memory Project of the Library of Congress online has a special collection of railroad maps for 1828–1900, located at: *http://memory.loc.gov/ammem/gmdhtml/rrhtml/rrhome.html*

Fire insurance companies are the other trove of maps. The fire insurance map gives such detailed information as construction material, height, and function of constructions and the location of lot lines. Since 1867 the Sanborn Map Company has issued detailed

Shtetl Seeker

www.jewishgen.org/Shtetl Seeker/loctown.htm
Sometimes those villages of Eastern Europe can be hard to find on a map. The Shtetl Seeker site searches for a village by Soundex and returns its longitude, latitude, and location from a large city in that country (such as Moscow, Berlin). You can then click to display a map showing exactly where that town/village is. If you're confused by boundary changes or only know the town and not the country name, you can search all of the countries in the databases.

plans of 12,000 American cities and towns. In 1967, shortly after the Sanborn Company discontinued its large-scale map series, the Census Bureau transferred 1,840 volumes of Sanborn maps to the Library of Congress. While the earliest atlas dates from 1867, most fall within the period 1876 to 1961. Although these maps are mostly offline, you might pursue a search just to find, say, an exact description of an ancestor's house on a tucked-away lane in turn-of-the-century St. Louis, MO.

Maps made by city fire departments are another resource. One for the city of Chicago resides online at *www.uic.edu/depts/ahaa/imagebase/firemaps/firemap.htm.* This map is detailed like those for Sanborn. You see not only each ward but whether the construction in each block is brick, wood, stone, or iron. A printout of this map would make a particularly interesting addition to your personal family history, if Chicago plays a role in it.

CHAPTER ELEVEN

Going to the Library

America has several major libraries devoted entirely to genealogical research books and records. These include the New England Historic Genealogical Society in Boston, the Newberry Library in Chicago, the New York Genealogical and Biographical Society, and the LDS Family History Library in Salt Lake City, Utah.

Every state sponsors a major library devoted to historical materials related to that state. These state history libraries are located in each capital city, but some have branch libraries elsewhere. Every state has its own historical society or division of state history, whose operations revolve around the state's history library. Such state historical libraries contain large collections of published books and local sources useful to genealogists.

Even most university libraries and several major public libraries have sections and librarians just for genealogy and family history. If you live near one of these specialized libraries, take time to go there and find out what genealogy holdings they have, if any, about each of your family lines, because contrary to popular opinion, you simply can't do your entire family tree on the Net. There is no substitute for on-site research.

After visiting the online library sites in this chapter, your next stop in your ancestral quest will be in libraries to locate microfilm of original documents mentioning your ancestors. Consult the online card catalogs of research libraries to see what's available, then plan your research strategies for your visit.

The Biggest of All: Family History Library

www.familysearch.org

The main Family History Library (FHL) in Salt Lake City is often referred to as the Mormon genealogy library, but your ancestors need not have been members of the LDS Church to have records of their existence cited in book, microfilm, microfiche, computer, or map format here. The FHL and its thirty-five hundred local Family History Centers (FHC) are considered the largest genealogical library system in the world. Since the centers are so close at hand, they're the most logical starting place to spend most of your offline time doing genealogical research. It's essential to learn how to use the FHL catalog of over two million rolls of microfilm and hundreds of thousands of books and maps.

Perhaps you've heard of the huge granite vaults where the original microfilms of church and court records are archived. At the FHL you may view a short video about the vaults at many local FHCs. The LDS Church became interested in preserving ancestral records in the late 1940s when the bombing of London threatened the survival of St. Catherine's House, a major records repository in Great Britain. Today over a hundred microfilming crews are out in the field at tiny churches and courthouses throughout the world. These volunteers are usually retired couples, who travel and maintain their foreign residence at their own expense. Considered on a special mission for the LDS Church, rather than proselytizing, these workers spend their days microfilming original records. Typically a copy of the microfilm is given to the archive or church where the originals reside—a great boon to preservation work throughout the world.

Why is this important to you? By viewing microfilms of original records at your local LDS Family History Center, it is literally possible to save thousands of research dollars. I did most of my German genealogical research from southwest Florida by ordering the microfilms for the churches in the Germanic states where my ancestors lived since the 1700s. I typically found church records and "family books" which had been microfilmed by LDS crews over ten years ago. Later, when I actually traveled to do research in Germany, I visited all the towns my ancestors were from and did on-site research for the records not yet available on microfilm.

FHC Research Process

Here's how you'll access the vast FHL resources, first online, then at a Family History Center:

1. Look for a Locality or Surname resource on the Family History Library Catalog online, *www.familysearch.org*
2. Print out the "View Film Notes" page.

Your local FHC

To find your nearest Family History Center, search for it at: *www.familysearch.org*

3. Take the printout to your local FHC.
4. Complete the order process if the item you require isn't already at the FHC.
5. View the microfilm/microfiche.
6. Obtain a photocopy (from film/fiche) of the entries mentioning your ancestor.
7. Evaluate the reliability of the information.
8. Computerize the data in your genealogy management program.
9. File the photocopy with other documents for that ancestor.

After clicking "Place Name" in the online FHL catalog, you are asked to specify the locality: A hit list of localities matching that name appears, which can be individually selected to see the records. For example, I searched for a place named Canton. After clicking the search button, I discovered there are 20 places in the FHL catalog with a Canton reference. In this case, they were all cities, from Canton, China to two Canton Townships in Pennsylvania and Washington.

In a different search, this time for Georgia, I received a listing covering not only the state of Georgia but towns in Nebraska and Vermont named Georgia, as well as the former Russian Empire of Georgia, and the Republic of Georgia. This will give you an idea of the scope of the locality search engine at this important site.

In another search, clicking the hyperlink for Germany netted a lengthy category list. I was happy to see that the German place names in this catalog follow the Meyers Orts gazetteer.

The "View Related Places" button lists the smaller localities in Germany. As you scroll down this page you'd read that there are 253 matching topics beginning with the "almanacs and archives and libraries" and ending with "social life and customs, societies and taxation." When I clicked on the topic "church records" I found a listing of evangelical church records that looked interesting. I printed out this page to take to my local Family History Center, so I can order the correct microfilm by number.

Keep in mind you can't see everything at an FHC. If the item you require is in CD-ROM, map, or book format, it may be viewed only in Salt Lake City at the Family History Library. However, if

View Related Places button

you know the author/title and publication information, it's entirely possible that you can locate the resource elsewhere. There are numerous online card catalogs to help you locate the book at another facility. Consider using the "inter-library loan" option if your local public library supports this process.

If you decide to visit the Family History Library in person, you'll be able to view most of the materials listed in the catalog. I recommend spending about 100 hours working on the Family History Library Catalog online before spending a week in Salt Lake City.

Although many folks think that the Family History Library has a copy of every book that has ever been published on family history, this is not quite true.

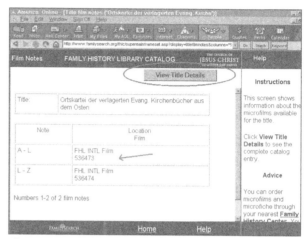

German Link

However, it's still the single largest genealogical resource in the world. Huge series of microfilms and books are kept in the vault, or back stacks. If you notice such a label in the FHL catalog, be sure to write in advance to have them pull the item for you to view when you arrive.

Growth demands more space. Since the FHL adds about five thousand new books, films/fiche per month, they are fast outgrowing their space on West Temple in Salt Lake City. A few years ago they moved the surname books (compiled family histories) across Temple Square into the Joseph Smith Memorial Building.

Great Genealogical Libraries
Allen County Public Library

www.acpl.lib.in.us

The Fred J. Reynolds Historical Genealogy Department of the Allen County Public Library in Fort Wayne, Indiana, was organized in 1961 by the library director for whom it was named. The department's renowned, ever-growing collection contains more than two hundred and twenty thousand printed volumes and two hundred and fifty-one thousand items of microfilm and microfiche.

This fantastic library is well known to experienced researchers for its incredible collection of genealogy and history magazines, indexed in

PERSI (PERiodical Source Index). This index is in book, CD-ROM and online database format. However, to access PERSI online you must use the library link to Ancestry.com or go directly to the site, as below.

PERSI

www.ancestry.com

The Periodical Source Index, or PERSI, is the largest and most widely used index of genealogical and historical periodical articles in the world. Genealogical periodicals (magazines, newsletters, journals, etc.) contain all sorts of valuable information about individual ancestors, entire families and lineages, and all types of genealogical records and repositories. Newspapers can also supply clues to historical events, local history, court and legal notices, obituaries, and more. The index includes nearly all English language and French-Canadian genealogy periodicals.

Articles are indexed in the following formats:

1. 1847–1895 (publication dates)
   LOCALITY (U.S., Canada, or foreign countries)
   FAMILY (major family names, not every name is indexed)
   RESEARCH METHODS (how-to type articles)
2. Annual updates
   LOCALITY (U.S., Canada, or foreign countries)
   FAMILY (major family names, not every name is indexed)
   RESEARCH METHODS (how-to type articles)

If an indexed article interests you, you have several options:

1. Search for the article in your local public library genealogy department's periodical collection.
2. Find a copy of the publication at the LDS Family History Library next time you visit.
3. Submit a request listing the article's index entry, complete with the code for the magazine title, etc., in a letter addressed to:

> Allen County Public Library
> PO Box 2270
> Ft. Wayne, Indiana 46801

Railroad Library

The California State Railroad Museum Library (*www.csrmf.org/library*) focuses on all aspects of railroads and railroading—historical, political, cultural, social, economic, and technical—with particular emphasis on topics pertaining to California and the West. Reference sources include a wide range of books, periodicals, railroad association and union publications, government documents, and trade catalogues. The Library also contains extensive photographs, drawings, and maps—including over 800 manuscript maps of the Atchison, Topeka & Santa Fe Railway Coast Lines, 1870–1970—manuscripts, and ephemera collections.

You may submit a maximum of six requests in each letter. You will be charged $7.50 prepaid handling fee for each letter, and 20 cents per page copied. Since the length of articles are not indexed, the actual photocopy fee will be charged after the work is completed.

Library of Congress

http://lcweb.loc.gov

In the subject areas of history, biography, and genealogy, the Library of Congress contains an incredible collection of books and typescript materials. Their card catalog of holdings is computerized and can be accessed throughout the United States. You can search the Library of Congress's holdings for genealogy books with your families' surnames. To do that, visit a nearby university library or large public library, which can connect with the Library of Congress's computerized card catalog, or look online.

As an aid to state library researchers, the Library of Congress has made it a lot easier to go online at individual state libraries and archives by setting up a page of links to these state facilities at: *http://lcweb.loc.gov/global/library/statelib.html.*

National Union Catalog of Manuscript Collections (NUCMC)

http://lcweb.loc.gov/coll/nucmc/nucmc.html

The Library of Congress provides access to the NUCMC (it's known as Nuck-Muck) database of over five hundred thousand hard-to-find manuscript records. Manuscripts are original documents—letters, diaries, photos, legal, and personal papers, etc., and as original documents they are of great value to researchers. The database excludes holdings of federal libraries and some state archives, so keep that in mind; those venues will have to be searched separately.

A recent search for "Gist" resulted in 31 hits, including a letter written in 1777 by Mordecai Gist. Clicking "More on this record" brought up the following details: "Letter, dated Baltimore Maryland, from Gist to Richard Peters, secretary of the Board of War in

Quaker Studies

The Friends Historical Library at Swarthmore College (*www.swarthmore.edu/ Library/friends/index.html*) is a depository for the records of Philadelphia, New York, Baltimore, and other smaller "Yearly Meetings." It holds in manuscript and microfilm the largest collection of Quaker records in the world. As a research library and depository of the Religious Society of Friends, the library doesn't lend collections either—to researchers or through inter-library loan. But they are open to the public, and you are welcome to make use of the resources, including a photocopier and a reader-printer for making copies from microfilm. (Bring official photo identification, e.g. driver's license.)

Philadelphia, concerning the detainment of 50 Highlander prisoners until their final destination could be determined; with further notes on the back giving instructions on where the letter was to be delivered." This manuscript is on file at the state Historical Society of Wisconsin, where one would get a copy of it.

New York Genealogical and Biographical Society (NYGBS)

www.nygbs.org

Since many of our ancestors came through the port of New York, the work of the NYGBS is significant for many researchers. The Web site features a list of New York State records on microfilm in the NYGBS Library; New York federal censuses, indexes, and other finding aids; the Vosburgh Collection of New York Church Records; and New York City Vital Records. Just the sort of things you need to know to unravel the mystery of your immigrants forebears.

www.nygbs.org

Besides New York records, the NYGBS selected bibliographies for genealogy research that are of great value. Bibliographies for African-American, Catholic, Eastern European, German, Hispanic, Irish, Italian, Jewish, Scandinavian, and Scottish research are online. As are the research categories Women in History, New York Dutch Families, and Using Artifacts and Family Heirlooms.

Daughters of the American Revolution Library

http://dar.library.net/

A research trip to Washington is not complete without several days at the DAR Library. A good time to visit is on Sunday afternoons, when the National Archives and Library of Congress are closed. The hours are Monday–Friday: 8:45 A.M.. to 4:00 P.M.; Saturday: closed; Sunday: 1:00 to 5:00 P.M. The best book to help you plan your strategy for using this library in person is *American Genealogical Research at the DAR*, by Eric G. Grundset and Steven B. Rhodes. It is published by and available through the DAR.

The focus of the library's collection is on Revolutionary War records of the federal and state governments, census records, and major indexes of records from eastern states. The on-line catalog of its holdings supersedes the three-volume printed set and includes much additional information.

Thousands of DAR members throughout the country are doing all they can to publish indexes to Bible records in their possession and provide a copy of these to the DAR Library. If you have Early American ancestry, you'll want to request a photocopy of the original applications for membership for women with the same Revolutionary War ancestor or patriot. The application may supply needed information.

Newberry Library

www.newberry.org

Recognized as one of the leading genealogy research libraries in the U.S., the Newberry Library has an online card catalog and a special genealogy section with how-to guides, as well as descriptions of services, publications, and collections. Although situated in Chicago, the Newberry collection has over seventeen thousand genealogies. It is especially noteworthy for coverage of colonial America, particularly New England, and also includes many rare titles covering gentry and noble families of the British Isles. This points up the need for researchers to look beyond local boundaries to find information on an ancestor. A great finding aid is Peggy Sinko's *Guide to Local and Family History at the Newberry Library*.

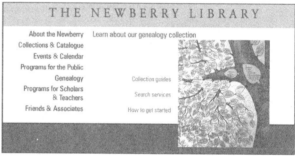

www.newberry.org

Municipal Collections

Many municipal libraries have superb genealogy collections. These are just a few of the most eminent with an online presence. Check your own local library—you never know what you'll find.

New York Public Library

www.nypl.org

The main genealogy section of the library is located in the Irma and Paul Milstein Division of United States History, Local History, and

Genealogy. Other divisions of the New York Public Library for genealogists include the Rare Books Division and Manuscripts and Archives Division, the Jewish Division, and the Map Division. The online catalog is at *www.catnyp.nypl.org*. It contains cataloging since 1972. Many special collections will not be found online.

Los Angeles Public Library

http://catalog.lapl.org

If you do a search for "genealogy" at the Los Angeles Public Library online, 12,563 records appear.

The *Los Angeles Herald Examiner*'s photo collection is part of the massive Los Angeles Public Library database. Do you have family who lived in LA? It's not all Hollywood there, and adding a vintage photo to your family history will enhance your understanding of how your relatives lived. I especially loved a horse and buggy fire department photo I found.

Detroit Public Library

www.detroit.lib.mi.us

Be sure to visit this library's special collections, including the widely known Burton Historical Collection, a large repository of historical and genealogical materials. The original collection was donated to the Detroit Public Library in 1914 by Clarence Monroe Burton, a Detroit attorney.

Members-Only
The New England Historical and Genealogical Society Library

www.newenglandancestors.org/index.asp

A membership (Individual, $50) entitles you to unlimited on-site use of the library, including access to the manuscript and rare book collections; unlimited access to online content on *www.newenglandancestors.org*; Circulating Library privileges; subscriptions to *The New England Historical and Genealogical Register* and NEXUS.

Examples of recent additions to the online library in April 2000 were: "Vital Records of New England Civil War Veterans Abstracted from

Organization Pension File Index: Part 2" and "Probate Records in Connecticut."

National Genealogical Society Library

www.ngsgenealogy.org/library/body_frame.html

The collection, located in Arlington, Virginia, includes about thirty thousand books, of which two-thirds are available in open stacks. The remaining materials are in active storage and can be retrieved by request. In addition to works of family history and local history, the library has an extensive reference collection. Vertical file materials include Members Ancestral Charts, Bible Records, and Family History Files. Other resources include FamilySearch, the GLO Land Records Series, and CD-ROMs, microfiche, and microfilm. The online catalog can be viewed at the site by non-members. Click on library, then online catalog.

The library loans 2–4 books for $10–$12. The borrower may keep the books for two weeks after receipt and must pay return shipping (cheaper book rate is fine). NGS membership is $40 per year and includes subscriptions to both the *NGS News Magazine* and the *NGS Quarterly*.

Getting Books from Other Libraries
OCLC Online

www.oclc.org/oclc/menu/home1.htm

This is the site for the card catalog your library uses to locate a book for inter-library loan. Learn how to find a book on it, and then locate a library willing to loan the book to your library. Print the screen that contains the information and take it to your local librarian (who will appreciate that in this time of cutbacks and diminished library hours, a genealogy researcher has gone the extra mile in expediting the locating process). At our library, there is no charge for the postage, though I've heard some libraries do pass this charge along. You may or may not be able to check out the book and take it home; it depends on the policy of the distant lending library. Don't be disappointed if a rare, out-of-print book is not approved for inter-library loan. At least you've managed to locate a copy. You can visit it on your next vacation!

Vertical Finds

At the Pennsylvania State Library, I worked all day on the "vertical files"—cabinets stuffed with file folders containing letters, typed manuscripts, and other documents. I looked up my major surnames, and discovered to my delight someone had done research on seven of my Pennsylvania lines. In 1956, he submitted these neatly written and partially documented* compiled genealogies, some as small as six pages, others amounting to over thirty pages. Since these were too small to be bound, they would not be found in the card catalog by author, title, or surname.

Documented means that source documents used to arrive at lineage assumptions are cited. An example: "Paul Forman's will is found in Will Book A, Lincoln County, Kentucky, page 46."

Global Card Catalogs

A friend prepared for his research trip to Scotland by viewing the online card catalog of the National Library of Scotland. This saved him a lot of time, because when he visited Scotland he knew which manuscript collections and books he wanted to look at in advance. More libraries come online all the time. Search for sites for the country you're interested in.

- National Library of Scotland—
  www.nls.ac.uk/
  Contains nearly two million records and covers all printed material acquired by the library since 1979. The online catalog covers the majority of the printed collections.

- National Library of Canada—
  www.nlc-bnc.ca/amicus/ecatalog.htm
  Here you'll be able to access the card catalog online in French as well as English. Although library access requires a membership fee, there is

an option to allow researchers free access using resAnet and Telnet.

- National Library of Ireland—
  www.heanet.ie/natlib/
  Find advice here on what you need to know about to begin your Irish ancestor research. The NLI provides a listing of qualified individuals you may contact to commission research, in case you're not planning a trip yourself. Genealogical sources at the NLI include church and valuation records.

CHAPTER TWELVE

Genealogy Societies

Lineage-Linked

The Daughters of the American Revolution (DAR) headquartered in Washington, D.C. is perhaps the best-known lineage and heredity society in America. To belong to the DAR, you need to provide proof that you are a woman who descends from someone who served on the colonists' side in the Revolutionary War.

The leading heredity and patriotic societies in America are:

General Society of Colonial Wars
General Society of Mayflower Descendants
Holland Society of New York
National Society of Colonial Dames of the XVII Century
National Society of Daughters of the American Revolution
National Society of New England Women
National Society, Sons of the American Revolution

There are dozens of other such societies in America. Here is a sampling of other interesting groups, just to illustrate the range of interests displayed by these units:

Children of the Confederacy
Descendants of the Signers of the Declaration of
     Independence
General Society of the War of 1812
Heredity Order of the Descendants of Colonial Governors
Order of First Families of Virginia, 1607–1624
Order of the Stars and Bars
Pennsylvania German Society
Pilgrim Society
Sons of Confederate Veterans
Sons and Daughters of Pioneer Rivermen
Sons of Union Veterans of the Civil War
United Daughters of the Confederacy

All of these societies require applications for membership, supported by genealogical records showing that the applicant is related

to an ancestor involved in the cause the group honors. These applications and accompanying genealogies are a rich pool of genealogical information. So, if you know of an ancestor whose activities relate to a cause on which one of these organizations is founded, contact them to see if that relative is in their database. If so, that database will also tell you of descendants of that person.

Local Clubhouses

Nearly everyone I meet in chat rooms belongs to a local genealogy society. Many have also joined a society close to where their ancestors lived, primarily to receive the society's newsletter.

Local societies concentrate on teaching basic research techniques useful to nearly all genealogy researchers. They also provide members the opportunity to share their successes and failures with each other and to learn new research techniques from guest speakers.

Your reference librarian can tell you about history and genealogy societies in the area. If you choose to participate in a courthouse or cemetery indexing project, as many of these societies do, you'll really be paying your dues.

Genealogy societies I currently belong to:

Genealogy Forum on AOL
National Genealogical Society
Genealogical Society of Pennsylvania (where many of
    my ancestors once lived)
Palatines to America (the ethnic group I am concentrating
    on lately)
Daughters of Utah Pioneers (seven sets of ancestors helped
    me qualify)
Manasota Genealogical Society (where I live)
Manasota PAF Users Group

The county adjoining mine is home to the Genealogical Society of Sarasota, whose members man the genealogy department at the

The Godfather: The National Genealogical Society

www.ngsgenealogy.org

Founded in 1903 in the District of Columbia, The National Genealogical Society (NGS) has been located at Glebe House in Arlington, Virginia since 1985.

The NGS is a nonprofit organization with a national membership of over seventeen thousand members. Most of its members are individuals, but its institutional members include genealogical and historical societies, family organizations, libraries, and other organizations.

Selby Library downtown. In Largo, Florida, the public library has a genealogy section, complete with several computers and CD-ROMs. The only way you can access the CD-ROMs, however, is if a volunteer from the local society unlocks the file cabinet that holds them.

Other libraries are larger and can devote staff to the genealogy reference section. Local genealogy society members raise funds to buy more books, or help with shelving a few hours a week. Our local LDS Family History Center is staffed mostly with volunteers from the local genealogical society.

It's a good policy to take a more active part in your online or local genealogical society. You'll meet a lot of wonderful people, and you may make a cousin connection!

Society Sites

The following list will give you an idea of the enormous variety of genealogy societies represented on the Web. Every site will offer links to related pages and the opportunity to network with other researchers.

African-American Genealogy Group—*www.libertynet.org/aagg*
American-French Genealogical Society—*www.afgs.org*
American Jewish Historical Society—*www.ajhs.org/*
American Historical Society of Germans from Russia—
    www.ahsgr.org/
Anglo-German Family History Society—
    http://feefhs.org/uk/frgagfhs.html
Anglo-Scottish Family History Society—
    www.mlfhs.demon.co.uk/AngloScots/
Cherokee National Historical Society—
    www.powersource.com/heritage
Danish-American Genealogical Group—
    www.mtn.org/mgs/branches/danish.html
Federation of Family History Societies (UK)—*www.ffhs.org.uk/*
Genealogical Society of Flemish Americans—
    www.rootsweb.com/~gsfa

Germans from Russian Heritage Society—*www.grhs.com/*
Hawaii Portuguese Genealogical Society—
    www.lusaweb.com/genealogy/html/phgs.cfm
Hereditary Society Blue Book—*www.members.tripod.com/~Historic_Trust/*
Holland Society of New York—*http://members.aol.com/hollsoc/*
Huguenot Historical Society—*www.hhs-newpaltz.org/*
Hungarian/American Friendship Society—*www.dholmes.com/hafs.html*
International Association of Jewish Genealogical Societies—
    www.jewishgen.org/ajgs
Irish American Archives Society—
    freeyellow.com/members7/ohioaoh/iaas.htm
Israel Genealogical Society—*www.isragen.org.il*
Jewish—Lenni Lenape Historical Society—*www.lenape.org*
Lithuanian American Genealogy Society—
    www.angelfire.com/ut/Luthuanian/balzekas.html
Manitoba Mennonite Historical Society—*www.mmhs.org*
National Huguenot Society—*www.huguenot.netnation.com/*
National Japanese American Historical Society—
    www.nikkeiheritage.org
National Society of Hispanic Genealogy—*www.hispanicgen.org*
Norwegian-American Bygdelagenes Fellesraad—*www.hfaa.org/bygdelag*
Norwegian-American Historical Association—
    www.stolaf.edu/stolaf/other/naha/naha.html
Palatines to America—*www.genealogy.org/~palam*
Polish Genealogical Society of America—*www.pgsa.org*
Portuguese Historical & Cultural Society—
    www.dholmes.com/calendar.html
Puerto Rican/Hispanic Genealogical Society—
    www.rootsweb.com/~prhgs/
Slovenian Genealogy Society—*http://feefhs.org/slovenia/frg-sgsi.html*
Société Généalogique Canadienne-Française—
    www.sgcf.com/anglais/welcome.htm
Society of Acadian Descendants—*www.acadian.org/sad.html*
Swedish Ancestry Research Association—
    www.members.tripod.com/~SARAssociation/sara/
    SARA_Home_Page.htm
Swedish Colonial Society—*www.colonialswedes.com*

CHAPTER THIRTEEN

Genealogy Cyber Communities

Newsgroups

By now you're probably ready for some of that online genealogical community you've been hearing about, and are eager to talk (well, type) and exchange ideas with your fellow researchers. No matter what your genealogy interest is, you'll find a discussion group, called a newsgroup, already organized with tons of messages you can read and answer. These public message boards are part of Usenet (which stands for Users Network). If you'll recall, organizing messages from genealogy newsgroups is how RootsWeb got started.

In all, there are over thirty thousand newsgroups, of which 50–60 are for genealogy. Newsgroups are divided into major categories, called hierarchies, each with many subcategories. The hierarchies, which are seen in the first part of a newsgroup's name, are rec (recreation), soc (society and culture), biz (business), sci (science), comp (computers), talk (controversial issues like politics), news (Internet and Usenet issues), misc (miscellaneous), and the famous alt (an alternative free-for-all with many unusual groups, many sexual in nature). For genealogy newsgroups the hierarchy is soc.

Let's look at a few examples for soc.genealogy:

soc.genealogy.computing
soc.genealogy.french
soc.genealogy.german
soc.genealogy.hispanic
soc.genealogy.medieval
soc.genealogy.surnames.britain
soc.genealogy.surnames.canada
soc.genealogy.surnames.usa

How to Find Genealogy Newsgroups

Before you look for newsgroups, you need software called a newsreader so you will be able to read and post newsgroup messages. No problem—both Netscape and Internet Explorer browsers include newsreaders.

If you have Netscape Communicator, click on the newsgroup icon to launch Collabra. If you have IE, click the mail icon (mailbox) to launch Outlook Express and select the newsgroup option, or go to the "Go" menu, then select newsgroups.

Click on different options to show the list of all newsgroups (a very long list appears, in alphabetical order), search for a newsgroup by keyword (all newsgroups that include the word appear), or look for brand-new newsgroups (new ones are formed all the time). Clicking on any one newsgroup will display the headlines (or "headers") for the messages, the users' names, and posting dates.

Once you know a newsgroup's name, you can reach it if you type "news:" followed by the name in the Location or Address box of your browser. For example, to reach the genealogy newsgroup called soc.genealogy.jewish, type "news.soc.genealogy.jewish."

You can subscribe to newsgroups you want to read and respond to regularly, meaning they will automatically appear when you open your newsreader, so you don't have to hunt for them. Click "subscribe" or the relevant menu option, depending on your browser, then click the newsgroup.

Newsgroups Made Easier

Because the names of newsgroups and the number of messages in each come up without descriptions in newsreaders, many people use the very helpful newsgroup directories on the Web, which are grouped by category for easy reference and include links to enter the newsgroups. For example, Liszt (*www.liszt.com/news*) groups newsgroups by their hierarchies—soc, biz, and so on—with many subcategories and descriptions. Deja News (*www.dejanews.com*) and CyberFiber (*www.cyberfiber.com/index.html*) use categories like "health/medicine," "business/money," "kids and parents" and "fan clubs and celebrities" and/or hierarchies.

You can search newsgroups in general, or a specific newsgroup, for a topic, writer, or posting date by using Liszt, Deja News, Reference.com, or Cyber Fiber or search engines like Alta Vista, HotBot, and Infoseek that search Usenet.

How to Navigate a Newsgroup

After you click on a newsgroup, its list of short topic headlines will come up. Click on a headline to read the messages, which are called postings. You'll often see clusters of responses to the same headline grouped in what are called threads. For example, messages with the header "re:SPIELBERG" in a genealogy newsgroup are threads.

You'll notice the number of unread postings in each headline because your browser keeps track of which postings you have already read to save time. You'll also note the name of the writer and date of each posting.

If you want to read a particular message, click on it. You'll see something like this (note how the surname is in CAPS):

Soc.genealogy.surnames.usa
Subject: DUBORD, Charles; NY, USA; 1861–1925
Date: Fri, 16 May 2000 22:03
From: doctordr1@hotmail.com
Newsgroups: soc.genealogy.surnames.usa

Looking for information on early history of Charles Dubord and Dubord family generally. John was born in Troy, NY, 1861, married Christine Healy, 1885.

A. Shaine

It's a good idea to hang around a newsgroup for a while and just read its messages—called lurking—to get the flavor of the group and the topics discussed. Many newsgroups have a FAQ (Frequently Asked Questions), so consult it before firing off a question about a topic that may have already been discussed at great length.

When you decide you're ready to post a message in response to a message—or start a brand-new topic and header—you can post it to the newsgroup at large, or you can send a private e-mail message to one person if your message refers only to them. You can print, delete, sort, and store messages as well. You'll probably want to create folders for different genealogy topics you're researching and store pertinent messages there.

Message Boards

Message boards, also known as bulletin boards or forums, are discussion groups for reading and posting messages on specific topics very similar to newsgroups. However, they are found on certain Web sites, commercial online services such as America Online or Compuserve, and bulletin board systems, which are networks of connected computers which predate the Web. Although anyone can post a message on a Web site message board, sites generally ask users to register first with their full names, e-mail and home addresses, jobs and interests because they hope to build steady audiences who will return and foster a sense of community. Some Web sites give users a trial run of their message boards. On commercial online services, however, only paid subscribers can use the bulletin boards.

Online message boards are in fact a lot like a supermarket bulletin board. With both, you leave a note with the hopes that someone will stop by and read your posting, and then respond to it. However, electronic messages don't get torn or fall off!

A lot of words are passed every day on the genealogy message boards on the Web. Following are some of the principal players.

RootsWeb's GenConnect

http://cgi.rootsweb.com/~genbbs

This message board (or bulletin board system as they term it) makes it easy for you to post your queries and share your data in the areas where your research is focused. The boards are divided into Location, Surname, and Special Projects, all of which are fully searchable. The Special Projects boards, about 25 in all, are on topics that range from Baptist Roots to Coal Miners Queries to Indian Captives. Well worth a look; you never know what category you might find more information in.

Another way to access GenConnect is through Web pages that provide a link to it. GenConnect provides search and posting capabilities on their message boards for many genealogy Web pages.

To navigate GenConnect, say for researching records in a specific county, you'd click on States, then choose the county—for

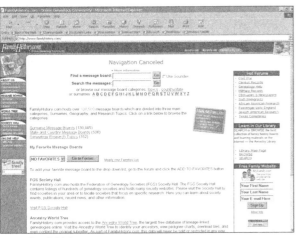

www.familyhistory.com

example, Pierce County in the state of Washington. You'd then see a list of messages, displayed in a list by subject. On this day, of the 53 messages, the subject you're interested in is Calvin Franklin Troup. You'd click on the red hyperlink to pull up the post made by Bill Rudy on Monday, 13 March 2000. You'd then be given the chance to respond to Rudy's post, and your response would be "threaded" as a subtopic of the original Calvin Franklin Troup.

A global search box helps you locate a message containing a word or name not specified in the title. In our sample, the title doesn't include the name of Calvin's wife, Sarah Moore, which is mentioned in the full message. You might not recognize the name Troup and miss the message. By using the global search, you can specify Sarah Moore, and the message will come up on the hit list. After reading the message, the next step would be to exchange e-mail with Bill Rudy to see what documentation or other information he might have on Sarah Moore. And, of course possibly discover that you share some names on your family trees.

GenForum

www.genforum.com

Here you'll find thousands of forums or message boards on surnames, U.S. states, countries, general topics, computers, and software, all searchable. The site is well designed and *fast*! Individual forums exist for surnames.

FamilyHistory.com

www.familyhistory.com

This site, which can also be accessed from Ancestry.com, hosts over one hundred thousand family history message boards divided into three main categories: Surnames, Geography, and Genealogy Research. Here you have the ability to create a set of your favorite message boards; browse through boards by topic, locality, surname;

and search for a word or name you specify. If you usually work off of your "favorites" list, do a monthly browse here of all the message boards for your major surnames. You don't want to miss anything new!

GenExchange Surname Discussion Forums

www.genexchange.org

Here the message boards are called Surname Discussion Forums. Click on the link at the top of the page to enter. You can search through all messages, or just pull up the ones you are most interested in. New surname forums are created once a certain number of posts have been made for that surname.

AOL Genealogy Forum (Members Only)

While many of the resources of the Genealogy Forum (GF) have a Web presence, the message boards are available only to members of AOL. Get there by going to AOL, keyword: roots, or keyword: gf.

When you first enter new message boards, you will see a button bar at the bottom of the message board window that says Preferences. It is here that you decide how you want your messages presented to you: Alphabetically (most researchers select this option); Oldest First, or Newest First.

Topics are threaded, but you can override this setting and set your personal preferences to view messages in an unthreaded format.

For offline reading, the maximum number of articles to download can be set to a higher number. If you set it to a lower number, you will not be overwhelmed with too many messages. If you want to see *all* of the postings, set the number of 9999. The GF recommends using this option so that you don't miss any postings, especially on your first visit to the boards.

The filtering preference comes in very handy to reduce the amount of unwanted messages. Select a filter type that you'd like to use, then supply the words or phrases that you'd like to block out. For example, select the Filter Type Subject Contains, then enter "Immigration" into the new filter box. Click Add Filter to add this filter to your list of current filters. This will block any messages with

DearMYRTLE's Weekly Genealogy Chat

www.dearmyrtle.com/chat.htm

Recent Dear MYRTLE Chat Topics

Ernst Thode's German Address Book
Five Things George Schweitzer recommends for German Research
German Biographies and Compiled Genealogies
German Naming Schemes
German Village Lineage Books
Hessian Research
How to Tape Instant Oral Biographies
What to do when you face a new locality for research
Jewish Records
Parish and Vital Records List
Passenger Arrival Lists—U.S.

the word "Immigration" somewhere in the subject line from appearing in the list of messages.

If you find a particular member's messages to be bothersome, select the filter type Author Is and enter that member's screen name into the new filter box. This will block any message from that screen name from appearing when you are reading messages.

Genealogy Chat

Chat is a way of meeting people online and talking to them in real time, faster than e-mail or newsgroups.

It can look a bit, well, chaotic. As you watch messages rapidly appear, almost by magic, in a box on your screen from a dizzying number of screen names, you'll have to scramble at first to keep track of who said what. In style and pace, live chat is different from the more organized world of newsgroups and bulletin boards, where you can read and answer messages at your leisure, often days after the original posting.

This means people in newsgroups and message boards, many of which have FAQs to create order, tend to think more before they type. The immediate nature of chat often means people blurt out the first thing that comes to mind.

But chat is very popular all over the world. Places to chat, called chat rooms—the room is virtual, as is everything else online—can be found on commercial online services, on Web sites ranging from some search engines to communities of common interests, and in Internet Relay Chat (more about this below). Chat rooms can be general or focused around one topic. Chats can be ongoing or scheduled at certain times featuring guest speakers, which can be very helpful to your research.

For me one of the most interesting parts of online genealogy research is the chance to get into a specialized genealogy chat room to discuss our current interests. I hold a genealogy chat weekly, and have been giving or participating in chats since the winter of 1984–1985. I've made many friends in this way, brought together by our love of genealogy. In fact, one of the first people I met in a genealogy chat room I got to know so well, when we finally met we picked the Family History Library in Salt Lake City as our meeting place!

There are lots of genealogy chat rooms in operation all over the Web. The most heavily attended by far are the genealogy chat rooms on AOL in the Genealogy Forum, but, as mentioned earlier in this chapter, you have to be a member of AOL to get in. Other chat rooms require some sort of software, or JAVA-capable Web browsers.

Chat room hosts tend to be helpful and understanding of "newbie" chatters. As in newsgroups or message boards, it's a good idea to hang out for a while and see what the others are saying in the chat room. Sometimes chats are informal, disorganized things. Other times, guest speakers make presentations explaining the assigned topic, software, book, or Web site, and questions are asked by members. Before too long you'll get the hang of it, but always respect the "rhythm" of a chat room to understand its goals—and to know whether you like it!

How to Chat: Software

Most genealogy chats on the Web require chat software.

Internet Relay Chat, or IRC, is a medium where people choose among thousands of channels, or different topics, worldwide and chat with this special software. Popular software includes mIRC for PCs, and Ircle for Macintoshes. Both can be downloaded free from the TUCOWS (*www.tucows.com*) Web site.

You need an IRC server, though most ISPs and commercial online services have them. If not, find the closest IRC to you through one of the biggest networks of IRC servers, such as EFnet (*www.irchelp.org*), Undernet (*www.undernet.org*) or DALnet (*www.dal.net*). Detailed information on using IRC, including lists of channels that you can search by topic—which show the names of chat rooms and numbers of chatters—and locations of servers can be found at their Web sites.

Extreme Chat

Generations: Find Your RootsWebCast— *www.sierra.com/sierrahome/ familytree/webcast* They call this "the Internet's only fully interactive genealogy talk show." Besides a computer with speakers, all you'll need is the current version of Real Player (available as a free download at this site) to hear the show. Listen to the broadcast and watch the special chat room screen, where you can read the threads of related conversations, see changing graphics, click to get to Web pages being discussed, and respond to an opinion poll. And, as with any radio talk shows, you can even call the 800 number and ask a question of the guest speaker. Guests are noted authors and lecturers, and editors and publishers in the field of genealogy and family history.

When you contact an IRC server, list the screen name you want to use for chats, and omit your full name and e-mail address if you want to remain anonymous.

Once you connect to the server, a list of channels will appear in a window on your screen. Click on one you want and people's screen names will appear along the side. All chat networks have channels for newcomers called "#newbies" (all IRC channels start with the symbol "#") or something similar. Genealogy chat rooms are called "#genealogy" or something in that category.

To get to my chat room, click on "#DearMYRTLE" on the channel folder listing and click the "Join" button.

Some Places to Talk Ancestors

- DearMYRTLE's Chats
  www.dearmyrtle.com
- Genealogy Forum on IRC
  www.home.flash.net/~gen4m. These folks have been around a good while, providing interesting chats to Internet users regardless of their ISP or online service affiliation.
- Genealogy on IRC
  www.genealogy.org/~jkatcmi/genealogy-irc/welcome.html. Be sure to check out the FAQ first. It helps unravel the mystifying confusion of Internet chats.
- International Internet Genealogy Society (IIGS)
  www.iigs.org/irc/index.htm.en. Exclusively for genealogy, the IIGS Internet Relay Chat is hosted by RootsWeb and is open 7 days a week, 24 hours per day so genealogists around the world can meet. If not many people seem to be online, "stay for a while, or try again later," is their advice.

Genealogy's Most Wanted Chat Page

www.citynet.net/mostwanted

This page is designed as a chat site to chat about a surname or a person who is "Most Wanted" in your research. Or you might come to the aid of another researcher requesting help. The researcher's e-mail address or snail mail address is provided should you have any information or leads to assist them in the search for his or her "Most Wanted."

Read some of the "Capture Stories" here about success in "capturing" a most wanted name or event. Another popular feature of the site is queries concerning adoption.

Family-Only: Private Chats MyFamily.com

www.myfamily.com

This is the place to set up a private family chat site, and invite members of your family to participate. There are two chat options, one involving voice chats, an innovative approach to family communication. No one but invited members may attend these chats.

Members Only: AOL's Genealogy Chat Rooms

Here you can visit six main genealogy chat rooms and an "auditorium" for special guest speaker events. The Genealogy Forum on AOL says: "Chats are hosted by our knowledgeable, experienced volunteer staff members. We now have over one hundred and forty such experts ready, willing and able to give you helpful advice."

It may seem partisan to say so, but AOL does seem to attract a huge number of online genealogists, and the chat rooms are very active and interesting. AOL keywords: roots or gf.

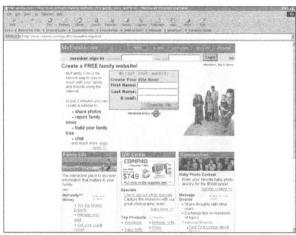

www.myfamily.com

CHAPTER FOURTEEN

Mining Mailing Lists

ailing lists are discussions on specific topics conducted entirely by e-mail. Messages go to all the people who subscribe to the list, which may be hundreds or thousands worldwide. Subscribers are usually passionate about the subject under discussion. If you crave a full mailbox, join a mailing list or two. But be aware, many are not totally open to the public and may be local, regional, or screened by a moderator who may want to know more about you before you join.

Genealogy mailing lists are a great way for you to join a group of like-minded researchers to focus on a surname, a locality, ethnic group, or even a software program. Although one is said to "subscribe" to a mailing list, there are no charges involved. They've got mailing lists for newbie researchers, for selling genealogy supplies and books, and for virtually every surname and locality you can think of. In fact, if no list interests you (and I would be surprised if that was the case) then by all means offer to be a volunteer host and create your own list topic. It's not that hard, and can be rewarding in many ways.

After subscribing to a list, it's always advised to "lurk" for a while. This means you'll just read the mail for a few days or weeks just to watch what types of communications are going back and forth. You don't want to come on like gangbusters and turn off everyone in the group. Be thoughtful in the composition of your list postings. It's considered bad netiquette to "flame" others, so keep your more fiery opinions in check. Remember that typing in ALL CAPS is considered yelling, but in genealogy e-mail it is acceptable to use CAPS for the surname in a query.

RootsWeb and FamilySearch are the main sites that service and index genealogy mailing lists, so we'll discuss them first.

How Mailing Lists Work
RootsWeb Mailing Lists Index

www.rootsweb.com/~maillist

The majority—over six thousand—of genealogy mailing lists are serviced by RootsWeb. Let's look at the steps for subscribing and

Mailing List Netiquette

WRONG

To: Smith-L@rootsweb.com
From: JohnDoeSmith12345@aol.com
SUBJECT: [blank]
I hear you've got some info on my Smith line in the U.S. and Canada. I'd appreciate your sending all you've got.

RIGHT

To: Smith-L@rootsweb.com
From: JohnDoeSmith12345@aol.com
SUBJECT: SMITH, Sidney Bailey, 1891–97
My deceased grandfather, Sidney Bailey SMITH (born 17 Jul 1891 at Norton Subconcourse, Norfolk, England) married 1st—Elise Mary SLOAN (born 22 Sep 1897 at Birkenhead, Chestershire, England. Died 4 May 1955 at Cardston, Alberta, Canada.)
Looking for proof that he is the son of: George and Emma (EASTER) SMITH, as it states in the Family Search Ancestral File, where his number is: (AFN: 46QG-V7).
Thanks, John

From the "right" example, the other members of the mailing list can see just how much work you've done on your own. Genealogists are usually quite open about sharing documentation and their ideas of how to go forward with research in a particular locality. Show them you aren't expecting it to be delivered on a silver platter.

unsubscribing from these mailing lists. Following is a list of key terms, universal to all mailing lists.

SUBSCRIBE—a single word sent in e-mail to instruct the mailing list "robot" to look for your return e-mail address and add it to the recipient list of the genealogy list you specified.

UNSUBSCRIBE—a single word sent in e-mail to instruct the mailing list "robot" to look for your return e-mail address, and remove it from the list of members of the genealogy list you specified.

LIST MODE: A preference: you'll receive each and every message a few minutes after it is sent to the list.

DIGEST MODE: A preference: you'll receive a periodic e-mail of several consolidated messages several times a week or so, depending on the level of activity of the genealogy mailing list.

Every mailing list really has two addresses: the list name, where posts should be sent, and the list name followed by request, where commands to the listserv (list server) software should be sent. For example, posts to ROOTS-L should go to ROOTS-L@rootsweb.com while "subscribe" and "unsubscribe" requests should got to ROOTS-L-request@rootsweb.com.

In other words, one processes your subscription, and another address processes members' e-mail to the list.

Let's say you want to join the GEN-NEWBIE-L mailing list (for genealogy newbies), here are the steps you'd take:

1. Go to Compose E-mail.
2. Type in the "To" portion the address: GEN-NEWBIE-L.
3. Type the word SUBSCRIBE for the "Subject" of your e-mail.
4. Type the word SUBSCRIBE in the text portion of the e-mail.
5. Click the Send button.

Be careful not to type anything else but the word SUBSCRIBE in the e-mail. If you wax poetic, saying something like "I'd really

like to exchange information with others researching the Elizabeth Hite and Paul Froman family, so please subscribe me to Hite-L"—it simply won't work. Remember, it's just a computer processing all of this, and that computer is looking for a single word command; in this case, the word is SUBSCRIBE.

In a few minutes, in most cases, you'll receive a confirmation of the SUBSCRIBE command. If you don't get it in a few hours, then perhaps you made a mistake in your e-mail request. You may have erred typing the name of a genealogy mailing list. To subscribe again, go to *www.rootsweb.com/~maillist*. Click on the hyperlink for the desired mailing list and an e-mail form will pop up automatically—correctly addressed. All you've got to do is type SUBSCRIBE in the subject line and in the text portion of the e-mail form, and click send.

When you receive the confirmation that you've successfully subscribed, it's a good idea to print out and file the e-mail, since it also provides information about unsubscribing as well as changing from list to digest mode or vice versa.

RootsWeb Mailing Lists Interactive Search

http://lists.rootsweb.com

Since the majority of genealogy mailing lists are serviced by RootsWeb, this search capability is essential. You'll be able to search the archive of previous messages, getting up to speed on what's already been discussed. Here's how it works:

1. On the Interactive Search screen type in the name of the mailing list; for example the surname list called WASDEN-L.
2. Once RootsWeb locates the correct archives, the next screen allows you to specify the word or phrase you want, and the year you wish to search. WASDEN-L has been around since 1996 so you've got the option of searching the archive for individual years '96, '97, '98, '99, or 2000.

In this way, you can locate, view, and print out any relevant messages you've missed, lost, or wish to view again. It works the same way for any "@rootsweb.com" mailing list.

A Few Things to Remember

- If you connect with someone on a mailing list who has documents to send, remember your manners and reimburse that distant cousin for photocopy and postage expenses.

- Don't ever give out your password or credit card to someone on a mailing list.

- As a security precaution, many active genealogists refer people only to a post office box or private mail service such as Mail Boxes, Etc. You can never be too careful.

FamilySearch

www.familysearch.org/Share/signon.asp
FamilySearch offers another huge group of mailing lists. After signing in with a user name and password you choose for registering on this free site, you'll be taken to the first mailing list screen. Here you'll be able to sign up for the genealogy mailing lists maintained by the servers at FamilySearch. If you want to add items to your list, click the tab for "View All Lists" and search for the surname you specify. Sometimes there is more than one related mailing list. Specify one, and click to join the list. Before long, e-mail will be arriving from other active members of the list. You can also elect to become a "list owner" by creating a new list, if there isn't one that covers your surname, locality, or ethnic group.

John Fuller's Page

www.rootsweb.com/~jfuller/gen-mail.html
The "mega listing" award for genealogy mailing lists goes hands-down to webmaster John Fuller. Though he is indexing, not actually servicing these lists, you can subscribe from this site. He also makes the announcements of new mailing lists for RootsWeb, the server for most of the popular genealogy mail lists. Even Web site indexing champion Cyndi Howells (of *www.cyndislist.com*) refers people to John's list.

His mailing list categories include virtually every country in the world, Cemeteries/Monuments/Obituaries, Computing/Internet Resources, Software, and Wars/Military.

"Read-Only" Mailing Lists

These read-only lists are actually electronic newsletters, sometimes called e-zines, which anyone can subscribe to and receive in e-mail on a daily, weekly, or monthly basis, depending on the author's or editors' whims. These differ from a conventional mailing list in that subscribers don't contribute to the content, they just read it.

(Although in most cases you can e-mail the author/editor on your own if you have a question or wish to comment on an issue.)

My own daily DearMYRTLE'S Daily Genealogy Column, is viewable daily at *www.dearmyrtle.com*, and can be subscribed to at the site. Here are some other newsletters of interest:

Ancestry Daily News

www.ancestry.com

Go to Ancestry's main page to subscribe to its free newsletter of family history tips, news, and updates. It's available on a daily or weekly basis; you make the choice when you sign up. Articles in June 2000 included: "Discovering Those Ancestors from Poland: Helpful Publications" and "Copyright Issues: An Open Letter from the Author of 'Old Calvary Cemetery—New Yorkers Carved in Stone.'"

USGenWeb Archives News

www.rootsweb.com/~usgenweb/newsletter/index.htm

This weekly newsletter describes the updates and newest submissions to the USGenWeb Archives. You may find such terms as wills, obituaries, letters, biographical sketches, county and township histories, censuses, cemeteries, etc.

Everton's Family History Newsline

www.everton.com

Everton's has been publishing the non-electronic *Genealogical Helper Magazine* since 1947, and are up to the ninth edition of the all-time favorite *Handbook for Genealogists*, so you certainly will want their five days a week e-zine. To subscribe, go to their home page, type your e-mail address in the box provided, then click the "Join" button.

Family Tree Finders

www.sodamail.com/site/ftf.shtml

Rhonda McClure, on staff at RootsWeb and former genealogy expert for MSN, sends out a fantastic daily column Monday through Friday each week. To subscribe via the Web, go to the URL above, enter your e-mail address, and click to check the newsletter you

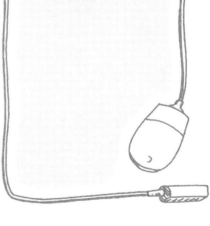

There are hundreds of genealogy mailing lists. To give you an idea of what's out there, see the Appendices for:

- Ethnic Groups Mailing Lists
- History Mailing Lists
- Localities
- Surnames

wish to receive. To subscribe via e-mail send a blank e-mail message to: *join-family-tree-finders@gt.sodamaillcom*.

Heritage Quest Newsletter

www.heritagequest.com

This newsletter is also very easy to sign up for. At the Heritage Quest Web site, click the "sign-up" button and just type in your e-mail address. You'll receive e-mail notices of the new offerings in the *Genealogy Bulletin* (their online newsletter), etc.

Missing Links

ftp://ftp.rootsweb.com/pub/minews

Long before their move to RootsWeb where they now edit the *RootsWeb Review*, Myra Vanderpool Gormley and Julia Case were the genealogy experts on Prodigy, producing the Missing Links e-zine. Back issues of Missing Links may be read online or downloaded from the ftp address above. For subscription info, see the next listing.

RootsWeb Review

ftp://ftp.rootsweb.com/pub/review/

To subscribe to *RootsWeb Review* or *Missing Links*, send e-mail with SUBSCRIBE in the message area to: *rootsweb-review-request@rootsweb.com*. The *Review* is edited by the same dynamic duo as *Missing Links*. Both come to your e-mail box once a week.

Treasure Maps Genealogy Newsletter

www.firstct.com/fv/sub.html

Robert Ragan of Jacksonville, Florida, has been the driving force behind this monthly electronic newsletter since 1995. A recent issue included the "Secrets of How To Use Bookmarks (aka Favorites) Effectively in Your Online Genealogy Research." Ragan calls his site the "How To Genealogy WWW Site"—so you'll be getting a lot of practical information from him. Condensed versions of back issues are available.

Offbeat and Unusual Mailing Lists for Genealogists

DISABLED-GENIES-L—A mailing list for genealogists who have disabilities that may make researching difficult. This is a place to meet and network, and find out about new devices and software that come into the market.

GEN-UNSOLVED-MYSTERIES-L—A mailing list for people whose family genealogies include "unsolved mysteries." Postings should include only mysterious disappearances or appearances, unsolved murders, questionable incarcerations, and other mysterious or unsolved events in an ancestor's life. Postings should not include "brick walls," since these would be repetitive in the context of other lists.

KISSINGCOUSINS -L—A mailing list for anyone whose families include same-name marriages (e.g., Smith/Smith) or more than one marriage between the same two families to discuss genealogical topics related to these occurrences. Additional information can be found on the Kissing Cousins in Genealogy Web page at *www.geocities.com/researchtriangle/forum/2288/index.html.*

LOST_NEWBIES-L—A mailing list for people who are new to genealogy and/or the use of the Internet in genealogical research.

MOMS_N_ME-ROOTS-L—A mailing list to aid moms of all ages, but especially those with young children, in researching their family. Also welcome are any ideas for helping mothers teach their children about their heritage and the importance of family research.

PSYCHIC-ROOTS-L—A mailing list for anyone with a genealogical interest in the coincidences that occur while researching. Are they just coincidences??

UFO-ROOTS-L—A mailing list for those whose ancestors arrived from outer space to make connections with others sharing this problem, discuss their ancestry, and provide advice on possible avenues for further research.

WORDS-L—Take a break from genealogy! This list provides a light-hearted discussion of English-English/American-English phrases and how they might have originated. These phrases have been passed down to us by our ancestors and have become part of our heritage (e.g., saved by the bell, turn the tables, the whole nine yards, the upper crust). Visit The Gene Pool's growing collection of phrases at *www.rootsweb.com/~genepool.*

CHAPTER FIFTEEN

The Family Database

Great Genealogy Software

For PC Users

Brother's Keeper
*http://ourworld.compuserve.
com/homepages/
Brothers_Keeper/*

Cyndi's List
*www.cyndislist.com/
software.htm*

Clooz
www.clooz.com/

Deed Mapper
www.ultranet.com/~deeds/

Legacy
www.legacyfamilytree.com/

For Mac Users

Reunion
www.leisterpro.com/

What a difference 50 years makes! A half-century ago, before computers and photocopy machines, a person would have to painstakingly handwrite or type a genealogy. After all this hard work, how did you make copies of the material for other family members? You had two choices: use carbon paper, making one or two hard-to-read copies; or, take the pages to a printer, be charged to have them typeset, and then pay huge sums to have it offset-printed on a printing press.

Today, you can publish your own family history book very easily. Self-publishing has now become a snap with computers. You can print as many copies as you want, or as you can afford at Kinko's. And, unlike even a decade ago, computers let you produce attractive fonts, page layouts, maps, charts, and quality copies of photographs.

But we're getting ahead of ourselves a little bit here, because you're likely still engaged in hunting down vital records or, more likely, haven't yet started because you're reading this book first! But as you accumulate your family's basic records, you'll be recording them. First on paper, then, as you move further into the cyber-age way to keep records, a genealogy software program.

In your note-taking stage, your computer can still help out. Printable forms can be found on the Web, ready for the down-loading. Let's take a look at these forms and what goes into them.

Saving Genealogy Records: Stage I
Family Group Sheets

You need to make crystal clear who the family group is that you will be presenting on each branch of your family tree. To do that, the names and descriptions of relationships should be recorded on a family group sheet.

Each sheet contains one family: mother (with maiden name), father, and children; their birth and death dates.

Blank forms for family group sheets are available online. Some of the forms are in Acrobat Reader format. If you don't already have Acrobat on your computer, just click the symbol on the site and it will be downloaded (it's a great free program from Adobe). Find family group sheets at:

www.familysearch.org/sg/FamGrpRe.html
www.ancestry.com/save/charts/familysheet.htm
www.everton.com/charts/freeform.html
www.sierra.com/sierrahome/familytree/gencorner/infosheets

Pedigree Charts

The pedigree chart, or ancestry chart, is your basic family tree. It begins with you, then shows your parents, grandparents, great-grandparents, great-great grandparents, etc. The charts usually go back four or five generations, although of course you can go back as far as you want if you can find the records.

Genealogy software programs make pedigree charts infinitely more easy to create—as far as drawing the chart goes and filling out the blanks, not finding the facts. Software also facilitates creating a pedigree chart based on anyone whose name is entered in the program.

In your basic research, however, you'll want to download some printable chart forms to keep track. Find pedigree charts in the back of this book or at:

www.familysearch.org/sg/PedChart.html
www.everton.com/charts/freeform.html

Other Records of Your Records

A correspondence record helps you keep track of those you have corresponded with in your research and whether or not you have received an answer.

When you research a relative, remember that other people were a part of your relatives' lives—living next door to them, attending the same school, belonging to the same church, or serving in the same military unit. Sometimes your ancestors' associates kept diaries, wrote letters, or recorded their own life stories in which they tell about the place and time when your relatives were there, too.

Laptop-Friendly Genealogy

The Master Genealogist—
www.whollygenes.com
When visiting a library or archive with a laptop, this is a handy, compact program, for Windows or DOS. The records for an individual are right there on the main screen in a scrollable list box. No more having to dig in your notes. The Web site has a feature that measures TMG against other popular programs across more than 350 feature categories.

Caveat Emptor

Here are some guidelines about secure Web sites and the protection of your credit card:

1. When in doubt, use the 800 number provided for sales. You'll usually find one listed near the bottom of a Web site's order form.
2. Look for the "Secure Site" logo on the page. This is the universally accepted code that the information you'll give about your address, phone, and credit card will be transferred from your screen to the Web site in a safe, hack-proof mode.
3. *Never* give out your password or credit card information on the Internet or in e-mail unless it is encrypted or protected from hackers.
4. Purchase items only from reputable retailers.

Those records often mention local people. Perhaps an associate of your relative wrote something about him or her by name. It takes a bit of work and correspondence to identify who these associates of your relative were. You can check censuses, organization membership lists, and property tax records of the locality.

You then need to locate living descendants of those associates, write to ask them if their ancestor who knew your relative left any diaries, letters, or autobiographical writings. Also check the library and the historical society near where the person you are researching lived, and find out if they have diaries, letters, or life writings for that location and time period.

A form for keeping a running record of your correspondence is available from Ancestry at: *www.ancestry.com/save/charts/correcord.htm.*

Ancestry also offers research calendar forms, to track by date every record source you have searched, and research extract forms, to summarize information that may be time-consuming or difficult to reread quickly.

Saving Genealogy Records: Stage II

Eventually the paperwork will get overwhelming with your folders, notebooks, family group sheets, and pedigree charts, and you'll realize you need genealogy software to keep track of all those great-grandparents and sixth cousins once removed. I've heard of researchers trying to record everything in a word processing program—a daunting task; doing it by hand is easier! Those more computer savvy have created Excel or Access databases to try to sort through the relationships. However, you simply can't beat a true genealogy software program for organizing data.

The single most important reason for using a mainstream genealogy program is the ability to type a name or date in once. Before computers, this data would have to entered *by hand*, several times in several places. Now software can plug the data into all the right places and print out a variety of customizable pedigree charts,

Preservation Tactics

Taking care of old documents and memorabilia is an important task for genealogists. You're not only preserving your genealogical past for this lifetime but making sure it's there for your descendants.

The National Archives and Records Administrations has a page devoted to the importance of archival preservation; read it at: *www.nara.gov/arch*.
Acid-free document boxes, sheet protectors . . . there is a whole industry devoted to keeping your papers and heirlooms from yellowing or turning to dust. Here are some sites that offer archival supplies for sale:

- 20th Century Plastics—*www.20thcenturydirect.com*
  Here you'll find acid-free top-loading sheet protectors for old photos in a zillion formats and sizes. They also offer archival-quality three-ring binders, including the hard-to-find legal size for those Civil War pension file photocopies.

- Light Impressions Direct—*www.lightimpressionsdirect.com*
  A good place to order acid-free tissue paper and boxes to store old family quilts or a christening dress. They've even got moldable acid-free Styrofoam-type cushioning to safely store 3-D objects, such as spectacles and porcelain figurines. They also offer excellent book titles on the subject of preservation.

- The Memorabilia Center: Genealogical, Historical, and Archival Supplies—
  http://members.aol.com/TMCorner/index.html
  This site offers a number of archival products.

family group sheets, as well as sorted lists—even a paragraph-formatted family history book.

Great Genealogy Software

I caution you not to use a program that is incapable of supporting the import and export of a GEDCOM (Genealogical Data Communication) file. When genealogists exchange these generic genealogy data files, the sharing of compiled research is expedited. For instance, in less than four minutes I can import a GEDCOM file of Cousin Rolland's data—even if he has a different genealogy management program from mine. If he'd sent me printouts of everything (about 350 people and 42 marriages)—I would have to type names and dates into my genealogy program, and not as quickly or as accurately. The import of his GEDCOM file frees me up to spot-check his documentation, and work on the brick walls he ran into that left holes here and there in his pedigree charts.

As with all things software, the number of genealogy programs has grown in leaps and bounds—close to forty are out there today. What follows is a review of the most well known and used of these programs, as well as a few others less well known but worth checking out at their Web sites.

All of these programs have a Web site, and ownership of some of them entitles you to online research privileges of their databases, as well as Web space on the site.

What's a PAF?

A PAF is a Personal Ancestral File, the official computer data form of the LDS Church. Originally a DOS program, it's now available, free, in a Windows version from *www.familysearch.org*. Click "Order Family Resources." PAF 4.0+ supports GEDCOM files, photos, multimedia, etc., and can be used in family Web pages as well as genealogy software programs.

Family Tree Maker

www.familytreemaker.com

One of the most popular and easy-to-use genealogy programs for Windows and Power Macintosh. You can download a 32 MB free trial version, or buy either of two versions—one with 12 CD-ROMs and the Deluxe with 20 CD-ROMs. Each provides a link to upload your GEDCOM file automatically to the FTM Web site for public viewing. Each version also includes a link to search in *www.genealogylibrary.com* as a registered owner of FTM.

For individual family member bios, you can scan in photos for different family events like marriages.

Family Tree Maker is also well known for an excellent collection of genealogy data in CD-ROM format, including the lineage-linked World Family Tree.

Family Origins

www.formalsoft.com

This well-designed genealogy program was created by Bruce Buzbee, who also wrote the companion book, *Getting the Most Out of Family Origins*. Unusual for programmers, Buzbee is a good writer, too. The book is full of shortcuts to speed up your data entry, and tips on his favorite options.

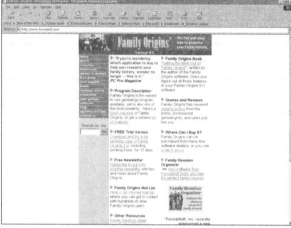

www.formalsoft.com

The Family Origins edit screen allows you to add an unlimited number of facts for every person (i.e. birth, death, marriage, occupation, religion, description, etc.). If you want to add a fact type that isn't in the predefined list, you can create your own fact types. Family Origins also allows notes and unlimited source citations for every fact.

The program claims to have the largest selection of printouts available in a genealogy program: pedigree charts, family group sheets, four types of box charts, six styles of family history books (the program writes the sentences for you!), 27 different lists, mailing labels, calendars, hourglass trees, individual summaries, five types of photo charts, and seven types of blank charts.

Family Origins works well with PAF files and the Mormons' TempleReady system (available at Family History Centers).

FAMILY-ORIGINS-USERS-L@rootsweb.com

Users of Family Origins can interact with other users with this mailing list, seek help in using the program, and exchange ideas and solutions regarding problem areas.

FO-etc-L@rootsweb.com—Another mailing list for Family Origins users. Expands beyond software-specific questions and issues to include assorted topics as they are associated with users' various projects and/or methodologies.

Ancestral Quest

www.ancquest.com

Ancestral Quest for Windows is built on the PAF database. Databases can be opened, saved, and edited equally by Ancestral Quest or PAF. Add-on programs and utilities designed for the PAF database—an LDS Temple Names Preparation module, along with some other LDS reporting options—can be directly used by AQ though it is also a stand-along program. It provides full GEDCOM export and import capabilities, so files can be shared with genealogy programs that support the GEDCOM standard.

You can also select an entire branch of your family tree, export a branch, use this to split databases, or even prune out unwanted branches that you imported from a relative or a public database. With the Hammond Maps of the World program (which requires a Pentium processor) you can view continents and countries of the globe and zoom in on a city/town and copy and paste it into your data.

Generations Millennium Collection

www.sierra.com/titles/genealogy

Windows users will appreciate the customizable pedigree charts created by this program. Although you can purchase a scaled-down version of this program titled Family Tree, I recommend the full package of 31 CD-ROMs, 350 million names and references, and four complete software programs.

Generations is the only genealogy software to provide access to the 200 years of data collected from Ellis Island. The list of titles on the CD-ROMs includes the Generations World Name Index with ancestor and living relative resources, exclusive Ellis Island records, immigrant ships to the U.S., land records, marriage records, 1800

Digital Image Census, records from the major ports of immigration, National Archives databases from the Revolutionary War up through the 20th century, Social Security Index, Civil War muster rolls, Census images, War of 1812, World War I, World War II, and the *Titanic* passenger list. (Although you are getting a lot for your money, note that a lot of these lists are available on the Web.)

You'll also find a video, *Remembering Ellis Island, Everyman's Monument* and a book, *A Guide to American Naturalization Records 1790–1900*, by John Newman, which explains how to wade your way through the various types of U.S. naturalization records.

www.sierra.com/titles/genealogy

Ultimate Family Tree

www.uftree.com

This program allows you to track your family's medical history, discover the average number of children per family group, note the age of parents at children's births, calculate the number of male and female children, spot the age of death, age at first marriage, etc., in its Heredity Statistics Report option.

I liked the spreadsheet-like Data Input, which lets you enter a large group of people associated with a single event or source into your database. For example, certain records, such as census pages, contain information on numerous people. Data Input lets you enter the information from the census document in one place and automatically updates each individual's record.

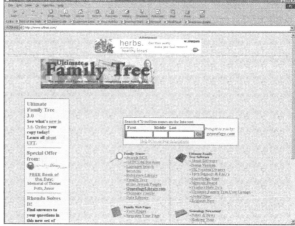

www.uftree.com

The Ultimate Family Tree offers an e-mail newsletter that updates recipients about the latest products and web site happenings. To subscribe, send an e-mail to UFT–L–request@rootsweb.com that contains the word SUBSCRIBE and nothing else.

A Jewish Genealogy Program

Available in English or Hebrew versions, ILANOT (*www.virtual.co.il/secure/bh/ilanot.htm*) allows you to store all types of information, including religious events, photos, video clips, treasured stories, etc. What's special to this program is the host of features designed for Jewish genealogy, such as Hebrew-to-English date converter, special fields for Bar/Bat Mitzvah dates and information, and a dropdown listing for all Torah portions. Through the software, you can submit your family's genealogical records for listing in the Douglas E. Goldman Jewish Genealogy Center at Beth Hatefutsoth.

Best Publishing Program
GENbook

www.foothill.net/~genbook

Let's face it, you're eventually going to have to put all this family history down in a book and publish it. GENBook is the ultimate software for creating printouts to take to your printer to be bound in book format. Although most genealogy programs have a "book" option, Rex Clement's program beats them all hands down.

Here's how it works: After you enter your family history into your genealogy software, GENBook reads your data directly from a Personal Ancestral File or a GEDCOM file—from Family Tree Maker (FTM), Family Origins (FO), or any other genealogy software that will make a GEDCOM file.

GENBook extracts the information into a Word or WordPerfect file and formats it into book form with a Title Page, Table of Contents, Chapter Headings, event notes, sources, and the all-important Index of Names. You can also generate a book of the descendants or ancestors of any person in your family tree. (Makes a swell gift for someone!)

Except for adding prettier graphics to the title page, this book-producing software has all the options and then some. In Rex's excellent manual, what the page will look like is shown for each of the options. Helps in making informed decisions! The Web site also shows sample page layouts.

I like the ability to index a woman under both her maiden name and married name. You can also specify that birth years are listed next to an individual in the index, which makes it a lot easier to distinguish between seven generations of James Smiths.

The book we're planning an index for? Read the next chapter!

CHAPTER SIXTEEN

Writing a Family History

P eople write life stories of their relatives for several reasons, ranging from obligation to recreation to curiosity. Some people have good collections of records and source materials, and decide they should write a history based on them. Others write for the opposite reason—they have no source material, know nothing about a relative, and want to do research to find out about him or her. Sometimes a special occasion prompts such a project— a major family reunion, a 50th wedding anniversary, an 80th birthday. Or, a person just finds he or she has extra time and chooses to spend that time putting together a history of the family or an ancestor.

Sometimes the productive genealogist finds him- or herself getting bushwhacked. To find and record genealogy information is satisfying, but it is also a bit dangerous. Just when you deserve to feel triumphant about finding the birth, marriage, and death details you've been seeking, you might start to feel a new and rising discontent. You start wanting to know more about the lives of the people listed on your charts: What kind of people were they? How did they live? What was life like for them, compared to your own life? You know their names, and now you want to know who these people really were. You wish you could find written biographies and life stories about them. Then you start to suspect that if their life stories are ever to be written, you might need to be the writer.

To write a biographical history about a family or relative is one of life's most rewarding—but also most challenging—projects. Unlike the genealogist, who is a finder and compiler of facts, this project requires that you put on the historian's hat and become not just a collector but a teller, or narrator, of the family story or a relative's biography.

Although the advice that follows is designed for a published book-length history, it can be applied to essay or chapter-length histories that you can use on your family Web site.

Family History versus Biography

Technically, life stories of relatives are biographical histories, not true biographies. So, whenever the term "family history" is used here, it really means a biographical history.

Biography experts have precise ideas about what makes a genuine biography. Their how-to books about biography writing are not designed to help you write a personal family biography. The true biographers assert that a biography must get inside the mind and soul of the person, and reveal his or her motivations and near-total personality. To do that, true biographers must have access to extensive introspective writings by the person or do many in-depth interviews with him or her.

Biographers warn against throwing in every detail about the subject, and they advise you to selectively use only the important information. But, those who write *family histories* are usually so glad to find any details at all about their relatives that they feel no hesitancy in including almost all of what they have discovered.

One lesson to learn from true biographers, however, is that you should do all you can to find and explain the "essence" of the person you are writing about. In other words, what is or was that person like? If at all possible, you should let the reader know what the main personality traits of your subject are or were.

Not Just the Facts

Just like 1 + 1 = 2, good history happens when you add good records to a good explanation of what the records say. Written as an equation, this is: *Records + Interpreter = History*

Therefore, your task as a family biographer is twofold. First, you must search hard and locate records that contain history information about the person. Second, you must study those records, decide what they tell you, and then write the story that your findings provide as well as you can.

Capture the "Essence"

If you had to describe your own mother by using only five adjectives, what ones would best do so? Not just any five adjectives—the very best ones. Then, using that list, can you tell a story about her or an experience of hers that illustrates each of the five descriptions?
When you do such an exercise, you get closer to what the true biographers say should be done—capturing the personality of the person.

Decisions, Decisions

- *Do you want to write an essay or book?*

    What final product do you envision? Do you hope to complete an essay or chapter-length history? Do you hope to produce a nicely bound book, a computer-printed booklet, or perhaps a booklet with scanned photos and text?

- *How many people or generations should you include?*

    Do you intend to write mostly about just one particular relative? About one couple and their family? About two or three generations of one side of the family?

- *Who is your intended audience?*

    Are you writing just for family insiders or also for the Web community beyond the family? Are you writing for the adult readers in the family, or do you want your history to appeal to teenage readers or even children as well? Your choice of audience will shape what and how you tell the story.

Once you've come close to answering those questions, you are ready to put on the historian's hat and get to work.

Chronological or Topical?

When writing about someone's life, you have to figure out when to deal with his or her life in chronological order and when to deal with it by topics. These two concerns, chronology and subject, constantly intersect through a person's life. For example, normally you would tell a life story in life-stage order, with each stage serving as a separate chapter:

1. Roots, or the person's family heritage up to his/her birth
2. Birth, including family setting into which the person was born
3. Pre-school childhood
4. Childhood, perhaps through grade school
5. Adolescent years

6. Coming of age as a young adult
7. Young parenting years
8. Later parenting years
9. Empty-nest years and retirement
10. Death and legacy

However, during each of these stages, a person is repetitively involved with the same types of life topics, such as:

A. Economics, income, work, career
B. Living arrangements
C. Family developments (birth of sibling, death of grand-parent, etc.)
D. Extended-family involvements
E. Health
F. Education
G. Hobbies, interests, talents
H. Church/religion
I. Annual holidays
J. Vacations
K. Friendships
L. Current events

Normally, you would write a person's life story using the chronological approach, and in each time period you would cover most of topics A to L, which are a part of every stage in a person's life. However, you'll probably do most of the life story in chronological, life-stage order, with occasional short detours to deal with some particular matter or topic that involves several time periods. For example, in one section you might choose to talk about the person's contacts with extended family (grandparents, uncles, aunts, etc.) during his/her entire lifetime.

One approach is vertical, the other horizontal. In chart form (see page 190), based on the two lists just given—the life-stage list (1–10) and the topical list (A–L)—here is what you face when deciding how to tell about a person's life:

Family History Filing

A typical family history file system contains a separate file for each of these groupings:

- Address file: names, addresses, and phone numbers for relatives, libraries, and contacts that are sources of information
- Leads to pursue, loose ends to tie down
- Genealogy charts and information (alphabetical order works best)
- File for each person or family unit in the study
- File for each place the family lived
- Map file
- Picture file
- File for certificates, documents, life stories, diaries, and letters

Biography Using Chronological Approach

LIFE STAGES	LIFE TOPICS A	B	C	D	E	F	G	H	I	J	K	L
1												
2												
3												
4												
5												
6												
7												
8												
9												
10												

Life Stages

1. Roots, or the person's family heritage up to his/her birth
2. Birth, including family setting into which the person was born
3. Pre-school childhood
4. Childhood, perhaps through grade school
5. Adolescent years
6. Coming of age as a young adult
7. Young parenting years
8. Later parenting years
9. Empty-nest years and retirement
10. Death and legacy

Biography Using Topical Approach

LIFE STAGES	LIFE TOPICS A	B	C	D	E	F	G	H	I	J	K	L
1												
2												
3												
4												
5												
6												
7												
8												
9												
10												

Life Topics

A. Economics, income, work, career
B. Living arrangements
C. Family developments (birth of sibling, death of grandparent, etc.)
D. Extended-family involvements
E. Health
F. Education
G. Hobbies, interests, talents
H. Church/religion
I. Annual holidays
J. Vacations
K. Friendships
L. Current events

The His and Hers Approach

To write the history of a couple, a standard formula that has worked well in hundreds of histories is:

Opening   The couple's engagement and marriage
Chapter(s) His growing-up years in his family
Chapter(s) Her growing-up years in her family
Chapter   As newlyweds and starting a family
Chapters Careers and child-rearing years
Chapter   Passing of the parents; summaries of the children as adults
Conclusion Assessments and observations about their lives

Family History Research Basics

In school you learned some basics about how to write a general research paper. Most of those principles apply here. In addition, history classes teach several ideas that pertain just to history research papers. Drawing from both approaches, here are some useful recommendations for working on your family biography project:

Organization

Before writing the history, round up materials that contain family information. What do you do when you obtain pedigree charts, photocopies of obituaries, photographs, newspaper clippings, and other source materials?

Your collection might start out as one pile of material, but sooner or later you need to divide the mass into separate groupings, each based on a separate aspect of the person's life you are researching. Typical groupings are by the life stages—childhood, teenage years, etc. Or, if the person you are researching lived in several places, you can group the records according to location.

Some people organize their materials into groupings by putting them in separate boxes. Most, however, favor the use of file folders, both computer and paper.

"But He's *Our* Black Sheep . . ."

The International Black Sheep Society of Genealogists (IBSSG) includes all those who have a dastardly, infamous individual of public knowledge and ill-repute somewhere in their family—preferably in their direct lines. This individual must have been "publicly pilloried in disgrace for acts of a significantly anti-social nature." Search the Black Sheep Archives for your candidate, or add one they haven't heard about through the mailing list, which you can join at the site. The purpose of the list is to discuss these individuals in order to learn more about them and share information about your "Black Sheep" with others.

Taking Notes

How does a record or source material become a history? That's where the historian, the interpreter, comes in. Records are not history—they are merely raw materials from which historians extract "the story" of what happened. So, at some point you will examine a letter, an obituary, or a life sketch; decide what information you need for the history; and write it down.

A generation ago, researchers wrote their notes down on index cards or half-sheets of blank paper. Today, more likely you'll be inputting your notes directly into computer files. Still, you must read the source materials; ask yourself, "What does this tell me?"; and then summarize your findings.

Four general rules about notetaking:

1. Summarize rather than copy a quote. It saves time later and gets the writing process started sooner if you render the information in your own words.
2. In your note cards or computer file carefully document where you found the information—copying down the bibliographic information of author, full title, publishing place, date, publisher, and the page number(s) you consulted.
3. When you do quote, copy the material exactly and put it in quotation marks.
4. When using note cards, write only one main idea per card and use only one side of the card. That way, your cards are easier to move from file to file, and you can see quickly what each card contains without having to refer to its front and back every time.

Sometimes the same information belongs in more than one file or section of your research. Computer notes are easier to copy and place in multiple files.

Back Up!

Because disks fail, computers crash, power outages suddenly make computers go dead, and tired people accidentally erase files, it is absolutely essential that every five or 10 minutes you make a backup or duplicate copy of whatever you are inputting. For security reasons, it also is good policy to store the backup disks in a place separate from the originals.

Honest History

History must be reliable, responsible, and committed to telling the truth. Dishonesty and errors can come from:

1. Improper reading of what the sources say
2. Not using all the sources available
3. Failing to know about contexts of time and place
4. Not double-checking family memories against other records
5. Censoring the story by leaving out pertinent information
6. Outright changing of the facts intentionally to mislead
7. Creating dialogue and fictionalizing an account

Sensitive Matters

When you write about your own family, you may feel uncomfortable presenting information about them that is negative. Withholding information might seem noble, and little harm is done when it involves minor matters. But leaving out significant parts of the real story is not the way to do it.

Because all families have sore spots, you face the problem of what you should or should not tell. You must demonstrate tact and compassion when facing difficult family problems such as illegitimate births, desertions, child abuse, adultery, crimes, alcoholism, disfigurement, or mental illness. You should not be in the business of sensationalizing human failings in order to tell a good story, but you shouldn't write sugar-coated biographies, either. Too many family histories deal only with a relative's upright character, righteousness, and goodness, and don't portray the real person who also has flaws and shortcomings. A sugar-coated history turns readers off.

To mix together equal parts of honesty with decency is to produce a commonsense understanding that some problems need to

Don't Believe Everything You Hear: Family History Department

Michael Girard had often heard that his grandfather's family the Girards had been "minor French aristocracy" who fled France for Canada at the time of the French Revolution, in 1789. Another tale was that they were descended from the 18th-century French mathematician Adrien-Marie Legendre—which made sense, since the paternal side of the family tended to be engineers and excelled in math. Michael, a geophysics professor himself, even named his daughter Adrienne, after this illustrious French ancestor.

Yet, thanks to the excellent records kept by French Canadians, the Girards found out that in fact, their family has been Canadian as far back as 1665. Indeed, the Girards were descended from the original "habitants" of French Canada. Which, of course, ruled out any relationship to Adrien-Marie Legendre!

Adrienne still likes her name, however.

be discussed and others do not. If a sensitive problem is not central to the history, you probably can ignore it. But if it played a key role in the course of the family, then you really should include it.

Most family sensitivities can be handled with tact and phrasing. When you need to deal with a sensitive matter, you can approach it from one of several directions:

1. Tell the story in full detail. Be as empathetic as possible—not necessarily justifying a behavior, but at least trying to indicate some understanding of why and how it came to be.
2. Include the story, but leave out names when appropriate so as not to damage someone else.
3. Touch on the problem generally and quickly, but don't give specifics. "Tom and Dorothy had a few rocky times in their married life, but . . ." "John got into a little trouble when he was a teenager." "She was ill for two years and could not work."
4. Tuck the problem into an endnote or footnote, assuming most readers won't read it.
5. Make no mention of the problem at all.

Source Reliability

Be skeptical about family versions of the past. The most reliable accounts are those written or told by firsthand witnesses with sharp minds for perceiving and remembering. Less reliable are stories told secondhand by those who heard it from someone else. For example, if Grandpa tells you about his life experiences, that's firsthand knowledge and can be relied on (but only so far as Grandpa saw it right in the first place and remembers it correctly). When Grandpa tells you things about his father that his father told him, however, you can expect some loss of accuracy in the transmission of the information.

Also, some people mistakenly think that because something is in print, it must be true. A lot of information printed in newspapers and books is incorrect, so always be skeptical.

Ask yourself this question about each source you read or hear: "How does this person know this?" In families, different relatives have different versions or understandings of an event or family reality. Watch for those differences and weigh carefully which one to trust. Often, historians can't determine which of two differing accounts is the right one, so they say something to the effect of "According to Aunt Mary . . . but Uncle Aaron disagrees and says that. . . ."

Balancing the Story

Even when writing about one particular person, you need to include the people who played key roles in each of his or her life stages. Histories too often slight the person's parents, spouse, or brothers and sisters. Sometimes a biographical history concentrates on the person's adult life and shortchanges the growing-up years.

Another imbalance comes from focusing most attention on spectacular, major happenings, and not including the everyday routine that was the heart of the person's life. In a similar vein, diaries often tell more about serious times and problems than happy and fun ones, so try to give a fairer, balanced view. Also, when dealing with controversial matters, be sure to let readers know of another explanation that a different family member may have.

Proving It

Document your assertions. Use endnotes, footnotes, or source notes to tell your readers where you obtained the information in your narration. Don't just expect your readers to trust you.

Raising Questions

Even with rich source materials about which a long history can be written, it is vital for you to stand back and ask commonsense questions about what any good biography of that person ought to include. Such questions will make you dig for new sources in order to find answers. What would you like to know about that person if a fairy godmother could grant you all your wishes? What should your readers know if your history is to be a complete and thorough one?

Analyzing Photographs

Photographs are good sources if they are labeled and studied. Questioning a photograph can make you gain some good insights into the person you are researching. Go through the journalist's who, what, when, where, and why questions. Who is in the picture? Why was this photo taken? Who took it? When and where was the photo taken? What does the picture tell you about such things as the community, the way people dressed, and how they lived?

Visiting Sites

It is both useful and exciting to visit the places where the person you are writing about lived. You can better describe it for your readers if you've been there. Visiting a site, you not only learn about the landscape, vegetation, climate, and landmarks, but you can research in the local library and talk to old-timers in the area. While there, you can videotape or photograph the family's sites for a multimedia history.

Conclusions

Decide to go beyond just the facts of what happened—seek to know how and why things happened. Analyze patterns in the family—health, personalities, occupations, talents, standards of living, religiousness, hereditary traits, etc. Make comparisons between siblings or between generations.

Surveying the Relatives

When you start collecting information for a family history, contact all your relatives to find out what they have. If the person or family group you are writing a history about goes back more than two generations, do more than survey just your immediate relatives—track down "invisible cousins" who descend from a common ancestor. If researching great-grandparents, for example, don't presume your branch is the only true line of the family. Very likely, another line of descendants from those same great-grandparents has more information about that couple than your side of the family has.

A law of physics applies to family objects: An object only passes to one person at a time. That means that if Great-Grandmother had a bundle of letters received from her mother, that bundle probably went to only one of the children. If you descend from one of the other children, your family by now does not even know about the letters that one of your distant cousins has. So, you need to tap into those other branches of the family to find out what those relatives might have.

The Many Kinds of Records

Don't ask your relatives a general question like "Do you have any records?" They usually have no clue what kind of records you need, and they might think you mean only genealogy information. Spell out what kinds of materials you are looking for. Survey each relative and ask if he or she has such items as the following, or knows where any are. With each relative you contact, run through as much of this list as pertains to the relative you are researching:

Genealogy information	Obituaries
Diaries	Letters
Scrapbooks	Property deeds
Marriage certificates	Death certificates
Photographs	Deeds
Wills	Financial records
Military papers	School records
Tape recordings	Objects, heirlooms
Clothes, uniforms	Cemetery/grave locations
Naturalization certificates	Passports

When you find that someone has source materials, ask to examine them to determine how they might be useful. If you need to use those materials, you have three choices: borrow them, have photocopies made of what you can use, or examine them and take notes at the person's home.

A Young Woman's First Diary Entry

"November 23, 1930. Yesterday I went to town and bought this book to enter scraps in, not a diary of statistics and dates and decency of spelling and happenings but just to jot me down in, unvarnished me . . . It seems to me it helps to write things and thoughts down."

Copying, Not Borrowing

When you find documents and photos at a relative's home, your first thought will be to ask to borrow them for your family history. I recommend taking that relative to lunch, right next door to the photocopy center in town. I have a friend who purchased a portable photocopy machine for about $300 to make photocopying easier. This way you won't have to worry about who you borrowed the materials from, or face the challenge of lost or damaged returned mail.

Oral Histories

A 70-year-old grandmother knows three generations of the living family, but she could also know two or three generations before her in time. This one witness could comment on six generations! It pays to tape-record or videotape the recollections of older members of the family, especially when you are writing about a person or family group contained within those six generations. Often, interviews are your best sources for the human-story part of the family.

Keeping More Personal Records

The importance of collecting, organizing, and writing down information from relatives and ancestors is crucial to a successful family history. However, it is equally important to record your own life stories to help future generations carry on the research you have worked so hard to compile.

Two very popular personal history activities are keeping a personal diary or journal, and writing one's own life story or autobiography. No hard-and-fast rules determine how to do either project, but by looking at how others have done them you can pick up some good ideas.

Diaries and Personal Journals

Of all the texts in the world, handwritten or printed, few are treasured as much as diaries or personal journals. We enjoy reading the

personal journals of notable people like George Washington and Charles Lindbergh, and the famous diaries of obscure people like Anne Frank and Samuel Pepys. In family circles, we cherish an old diary passed down to us by a grandparent or other forebear.

Today, the terms "diary" and "journal" mean essentially the same thing; clear distinctions between them can not be drawn. A good definition of a diary or journal is:

A personal record, kept daily or quite regularly and by date, wherein a person tells about his or her own experiences soon after they occur.

The key words in this definition, the characteristics that make diaries and journals distinctive, are: "personal", "quite regularly", "own experiences", and "by date."

Nearly everyone who can write eventually toys with the idea of starting a personal journal or memoir. And the number who do try it is surprisingly large. Journal-keeping is popular. People of all ages are writing in diaries today for the same reasons people have done so for centuries. In our day, we have paper, pens, and computers readily available—not to mention more schooling than people in the past—which make the activity much easier these days.

What is a Journal or Diary?

Libraries contain published and unpublished diaries that have survived the ravages of time. They are hand-printed, handwritten, typed, legible and illegible, narrative and shorthand, tall, tiny, thick, skinny, and of various colors of paper, ink, and bindings. Their entries are impersonal, deeply emotional, mundane, exciting, aloof, conceited, literary masterpieces, and barely literate. There are long and detailed entries as well as brief ones, regular as well as irregular ones, and gaps and interruptions lasting days, weeks, or months. Some diarists penned 30 or more volumes during a lifetime; others wrote only a few pages.

Surviving diaries show that journal-keeping is a highly personal activity—journals are as unique as the people who pen them. Part of the satisfaction diarists receive comes from complete freedom to fill up the pages in any way they wish.

Emotional Diary Entry of a Colorado Father Whose 11-Year-Old Son Was Dying of Diabetes

"Dec. 10, 1884. Oh dear God, I wish the doctors were smarter and could discover something to cure this awful disease. They will someday, but it will be too late to save my little boy."

Two myths about journal-keepers are prevalent; first, that diaries are mainly the work of adolescents; second, that journal-keeping is primarily a female activity. To the contrary, library lists of published and unpublished diaries show more adult than juvenile diaries, and more men's than women's. Journals are personal thoughts penned by young and old of both sexes. Anyone who can read and write is a potential diarist. And, with the easy availability of tape-recorders, anyone who can talk can be a diarist without writing a word.

Why Keep a Personal Journal?

We are all busy people. Journal-keeping can be quite time-consuming. Why, then, do people continue to do it? Put simply, it brings personal satisfaction for a variety of reasons. There are several purposes or needs that journals fill.

Recording Special Experiences

Tourists at Gettysburg click cameras constantly. Photographs allow you to record special scenes. Diaries also record special experiences, but as word "pictures." And, as an advantage over photographs, words can quickly span a sequence of happenings, trace an experience from beginning to end, detail the role played by each participant, describe feelings and reactions, and explain complex factors invisible to a camera's eye. Innumerable diaries were begun because someone witnessed or participated in something special, unusual, or extraordinary, and wanted to remember it.

Some events lack historical importance but are full of vital personal importance. Of such matters as these, diaries are filled; making a goal in soccer, passing a tough exam in high school; dating, wedding plans and details, pregnancies, divorces, deaths, new jobs, special vacations, major illnesses, moving, military experiences, intellectual discoveries, and so on.

A Friend

A journal is a friendly, listening ear—something we all need from time to time. Robinson Crusoe needed Friday to keep from going mad. Diarist Anne Morrow Lindbergh observed, "In our family, an experience was not finished, not truly experienced, unless written down or shared with another." Loneliness produces some of the finest diaries because people of all ages, away from loved ones or surrounded by uncaring strangers, need to tell someone about their lives. Diaries, then, become their listeners.

Expressing Feelings and Emotions

Experiences can be powerful and deeply felt. Some events or emotions can be too overwhelming to share fully with other people. We could compile a long list of people whose journals served as emotional safety valves for expressing such emotions as anger, frustration, fear, worry, deep sorrow, pride, hope, and love.

A Record Book of Everyday Doings

Lawyers, sales representatives, and businesspeople use appointment books not only to plan ahead, but also to refer back to past work. Doctors and dentists keep records of their patients' health. Car owners have vehicle maintenance books so that they can know when to change the car's oil or get it tuned up. Parents record immunization histories of their children. PTAs, corporations, religious groups, and government agencies keep minutes of their meetings.

Diary-keeping is a personal application of this need to record normal activities. Diaries serve as minute books for the individual. Because memory is fallible, journals prevent the loss of information that could be easily forgotten. In time, such a faithfully kept record of everyday doings becomes a valuable reference book—a data bank filled with useful information about past experiences and associates.

A Family Record Book

Some parents keep journals to serve as their family unit's minute book or history. Important developments are noted therein, such as births, deaths, marriages, moves, vacations, and accomplishments. As adults, the children often love to hear what their parents wrote about them in earlier days.

Useful Mirror of Oneself

A journal, if frank and forthright, provides you with a fairly accurate picture of what you are like. It records your personality, behavior patterns, habits, tastes, interests, and progress. It also shows your strengths and weaknesses. Memory plays tricks on people. It sometimes blanks out negative things you do, making you see yourself in the most positive light. Or it does just the opposite: It focuses on only the bad and blots out your good qualities. Your journal serves as a record of how you change over time, offering you perspectives for judging development, attitudes, strengths, weaknesses, and worth.

The journal acts as a soul-mirror, offering strength in times of trouble and recalling positive parts of your life during times of depression and self-doubt. For some it helps trace out the meaning and understanding of life's purposes. It therefore is a good place to make resolutions and plan improvements for oneself, and then to record how well those goals are reached.

An Enjoyable Hobby

As noted earlier, people keep journals because they enjoy it. Journal writing can be like conversing with a close friend, one of life's genuine pleasures. It involves creativity when artwork, poetry, clever narration, and word play are attempted. Diary writing is a quiet, private time, when the person is alone with himself and away from other demands. These peaceful moments provide healthy interludes for rethinking, self-assessing, planning, relaxing, and reminiscing. Good things are experienced twice when written about in a diary.

Additional pleasure comes from reading the journal later. This is a person's very own creation, a personal contribution to literature and history, his or her own thoughts and feelings. To read your diary is to relive old times, remember old friends, and see turning points in life that at the time seemed insignificant.

For Assignments

In some college classes, instructors use personal journals as learning tools to help students discover their own reactions and ideas about the course's subject matter. Military officers, ship captains, explorers, and foremen—involved in ventures that require strict

accountability—keep daily journals for their professions. Ministers, missionaries, and church workers often feel obligated to keep a record of their stewardships. And more than one person became a diarist simply because so-and-so gave them a blank diary as a present, and they knew the giver would be checking to see if the receiver used the gift.

For Partial Immortality

Anne Frank may have passed on, but she is still able to share her thoughts with countless new generations through her diary. Her case shows how diaries provide a degree of immortality. Some diarists write intentionally for unknown readers yet to be born. Parents sometimes record advice for children or grandchildren to read many years later. Wars, accidents, and sudden misfortunes force people into desperate situations in which hopes of escaping grow dim. Such despairing people sometimes use diaries to detail their plights so that others can know what happened to them.

For Whom is a Journal Written?

Diarists seem to have in mind one of four audiences. These are:

- **The Private Journal:** Most journals are likely written for the eyes of the writer only. Either the diarist believes that no one else would be interested in it or he or she is recording things others should not see. The sense of privacy in journal-keeping allows for free and uninhibited discussions. A private dairy, then, needs to be kept in a safe place where others can not read it.
- **The Semi-Private Journal:** Even if no one sees the journal but you, it has filled its purpose. Keeping a semi-private journal means that you don't mind if someone else reads it, but you are not really writing the journal for others.
- **The Semi-Public Journal:** This type of diary is written especially for someone other than yourself: a spouse, child, friend, or unknown future reader. In writing a semi-public

Mary Boykin Chestnut's Diary's Opening Entry, Two Months before the Civil War Broke Out

"February 15, 1861. I have always kept a journal, with notes and dates and a line of poetry or prose, but from today forward I will write more. I now wish I had a chronicle of the two delightful and eventful years that have just passed. Those delights have fled, and one's breath is taken away to think what events have since crowded in."

journal, you therefore tend to be careful how you tell things so that your self-image and the reputations of others are protected.

- **The Public Journal:** Written for wide public consumption, even perhaps publication, a public journal tends to say too little or too much. It often says too little when it emphasizes the positive, gives satisfactory explanations for questionable behavior, and avoids negative admissions. Consequently, the full, unvarnished story is not told.

  It may also say too much when more truth is told. Sensational materials designed to shock and excite the public are intentionally added, or lies are inserted to enhance the marketability of the journal or to damage the enemy's reputation. Even with the public as the intended audience, though, a diarist can write a reasonably honest account–and many do.

Not surprisingly, there seems to be a direct correlation between how private a journal is and how honest its content is.

Children's Diaries

Some five- year- olds have written simple diaries, but at age nine or 10 is a more typical time for children to start keeping a diary. It is a good idea for parents to give a child a blank-page or lock-and-key diary as a gift. That may encourage a child to start a diary, or it may simply be there when some interest sparks a while later.

Some parents keep a diary for a child who is too young to be able to write. They ask the child what should be written down, and then they do it. In the middle grades, some teachers require students to keep some kind of journal containing reactions to reading materials or class projects.

Parenting experts overwhelmingly agree, however, that parents should never read a son or daughter's diary without permission. Respect their privacy. After all, that's what most journals are about.

Keeping a Computerized Diary

Lots of people have taken advantage of advancing technology and they have decided to keep computerized journals. Three cautions need to be heeded by those keeping diaries on computer: First, make a backup copy for each entry and keep it on disk. Second, print out the diaries after each month or two of entries, creating a hard copy on paper in case the disk becomes damaged. Third, when you upgrade to new word-processing software, upgrade past diary entries into the newer software from the old disks.

Typed entries are easier and less time consuming than handwritten ones, so they tend to be longer, more detailed and more legible. On the down side, they are a little less personal than those written on paper. But in this day and age, a computer is something we deal with daily and with the advent and popularity of e-mail, a computerized diary is much more acceptable.

Put Your Diary Online

A diary or journal would be a great addition to any personal family Web site. Not only is it a way to keep your family apprised of what is going on in your life it is also a way for you to express yourself.

If you don't want the whole Internet world reading about your personal life, consider writing a fictionalized diary. In this type of atmosphere you can take on a new persona and conquer new worlds that would otherwise be rendered impossible. Become a Civil War hero or a champion pole vaulter. The options for adventure are limitless.

How Often to Write

Daily journal entries are best. They tend to capture more of the actual feelings and emotions in a situation. Details can be forgotten in a few days, so daily entries help to ensure accuracy. Habit helps in writing regularly. Some diarists sign off the day by reviewing it in their journals. Others use early morning hours or lunch breaks for the task.

Sometimes a daily entry seems unwarranted because nothing of importance happened that day. If so, the diary habit is

Children's Diaries

Unfortunately, very few children's diaries are preserved. Too often the child diarist grows up, is embarrassed by his or her juvenile jottings, and destroys the diary.

In your family, if possible, encourage children to keep their journals and diaries.

maintained if you do nothing more than just jot, "Nothing of note happened today."

Dear Diary: Ideas for Writing

A few journals are specialized, focusing on only one aspect of a person's life. There are single-subject diaries dealing with such things as a childbirth experience, a military career, a political campaign, a love affair, a vacation, a writer's thought process while creating a novel, and a business operation. But instead of specializing, most journals treat a wide range of subjects, often randomly.

News of Your Day

You may ask yourself when ready to write: "What was new today?" Some days deserve but one line, others many pages. Write about the sort of things you readily share with a close friend or relative. But also tell important developments that are too personal to tell anyone else. Some events, though not historic, are of vital personal importance, and diary after diary is filled with them. It sometimes helps to select a half-dozen categories that cover your main daily activities—work, school, personal matters, family happenings, leisure, finances, etc.—and to review each one every time you make a journal entry.

Writing about big events seems obvious, but that task bedevils many diarists. The problem is, the more important events in our lives occur at the times when we have the least chance to write about them. Yet those are the very happenings that most deserve diary treatment, the ones which, if preserved, produce lasting value for your journal. Those fast and busy times are the ones that really merit being recorded. This is because the mind is so busy then that the memory misses much, and too many details of that major happening are quickly forgotten.

Travel

Travel is exciting for most people, whether for business or pleasure, and a journal record of the trip often is appreciated later. Write in a

travel journal such things as transportation methods, accommodations, travel mates, sites you see, people you meet, new customs encountered, new foods you taste, and what you really like and dislike about your visit.

Current Events

Journals often disappoint when they fail to pay any attention to major national or local news events. If happenings of the magnitude of the Kennedy assassinations, man first walking on the moon, presidential elections, Watergate, the collapse of the Soviet empire, or the abortion and gay rights debates trigger responses in you, why not describe your reactions in your journal. Tell about the broader forces that are disturbing your personal world, such as national economic trends, local protest movements, government regulations that affect you, matters being decided in current elections, local celebrations, new construction or demolition, crime in the neighborhood, and natural disasters.

Religious Experiences

A person who is in love has a dimension added to his or her life that was missing before. Likewise, a religious believer has a world of thoughts, feelings, and experiences than nonbelievers lack. Religion, like love, being a more private than public matter, is a topic many diarists write about.

New Ideas and Insights

New knowledge, new ideas, new "truths" of which diarists become aware deserve some notice. School situations produce many new insights through science, philosophy, history, and other classes. Speakers stimulate minds, as do books, magazine articles, discussions with friends, and quiet moments of meditation. Being a parent triggers much thought about what the role truly means and how to fulfill it. Being a leader or having contact with large groups of people is enlightening. Observations and conclusions about man, society, and the world make good ingredients for thoughtful journal entries.

Diary Entry of a Young Teenager

Helped Grandma with the weekend shopping. She was dead fierce in the grocer's; she watched the scales like a hawk watching a fieldmouse. Then she pounced and accused the shop assistant of giving her underweight bacon. The shop assistant was dead scared of her and put another slice on.

From Sue Townsend's *The Secret Diary of Adrian Mole* Aged 13¾

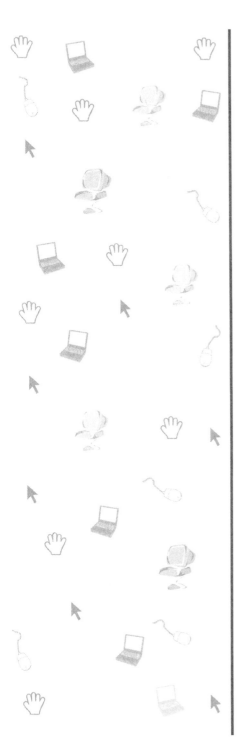

The Routine, Everyday Life Matters

Something need not be new and exciting to merit journal attention. Even newspapers carry "non-news" items about everyday living like those found in feature articles. If a journal deals only with the unusual or exciting turn of events, and makes no mention of normal, routine, everyday type doings and contacts, it presents an incomplete picture of the diarist's life. While it might be absurd to tell in detail what the breakfast menu is every day or how the business is run hour by hour, it seems equally foolish to write a journal without at least once detailing the commonplace activities and everyday acquaintances occupying so much of your time and concern.

Opinions

Like the editorial page of a newspaper, why not take the time now and then to express your opinions about politics, religion, moral issues, the economic system, your boss or employees, your neighborhood, and current music or television shows or movies? Newspaper editorials sometimes eulogize prominent people for accomplishments. Why not pay tribute to the success of a close friend or relative? If you write an opinion letter to your local newspaper or congressional representative, why not copy that into your journal? Why not express some of your value system in writing your diary? Why not editorialize sometime in your journal about what you stand for in life and why? Write about what you like and dislike about your life right now. Or, be introspective about life and its meanings and changes.

Want Ads; Hopes, Plans, and Goals

People who pound the positive-thinking drums assert that the mere act of putting one of your goals into writing increases the chance of the achievement of the goal. If you are not where you want to be today, why not indicate in the journal what situation you are hoping for or working toward? You can also record there your resolutions to change—to live better, to lose weight, to take lessons, to control a temper, to get out of debt, to quit smoking, or whatever. Subsequent entries can trace how well or poorly such resolutions are fulfilled. This gives the journal a forward-looking, blueprint role in the diarist's life rather than only a backward-looking, recording function.

Humor

Some jokes are too much in bad taste to be written down. However, many jokes reflect the society and culture of the times. So, why not include selected jokes and humor in your diary? Many political cartoons also brilliantly capture opinions and values, and current humor tastes, so why not photocopy a few favorites and include them?

Feelings

Humans are not emotionless machines or animals—we are creatures who feel and react. Feelings are the happenings inside the human soul. Therefore, a journal in which feelings are not expressed is seriously deficient. Too many journals are matter-of-fact about emotional situations: "I was fired today." "My daughter ran a 104 fever last night." "I had another date with Tom this weekend." In these cases, strong feelings are not being recorded. Why not use your journal as a place to tell off the boss that just fired you? To worry or cry about your ailing child? Or to be thrilled or discouraged by Tom's affections?

Autobiographical Flashbacks

Days when nothing particularly important happens are good times for writing non-news entries, such as expressing opinions or thoughts about everyday living. Another possibility is to record autobiographical information from the years prior to when the journal began. Some diarists try to begin their journals with a summary of their life to that point. But all too often that task looms so large that it sinks the whole effort to keep a journal. Perhaps a better way to record autobiographical passages is to sprinkle them here and there throughout the journal whenever there is a newsless day.

Journal Hints

It helps to compare a diary or journal to a newspaper. A newspaper has sections or subject areas: national and local news, society, entertainment, editorials and opinions, etc. Your diary can deal with similar matters as well, and not just big news items.

Touches That Add Interest

A meal tastes better with salt, pepper, and seasonings. Likewise a journal becomes interesting when some nonreporting kinds of "seasonings" are stirred in.

Details and Examples

Columbus, regarding his first day ashore in the New World, did not shortchange his journal by writing something brief like "Visited new island today and saw some strange natives." Instead, he recorded many fascinating details and descriptions (see the sidebar)

Conversations

Actual dialogue, as accurately written as possible, sometimes captures reality better than descriptions alone. Anne Frank provided this example dated March 13, 1944 in her now famous diary:

> Peter so often used to say, "Do laugh, Anne!" This struck me as odd, and I asked, "Why must I always laugh?"
>
> "Because I like it; you get such dimples in your cheeks when you laugh; how do they come, actually?"
>
> "I was born with them. I've got one in my chin too. That's my only beauty!"
>
> "Of course not, that's not true."
>
> "Yes, it is, I know quite well that I'm not a beauty; I never have been and never shall be."
>
> —From Anne Frank: The Diary of a Young Girl (Translated B.M. Mooyaart, Doubleday) NY: Pocket Books, p. 166.

Drawings and Poetry

Many diarists doodle in their journals. Those with artistic talent put good samples of their work there, too. If you have access to a scanner, it will make it all the easier to incorporate these images to a Web site that you have set up. Poems, either original works, or those of a favorite poet, will only serve to enhance the diary entries.

Maps and Charts

Among other scannable items are maps and charts. These can be maps of the neighborhood, showing who lives where, or floorplans of a house or office. Diagrams can show genealogy or how an organization is structured. Some diarists even include a mood chart, tracing highs and lows over time.

Letters

Either received or written, letters can be included on a limited basis.

Problems and Dangers

Getting Behind

Rare is the diarist that does not fall behind! When this happens, you face three clear cut choices. The first and easiest is to quit. A second choice is to catch up on the missed days and events, relying on memories and notes. The third choice is to leave a gap.

Most journals have gaps. Gaps are all right. They are certainly better than quitting the journal all together or reconstructing the events haphazardly.

Balancing Moods and Tones

It's a fact that diarists record more about discouraging times than happy ones, so their journals present a distorted view of their personalities. Being overly negative as well as being overly positive misrepresents the truth. Seek balance and fairness.

Writing Too Cleverly

Trying to write too well—in a clever style with carefully crafted sentences, meticulous organization, and judicious selection of topics—may make journal-keeping more of a dreaded task rather than an enjoyable hobby. Most diarists, being in a hurry and not having to worry about critical eyes, write freely as ideas strike. Like making a vegetable soup, they dump a lot of different items randomly into their journal broth.

Current Prices Listed in a 1970 Diary

"Eggs down to 41 cents this week from 53 a few weeks ago. Gas up to 34 cents from 26.9 a month ago. Bread 44 cents, milk (2%) 1.03 a half-gallon, bacon 90 cents a pound, Life Savers 7 cents, 2 pounds Hershey's cocoa 78–79 cents, margarine 31 cents, bologna about 80 cents a pound, hamburger low of 59 cents, usually 65 cents a pound. Cold cereals large box like Wheaties and Cheerios near 60 cents."

Full Identifications

To avoid confusion, loss of time, and loss of name recognition be sure to identify everything fully. That is, be sure to include full dates, complete names, children's ages, and proper locations.

The Completed Journal

While making entries, the diarist can greatly improve its readability and usability by adding some simple touches.

Page numbers
Table of contents
Underlinings of dates, names, important events, and keywords
Index
Summary of the main happenings during each year

Writing Your Own Life Story
"By Myself, I'm a Book!"

You cherish life stories written by a grandparent or other ancestor. You can read them however, only because those people took the time and wrote an account of their lives. Many people write their own life stories. By seeing how others have done it, you can gain some useful ideas about how to write your own story.

Why Bother?

Most people do not take the time to document their life stories. Writing workshop polls indicate that, on average, only two out of a person's parents and grandparents have written even one page of a life sketch or story. Indications are that, among the general public, probably less than one adult in 10 writes a page or more about his or her life.

However, in our age of inexpensive paper and pens, tape-recorders, word processors, and computers, more and more people are writing their life stories. And you can join in the fun.

Life stories found in libraries and in families range in length from one or two pages to one or two volumes. They can be hand-written or typed; but again, this is a great idea for a way to get more of your family's history online. Perhaps after putting your own story on a family Web site, you can then branch out and write stories about other family members. This way your heritage will not be lost for future generations.

People fail to write personal histories for three main reasons, lack of interest, lack of know-how, and discouragement caused by the amount of work such a project entails. The following are some reasons to overcome these hesitations in order to write a good personal history.

If you are reluctant, is it because you don't think your experiences are important enough to write about? Every life is of priceless value. So much time and so many resources go into making a human being a healthy, capable person. Why not leave some account of your life as a way to perhaps credit those who had a hand in your develop-ment as an individual? Are there not some insights and lessons of life you can pass along to the next generation?

Another reason for creating a personal history is that the effort is highly beneficial to the one doing it. In the process of reviewing your life, you end up learning a great deal about yourself. You also remember things about your youth that may help you better under-stand and raise your own children. You discover things about your parents that can enhance your relationship with them in their older years. You remember old friendships and may even renew or strengthen old ties.

Writing a life story is also an enjoyable experience. It can be a creative, fun hobby because it combines the best elements of detec-tive work, collecting, nostalgia, and creative writing.

If you record your history yourself it will be more accurate than accounts others may write about you. You can save your life story from errors of commission and omission that may be inflicted upon it by well-meaning descendents who will try to tell—and may end up mis-telling—your history.

Christopher Columbus' Diary, October 12, 1492

They are the coulour of the Canary Islanders (neither black nor white). Some of them paint themselves black, others white, or any other color they can find. Some paint their faces, some their whole bodies, some only the eyes, some only the nose. They do not carry arms or know them. For when I showed them swords, they took them by the edge and cut themselves out of igno-rance. They have no iron. Their spears are made of cane. Some instead of an iron tip have a fish's tooth . . . They are fairly tall on the whole, with fine limbs and good proportions.

Why Did You Write Your Life Story?

I have regretted many times that my parents and my grandfathers and grandmothers did not leave a more complete record of their lives.
Wayne B. Hales

My children, for several years, have been asking me to write a story of my life. Since I am now 84 years of age, if I am ever going to do it, I must start now. I have decided to make an effort before I get any older.
Jesse A. Udall

In this biography, I have tried to express my own philosophy of life in my own words, reinforced by the words of others, and I hope that in what is written here those who come after me may see a picture of their own lives lived at their best.
Sterling Sill

Starting to Write a Life Story

Writing your life story is a very personal enterprise. Only you can decide what to tell and how to tell it. However, you can learn much by taking a closer look at how others have written their personal stories.

Even short life stories have great value. When such histories are less than five pages, they are not so much a story as a chronicle or listing of the main facts and happenings—somewhat like an encyclopedic summary of your life. Certainly, the more information there is the longer the story.

Let's consider some ideas for writing a fairly full life story of maybe thirty pages or more. This history should contain at least a handful of interesting sections or small chapters.

Begin by making a time-line outline of your life. List on paper or computer the major events of your life with dates. This outline will become more detailed as you further explore your life story.

Next create a very simple filing system in which you can organize bits of information you collect. Possible filing systems include binders, with sections set off for a specific subject or topic; and index cards similarly divided. If you are using a computer (which you likely are if reading this book) you can create the same kind of files in your computer file systems.

The keys to a successful filing system are the categories or sections of your life into which you divide the pages, folders, or cards. Each of the following useful categories could later be the subject of a separate section or chapter of your final history, such as "Life Stages":

Roots and family heritage
Childhood
Youth or adolescence
Early adulthood
Middle or prime adulthood
Later years

Some people file by geographic location. This division is extremely useful if you have moved a few times every couple of years. Set up a separate file for each place where you lived, and put into it information about that time period in your life.

You can also create files for special topics. These may be separate files even though they may cut across chronological or geographical periods. Such topics could include work experiences or careers, parenting, religious beliefs and experiences, influential people, humorous experiences, and health and medical matters.

Rounding Up Information

With a filing system in place, you can start gathering information about your life—from your memory and from other sources. Jot down brief notes whenever important memories come to mind. Some people even go so far as to keep index cards in their pockets or purses for this purpose. Then, put notes into each appropriate file.

Your memory is your primary source of information, but it's not the only one. Because the memory sometimes muddles the fats, other records may need to be checked in order to ensure accuracy.

Memory

An amazing instrument, a person's memory contains a conscious and unconscious record of everything that individual ever did, thought, or experienced. However, only bits and pieces are ever recalled easily and readily. Other memories require some work to dislodge, but such efforts pay off royally. Here are ways to mine your memory.

Brainstorm by Yourself

Devote short blocks of time—during a bus ride to work, just before falling asleep, while doing dishes or mowing the lawn, sitting at your desk or kitchen table—simply thinking hard about only one topic. Brainstorm like this a number of times on each topic. Note ideas that occur.

Anything Worth Saying About . . .

Good humor, jokes
Your health
Emotional high or low
Work, job, coworkers
Homemaking, housework
Happenings to family members
Best friends
Romantic interests
Money, finances, purchases
House, home, yard
Pets, animals
Neighborhood, neighbors
Weather, seasons
Important phone calls or
    correspondence
Church or religious beliefs
New insight, idea
Sporting events
Community service, good deeds
Historic happenings
Headline news
Decisions made, new plans
    or goals
Entertainment
Habits
Celebrations
Travel, tours
Deaths, birthdays, weddings,
    divorces

Use Memory Triggers

The following topics are meant to trigger a flood of memories as a person carefully ponders each one. The list will hopefully help you to recall lots of things you otherwise might forget to include in your history.

Life Story Topics and Questions

Briefly tell about your ancestors. When did they come to America and why? What family stories survive about individual relatives? What about family traditions, celebrations, and heirlooms?

Describe each community you have lived in or near. Tell about each community's geographic features, climate, economic activities, size, and the types of people living there. What are some of the community landmarks? Who were some of the leading families?

Tell about the different neighborhoods you have lived in. What part of town were they in? Why did or didn't you enjoy living there? How did the neighborhood change while you were there?

Discuss each house or apartment you lived in: Where located? How old? Main features. Tell why you moved and what effect moving had on your family. If raised on a farm or a ranch, tell about the fields, orchards, equipment, animals, and crops that were produced.

Childhood

Tell about your parents' physical characteristics and personalities. Was either previously married? How are your parents alike and how do they differ? What was each parent's respective role in the family unit? What were the main contributions they made to your life?

Name, characterize, and describe each sibling. Tell about the things you did with each other. Tell about adopted children, foster children, or other children living in your parent's home.

Name, describe, and tell about grandparents, aunts, uncles, cousins, and other relatives. Who among them were important to you as you grew up? Relate family stories about each one.

What were the religious preferences of your parents? What church or faith did you belong to? What were your parents' beliefs about social issues, politics, current affairs, education, and race relations?

What schools did you attend and when? Public or private? Mentally walk through rooms and halls. Try to remember favorite teachers or classes. Have any of them influenced you in your career? What serious, fun, silly, or embarrassing experiences come readily to mind?

Describe your high school years. How well did you do academically? Were you involved with sports or clubs? How did you interact with your peers? When did you succumb to peer pressure and what were the consequences of your actions? Tell about schoolmates and any rivalries that may have developed. Are you still in touch with these individuals today? What activities did you enjoy most as a teenager?

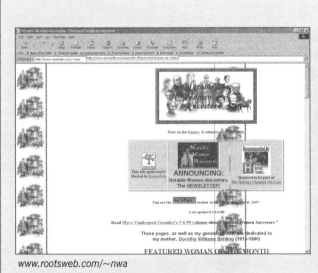

www.rootsweb.com/~nwa

The Notable Women Web Site

Notable Women Ancestors—
www.rootsweb.com/~nwa

Consider submitting an ancestor's picture and bio to Susanne "Sam" Behling who maintains this notable site—an excellent way to spotlight your female ancestors. Maybe you think she wasn't famous enough? The webmistress says, "There was nothing 'ordinary' about our female ancestors who risked their lives traveling in tiny ships across the ocean, living on the frontier and giving birth to numerous children..."

How did you learn the "facts of life"? Discuss your first dating experiences. Tell about serious romances or going steady. If you did not date much how did you feel about that?

Adulthood

How did you and your spouse meet? What common interests do you share? What things do you argue about most often? What marital adjustments were made? What has strengthened or weakened your relationship? What do you like best about your spouse?

Tell about the birth of each child and how names were selected. If childless, discuss your feelings about it.

Tell about jobs and promotions you have had. Have you made any career changes? Did you have any special training or additional education?

Tell something about your financial affairs as an adult. Which family members helped with the household earnings.

What experience did you have in domestic skills before marriage? Tell stories to illustrate how you handled household jobs such as meals, care of clothes, care of children, cleaning, and home maintenance. How did you feel about each house you lived in: its space, conveniences, and appliances?

If you are not married, explain your feelings about being single. What are the advantages and disadvantages of being single?

If you are divorced, tell something about what caused the divorce, how you and your spouse reacted to it, how you worked it out, and what the settlement was. In the long run was it a wise decision?

When and how did your spouse die? How did you deal with it? What readjustments were required? Tell about subsequent dating and relationships with other couples and former friends and family of the spouse. How soon after the divorce or death of your spouse did you think about remarriage?

Comment on your general physical condition and health from about age 18 to the present. Note any major changes or problems.

How did you feel about important political issues over the years? What presidents have you liked? How did you feel about America's involvement in the wars?

Comment on your adult hobbies, favorite recreational activities, athletics or exercise programs, talents, groups you belong to, typical weekends, cultural events, etc. What hobbies or activities would you have engaged in if you had had more time or if your spouse had let you? Tell about volunteer work or charitable work you participated in. What service organizations or auxiliaries did you join?

Of all the people you meet and work with during a lifetime, only a few become really close friends to you. These usually include a few fellow workers, employers, employees, classmates, neighbors, and people met at various activities and through organizations you belonged to. Comment on longtime family friends and close personal friends and some of the memorable things you have done together.

Discuss your feelings about each of your children and their families. What has been your relationship with your grandchildren?

Tell why you retired and how you feel about it. What have been your main worries and concerns? What new interests have you developed? What keeps you motivated?

Discuss your life beliefs, standards, values, religious convictions, feelings about your family's progress, and judgments about how the nation and society have changed for the better or for the worse. Evaluate what have been the most important ideas you have accepted, and the best things you have enjoyed. What would you do differently if you had the chance? If you had to honestly characterize yourself in one paragraph, what would you say? What are your feelings about death and dying? What suggestions would you offer to the upcoming generations about living successfully, finding happiness, raising children, practicing religion, helping society, and choosing careers?

As you can see, the topics and questions are endless. Your story spans your entire lifetime. And your lifetime is unique, so there are many facets that can be shared with others through closer introspection. Don't be afraid to open yourself up and share the details that have made you into the individual that you are today.

Family History

Within our family there was no such thing as a person who did not matter. Second cousins thrice removed mattered. We knew—and thriftily made use of—everybody's middle name. We knew who was buried where. We all mattered.

From Shirley Abbott's
*Women Folks:
Growing Up Down South*

Brainstorm with Others

Talk with others who can give you information about your life and experiences: parents, siblings, old school friends, neighbors, coworkers, former roommates, or your own children. If necessary, set up a meeting just for this purpose. Again, jot down ideas that are generated by these meetings and file them.

Visit Places from the Past

Visit old sites such as childhood homes, schools, and stores (and take pictures while there; you can scan these to a Web site later on). Listen to old songs. Read books and magazines that tell about past decades. Watch movies that recreate older time periods. In attics, family trunks, storage boxes, or museums, examine objects common to your youth, such as toys, clothes and fashions, furniture, and cars.

Use the Materials that Are Available to You

Some records exist and are usable; others have to be created, located, or made usable. Such records as the following may be your own or belong to relatives or friends:

Diaries: These are probably the most accurate source of history that you can use, especially for names, dates, and feelings. Locate any diaries (those you own or those of a close relative) that might tell about your world at some time or another. Select key quotes to include in your written account or to read on tape.

Letters: Any letters you have received and saved will contain data useful to understanding your past, as will letters you sent. See if you saved copies of letters you sent or contact someone who received and saved them (such as old boyfriends, girlfriends, or relatives).

Snapshots, Photographs, Slides, Movies, and Videos: Sort through your own pictures in order to label, date, and group them. Have others look at pictures or films with you to help you recall events, names, and feelings. Arrange to look at similar collections belonging to friends or relatives.

Scrapbook Materials: Thumb through scrapbooks or any envelopes, boxes, or drawers containing clippings, report cards, samples of school work, special event programs, certificates, cards, and letters.

Official Records: Many organizations keep records that may include you or your activities. You can consult local, state, or federal government records, military files, church records, organization membership lists, medical records, and family genealogy charts.

Published Materials: Examine old school yearbooks, newspapers, magazines, printed histories about your community and about organizations to which you belonged, and yearly almanacs that list current affairs.

Tape Recordings: Locate and listen to recordings of letters, family gatherings, current events, and oral histories.

Autobiographies and Life Sketches: If relatives or friends have written some of their life stories, their writings could tell about you or about relatives or events that were important in your life.

Putting the History Together

When compiling a life story, it is easiest to do one section at a time. Select one of the topic files and thumb through all the notes you have deposited there. Organize and group them. Develop a tentative outline to follow when writing or tape recording your remembrances about that subject.

For example, let us assume one of your files is labeled "teenage years," and that you have in it a variety of notes about your life back then. These notes can be grouped into sections dealing with high school, family, friends, work, hobbies, or religion. Using the notes and ideas you've jotted down, just start writing.

Never try to make your first version be your final version. The first version needs to be a working draft, not a perfect product. In working drafts you should try to get your facts and details straight and the basic information told accurately rather than perfectly. Polishing your work should come later in the process.

To give life to your story and make it more compelling, give details about what you did. (For example, in addition to saying that you were employed at a drug store as a teen, share some of the experiences you had while working there.) It is important that you

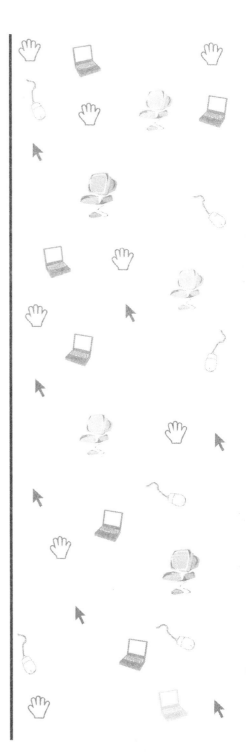

Why Did You Write Your Life Story?

To entertain the descendents of the Joseph King family, to help others remember their own growing years.

Mary King Timothy

To inform my children, grandchildren, brothers, and sisters of my life work.

Orson W. Israelsen

Chiefly for my family and friends . . . Life has been good.

Andrew Karl Larson(l)

tell not only *what* occurred but also *how you felt* about it as well, and some explanation as to *how* and *why* things happened.

Avoid the temptation to leave out problems or unpleasant events. Deal with them if they have played a major role in your personal development. To sugar-coat your history is to be dishonest. Everyone encounters problems in their lives and your history should show that you are no different than the next person.

If you are willing, let another person or two read the first draft and make suggestions for improvements. Then begin your revision. To polish up your working draft, rewrite to improve its organization, punctuation, grammar, and content. Strive for better sentence structure and more cohesive paragraphs. Missing information will need to be located and added.

Sites to Help Your Writing

Cyndi to the rescue once again: she has two pages—one on biography: *www.cyndislist.com/biograph.htm*, the other on Writing Your Family's History: *www.cyndislist.com/writing.htm*.

Family Tree Maker's Biography Assistant at *www.familytreemaker.com/bio/index.html* helps you decide what to write about. That leaves you free to concentrate on the most important part—telling the story!

Go to LiveStory Institute *www.kansas.net/~lifestor* for advice from magazine editor Charley Kempthorne. His essential message to family historians is to write the way we talk: "We learn how to write essays in high school and college, and we learn to hate doing it. Fortunately, history is not an essay but a narrative. Though we do not learn to write narratively in school, we do learn to speak in narratives on the playground and everywhere else, and we are constantly telling stories in our homes, at our jobs, and in every part of our daily life." He shows people how much they already know about writing.

CHAPTER SEVENTEEN

The Family Home Page

E nough surfing around other people's surname sites. You want your own to showcase your family history and your life story. But how much will it cost and how hard is it? Some of the sites you've seen are pretty awesome.

A family Web site can cost anywhere from nothing to a couple of hundred dollars—or several million. It can be short, a page or two, and it can be simple—text-only on a colored background—or elaborate, with images, animations, sound and video clips, and many links within and outside the site. These factors influence the cost and complexity of building your site.

Designing Your Family Page

If you have a basic knowledge of HTML and a graphic design background or flair, you may want to take the plunge and design it yourself with software tools you buy or download from the Web. If you don't—and want your page to be as simple and cheap as possible—take advantage of the free Web site creation services around. Let's look at these choices, starting with the free version.

Free Sites

Free home pages are available from some community-building sites on the Web, such as GeoCities, Tripod, and theglobe.com, NBCi.com, and from online services such as America Online, Compuserve, and some ISPs. You'll be given free, easy-to-use tools and instructions to design your own Web site (without knowledge of HTML, if you choose), select images, background, and text colors, or upload those you already have from your hard drive. You can create and edit text, and create links within or outside your site. The community, online service, or ISP will then publish your site, which will be hosted on its server, and your site's URL will include its domain name.

For example, Yahoo!/GeoCities (*www.geocities.yahoo.com*), the biggest such community on the Web, features over one million home pages in over forty "neighborhoods" centered around shared interests such as arts, family, sports, travel, and music. Heartland is for family pages. GeoCities will register your site, based on the keywords you select, within its community and in online directories of personal Web pages, which are segmented by geography and topic, so you can be found. GeoCities will throw in a free e-mail account to anyone who signs up for a home page.

Members, called homesteaders, must be willing to accept banner ads, which may promote an interest area or specific site in GeoCities or a sponsor. If you wish, you can have forums, search, and e-mail functions on your site, which can be up to 11 MB in size. (Don't forget that photos and graphics take up a lot of room.)

Tripod (*www.tripod.com*), a community site geared mostly to people in their 20s and 30s, has over eight hundred thousand members in over thirty communities of interest (or pods). "Home and Family" is the pod for family genealogy pages. Tripod members also get 11 MB of free space and free e-mail accounts, so they can pick up and send mail from its Web site.

At theglobe.com (*www.theglobe.com*), a community site with over one million members, about half under age 30, there is a strong emphasis on meeting people through chat and bulletin boards. Interest groups, called clubs, include Humanities & Thought and People & Lifestyles for family pages. Members also get free Web-based e-mail accounts and 25 MB of disk space.

If you want to see what other people's family home pages look like for inspiration, check out GeoCities, Tripod, and theglobe.com. All offer additional storage space for a more elaborate Web site and other extra features, if you are willing to pay a small amount for premium services.

RootsWeb.com

www.rootsweb.com

Probably the most spectacular entry in the free Web space arena came from RootsWeb in early 2000. They have offered unlimited free space to one and all—and as the largest genealogical entity on the Web, they have the room.

In addition, each RootsWeb Webmaster may use the space to host multiple Web sites, with each Web site located in a different

HTML stands for HyperText Markup Language, the major language of the World Wide Web. Web pages are written in HTML, which enables you to bring together text, pictures, sounds, and links. An HTML file itself is a plain-text file that can be edited on any type of computer. Web authoring programs make it a snap.

section of RootsWeb. This means that in addition to keeping track of your family, you could add a Web site to display anything, even your Tiki mug collection!

Robert Tillman, CEO of RootsWeb, even encourages users to store video on their Web sites: "If an individual wishes to share his personal experience of being at Pearl Harbor on December 7, 1941, he can—in a video message to his family. Similarly, those who have survived the Nazi Holocaust or WWII camps can share their stories so future generations can learn firsthand from the mistakes of past generations."

To obtain free Web space, go to *http://accounts.rootsweb.com/* and select free pages accounts. RootsWeb will provide free Web space for any non-commercial use that is not offensive, discriminatory, or promotes violence.

Family Shoe Box

www.familyshoebox.com

If you're looking to set up a personal Web page for your family affairs, this is one of the first hosting services you should check out. Though they do offer you the opportunity to build your own page using HTML, they also offer an easy way out for HTML novices. Editing pages on this site is as simple as cutting and pasting text and photos, and placing them where you would like them to go. This site is truly elementary for those who want it to be, and it's a good thing too! You can choose to edit text and fool around with the placement, size, font type, and color. It takes very little work to get your Web page to look just so with the help of this site. Bonus features that come free with registration include an "About Me" section along with a site calendar, photo album, resume section, favorite links page, feedback form, guestbook, and game center. They really anticipate *any* kind of Web page at Family Shoe Box, and are well-prepared to handle whatever comes their way.

FamilyBeat.com

www.familybeat.com

FamilyBeat.com claims that, in just two minutes, you can be on your way to running your own family Web site. As one of the initial steps in registering, they allow you to send out up to 10 e-mails to family members, and invite them to join your site. This is a great way to get your site off and running—with visitors—in just a matter of moments. A free message board comes automatically with registration, as does a family calendar and photo album. This is a great way to let family—wherever they are—know about upcoming gatherings, school plays, birthdays, or just about anything else you think may interest them. Some other great features that are unique to this site include the ability to have your site automatically updated every five minutes, a log of the last people to visit the site, and an area to post family food recipes. You'll never have to wonder just how mom got her meatloaf to taste so good again!

FamilyStreet

www.familystreet.com

Here's another Web host that specializes in helping to create family-oriented Web sites. Whether you're looking to find long lost family members, or keep in touch better with those you know of, this host can help. Best of all, they're one of the few sites out there whose main concern is your own privacy. By registering with them, you're assured your own private Web page that comes complete with a photo album, calendar, and message board.

More Options for Building a Family Web Site

You may want to consider some of the other Web hosting services which are described below. The majority of these sites are free for a basic site. If you are looking to have a top-level domain name (i.e. *www.domain-name-of-my-choice.com*), there will be costs associated with your site. However, if you are willing to add a "backslash dot this dot that" to your site name, you shouldn't have to part with any of your hard-earned money.

How to Sign up for a Free Site

To take advantage of free Web site creation services at *www.theglobe.com*, just type your name, e-mail address, and other information, and pick a user name for your new e-mail account on the home page.

That's it. You're a member now. Over the next few days, you'll get a series of e-mails urging you to try out different features, which are described in detail and include links so you can immediately reach these parts of theglobe.com's site. You can find chats by interest group and read more about members who are chatting and their home pages.

Members building their own sites have free access to over two hundred and fifty multimedia files to add interactive and jazzy designs, plus a trial version of a simple Web authoring tool which requires no knowledge of HTML, Parable's ThingMaker.

00server.com

www.00server.com

Register with this free Web hosting site and, within 10 minutes, you're on your way to your very own Web site. 00server.com lets you choose everything from your page layout (there are 10 different options), to the actual pages that you would like to include on your site (i.e., home page, about page, links page, contact information page). Additional features of the site include instant messaging, free e-mail, and the ability to upload files. 00server.com offers 20 MB of space, which should be more than enough space to get your site up and running.

20m Free Web Space

www.free.20m.com

Like 00server.com, 20m Free Web Space offers a plethora of free options when it comes to building your Web site. In addition to free e-mail and a choice of page layout and pages to include, 20m Free Web Space offers instant messaging as well. If the name didn't give it away, the allotted amount of space is 20 MB. Estimated time to register and set up? Approximately 10 minutes.

321 Website

www.321website.com

If you're looking to build a Web site that provides a truly inter-active experience, this is the host to use. Best of all, you don't need to know any HTML to get your page up and running, and almost every one of their many services is provided free of charge! Some of this site's great features include online chats, bulletin boards, a calendar, free e-mail, and a guestbook. Choosing default settings such as color has never been easier; all you have to do is point and click!

50Megs

www.50megs.com

It seems amazing that this much Web space can be yours in less than 10 minutes, but it's true. With just about a half million registered users, this place is certainly popular for a reason. 50Megs lets you choose just about every option imaginable when creating your page, from the file and page name to the page description and background color. A preformatted text box makes it easy for you to just cut and paste your Web page information.

Above World

www.aboveworld.com

It takes less than 10 minutes to claim your 25 MB of free Web space on Above World. Like 50Megs, Above World lets you create a page by simply choosing and typing in a file name, page name, page description, background color, background image, text color, link color, and visited link color. A similar preformatted text box allows you to cut and paste the text you would like to appear on your Web page.

Freeservers.com

www.freeservers.com

Hosting more than one and a half million Web sites would take a toll on some sites; not on Freeservers.com though. This site just keeps getting better. The steps couldn't be simpler: pick a name, choose a layout style, paste your own words in and you're done! This site offers lots of great extras like Web site statistics, counters, photo albums, and message boards. Inexperienced Web builders will be able to create a great-looking site in no time, while those with a bit of HTML experience can enhance their site through many of the advanced Web tools offered by Freeservers.com. Freeservers.com will even help you direct traffic to your site. You couldn't ask for much more from your Web host.

Freetown

www.freetown.com

Though it can be a bit frustrating when trying to register your site, one of the neat things about this site is that they actually treat their online community as if it were a town all its own. You have to "move in" to a specific address. And don't be surprised to find that some of the more desirable areas of town—Soho and The Waterfront, for example—are already booked up. You can't be guar-

anteed a vacancy. Once you do find a place to live, it's time to begin building your home page. Freetown does a great job of presenting you with all your options. They even go so far to show you the different sized fonts you can choose from. If you're not sure of where to find artwork on the Web, they'll connect you to loads of clip art. All in all, this is one community that it's great to be a part of! Additional services of Freetown include live chat rooms, free e-mail, and online forums.

GoPlay

www.goplay.com

It only takes a few minutes of time to have your site up on GoPlay. After a painless registration process, you can start building your page immediately. The site offers you 10 separate Web pages, and creating each one requires a point of the cursor and a click of the mouse. They give you a good number of choices when it comes to picking backgrounds and colors; you can choose to stick with an all-white background, or have your words plastered across a brick wall. Nothing is left up to the computer to decide. You can even add up to 10 links simply by typing in the site address and a brief description; there is no HTML programming involved. If you have pictures you would like to add, GoPlay will upload them for you. If you have no graphics available, but would like to include some, they even offer a small clip art library. Nothing is left up to you! Additional features of the site include a counter, guestbook, and e-mail feedback form.

Homestead

www.homestead.com

From the very first step of choosing the type of home page you want to create, Homestead offers you step-by-step instructions on how to do it. Decide whether you want to build a personal home page, a site for your small business, a Web page dedicated to your hobbies and interests, or a home for your club or organization. They even devote a section of their site to teen pages, and work hard to ensure the privacy of all who build there. On average, you are given 16 MB of Web space. You start by choosing the layout you would like for your site. But these aren't just any layouts, they are some of the most professional-looking around. From there, it only takes three easy steps to get you up and running: choose the elements you would like to include on your page; edit your page and its special properties; and preview! It's as simple as that. Message boards and counters are just a few of the advanced options available to you. Though there are plenty of great sites out there, this is one of the best!

JustWebit.com

www.justwebit.com

This site is dedicated to helping small and medium-sized businesses find a larger market on the World Wide Web. They offer free Web hosting, along with a variety of free ways in which you can draw more visitors to your site and—hopefully—increase your client base. A secure shopping cart and enough memory to store up to two thousand products are just two of this site's great features.

NetColony

www.netcolony.com

If 100 megs of Web space isn't enough to get you excited about having your site hosted here, how about these extras: unlimited bandwidth, guestbook, or bulletin board? All that and the low, low cost of $0.00!! The folks behind this site even take the time to give honorable mention to some of their members. There's no better way to drive traffic to your site than having that kind of publicity. Don't be surprised if you start hearing more and more about NetColony; it's one of the Internet's fastest growing Web sites.

TheRecord.Net

www.therecord.net

TheRecord.Net is one of those sites that specializes in a particular type of Web site, and succeeds at it. This is the place where, if you're looking for a place to publish your creative vision, you'll be welcomed with open arms. In addition to basic personal Web pages, TheRecord.Net is a site that welcomes you to make your writing, poetry, photographs, films, and audio recordings. But wait,

here's the best part. Because registering and creating your site on TheRecord.Net is free, you can imagine that there's lots of advertising. To keep you from thinking of these banners as nuisances though, TheRecord.Net will pay you 50 percent of the advertising revenue that is generated from your site. That's right, *you* can be the one making money here.

TopCities.com

www.topcities.com

With 50 MB of free Web space, this site gives you enough Web space to do just about anything. Also included in your free registration is an unlimited amount of bandwidth, friendly technical support, guest books, message boards, chat rooms, and e-mail. TopCities.com's EZ Web page builder makes creating your own home page a cinch. They also make it easy for you to publicize your site. One of the key steps in making any Web page successful is to submit it to various search engines. With just the click of a button, TopCities.com will submit your Web site for review to some of the World Wide Web's top search engines including AltaVista, Excite, Infoseek, and Webcrawler.

Webspawner

www.webspawner.com

Whether your Web site needs are business-oriented or personal, Webspawner can help have your site up in no time, without the hassle of having to learn any HTML. They host sites in a variety of disciplines, from business and money to society and culture. They even offer a special section for teenagers and offer all sorts of advice on dating, relationships, and the issues facing youngsters today. All you need to do is choose your colors and backgrounds and type in your text, and you're ready to go!

On the Cheap: Web Authoring Tools

If you really want to create your own site from scratch, you'll need a Web authoring tool. Many Web authoring tools include collections of images you can use, design templates to follow, and toolbars or menus that are fairly easy to use. Many are geared to amateurs and are about $50, but can range up to $400.

Some popular Web authoring tools come with your browser, like Netscape Communicator's Composer and Internet Explorer's FrontPage Express. Each shows you what your site looks like on the screen as you are composing. (This is called WYSIWYG, which stands for "what you see is what you get," and is a nice feature for an authoring tool to have.)

Shareware Web authoring tools are even cheaper, often requiring a registration fee. Shareware is software that is free for a trial period, often 30 days. If you plan to keep using it, you are expected to pay a registration fee to the developer and you are entitled to free upgrades. It's found in many places on the Web, and sometimes is available on CD-ROMs or floppy disks.

Classes in basic and advanced HTML and Web design are held by universities, continuing education programs, art schools, organizations, and some ISPs. Some are as low as $10–$25 per course.

You can also take free Web design classes online.

Even Cheaper: Free Lessons

These Web sites offer clear lessons on learning HTML and designing a home page:

- A Beginner's Guide to HTML—*www.ncsa.uiuc.edu*
- CNET's Builder.com—*www.builder.com*
- Creating Killer Web Sites Online—*www.killersites.com*
- How Do They Do That with HTML?—*www.nashville.net/~carl/htmlguide/index.html*
- Introduction to HTML—*www.cwru.edu/help/introHTML/toc.html*
- Lynda's Homegurrlpage—*www.lynda.com*
- WebMaster Resource List—*www.shoshin.uwaterloo.ca/wwres.html*

- Dave's Site—*www.davesite.com/webstation/html*. This is a "hands-on" tutorial . . . you get to test your new HTML skills as you learn them online, within your browser.
- Cyndi's Genealogy Home Page Construction Kit—*www.cyndislist.com/construc.htm*. Besides being a terrific page for learning the basics of Web design, many useful links are provided to similar sites.

In fact, there are so many pages on the Web devoted to teaching HTML and Web design that one is titled "Yet Another 'How to Create Your Own Home Page' Home Page—Or, How I Learned to Stop Worrying, and Love HTML"! Find it at *www.intergalact.com/hp/hp.html*.

Making Your Site Searchable and Linkable

1. Register your site with search engines. Click on the "add URL" button on the home page or relevant category page of most popular search engines for this free service. Fill in the title of your site, URL, short description, and keywords—which for the purposes of genealogy would include your surname and all its variant spellings, as well as special family history areas of interest dealt with on your site.
2. Link to related sites. One of the best ways to connect with others researching the same areas is to link to their sites and have them link to yours.
3. Research sites genealogy researchers will want to visit. Add those links to your site.
4. Use newsgroups, message boards, and mailing lists to announce your site. Join discussions and make relevant or instructive points. Observe Netiquette of the site or list first, so you don't get flamed for tooting your horn too loudly.

5. Add your URL to your e-mail signature. A link to your site others can click on is a good way to connect with fellow researchers.

Only for the Family: Private Sites

Why have a private family Web site, when as genealogists we hope to connect with others searching the same family lines? Well, because these private sites are just for your living family members. Here you can have a family calendar, post photos from the last birthday party, write private messages, and chat without worrying that someone outside your family will barge in uninvited.

"Being invited" are the key words here. If you set up a private family Web site, it will not show up on search engine hit lists. People who do somehow learn of the Web page address won't be able to sign in because the entire site is protected: passwords are given to each individual you've invited to be part of the group.

So if what you'd like to do is enhance the camaraderie and build esprit de corps among distant family members, then creating a private family Web site is the way to go. And as in "public" home pages, you don't need to know advanced Web page design to create the pages. The two sites discussed below have user-friendly click-to-choose options.

MyFamily.com

www.myfamily.com

Perhaps the easiest way to create a family Web site is to use the facilities at MyFamily.com, provided free of charge.

Here are the three easy steps to create a family Web site:

1. On the main page, register and click "Create My Site."
2. After completing the fill-in-the-blank Site Information questions, click the "Create Site" button again on the bottom of the screen, and in just a few seconds enter your user name and password.

3. You are next asked to invite six family members to join the site. To do this enter their complete e-mail address in the box for Step 3. MyFamily.com will now notify them about this private family Web site via e-mail.

At MyFamily.com you can:

Choose or change the family photo on the main page
Set up a family address book
Create a photo album
Make entries in a family events calendar
Post family history items
Upload the family tree, to be searchable
Place documents in a "file cabinet"
Send e-mail to any and all members of the family list
Post newsworthy items
Post family recipes
Chat—yes, a private chat room just for your list of
    family members!
Voice chat—an innovative addition
Find out who's online
Add new members
Create a new site

By clicking around and experimenting on my own site, I was able to add some birth dates to our family calendar right off the bat. I also uploaded five pictures and changed the opening picture to one of our 6-day-old Aubrey! I posted a "news item" requesting other family members to update the calendar with birthday and anniversary listings. Finally, I uploaded by complete family history database, so immediate family members could browse and download information at will.

The entire process took less than 10 minutes.

Ecircles

www.ecircles.com

A colorful, spunky private Web space to start a place for your family group. Has all the amenities: share photos, plan events, hold discussions, make announcements, and more. As the site says, "Keeping in touch is easy with everyone just a click away."

Online Family Reunions

An extension of our genealogical research is to share the information we have gathered with other family members. Some families hold regular family face-to-face reunions on an annual or biannual basis. Often significant anniversaries and birthdays are cause for bringing the family together. All too often we wait for weddings or funerals to realize how important our connections with living family members are to us.

Family Reunion Ideas

If you'd like to plan a family get-together, here are some Web sites that provide reunion planning tips and ideas for family activities:

- AOL's Genealogy Forum—
  www.genealogyforum.com/gfaol/reunions.html
  As the site says, well-planned family reunions don't just happen, and you'll need to enlist others to help you. The Reunion Center here has tips on forming family associations and a handy list of family associations that already exist.
- FamilyReunion.com—*www.familyreunion.com/*
  This site provides announcement space to advertise your upcoming family reunion.
- ReunionTips.com—*www.reuniontips.com*
  Provides planning tips and information on family reunions.

Take with a Grain of Salt

Just because you find it on the Internet doesn't necessarily mean it's true—especially when family Web sites are involved. The folks who put up that family site might have used a family Bible that was full of date errors, or may have relied on one of those boilerplate genealogical histories that are offered in the mail: "Learn the History of the Larsen Family!" If there's no scanned document or other citation to back up a fact you find on a family surname site, double-check it yourself.

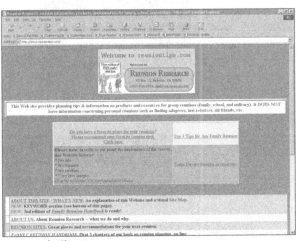

www.reuniontips.com

Doing It Online

If distance and time constraints do not permit an in-person family reunion, schedule an online family reunion. We did this once to celebrate my dad's 78th birthday. He has everything he needs, and loves it whenever our family gets together. Making the effort to sign online and visit together in a chat room all at once was just the surprise to make his birthday special.

- AOL's Genealogy Forum—Keyword: roots or gf, or *www.genealogyforum.com*
- All members of your family must belong to AOL in order to get into the chat rooms on AOL. Go to the Genealogy Forum and click on the "Reunions" button. Then read about how to schedule an online reunion, by sending an e-mail request to the Reunion Center Coordinator. Jill will get back to you as soon as possible, with a date and time set aside for your family's exclusive use of the Reunion Chat Room.

Announcing Reunions Online

RootsWeb provides a grand Calendar of Family Reunions. Go to *http://resources.rootsweb.com/~calendar*. There you can access a list of all reunions coming up (click "Index") or add your own on the schedule. Simply click the icon for "Add Event." Events are listed by surname, with dates, place, and contact info.

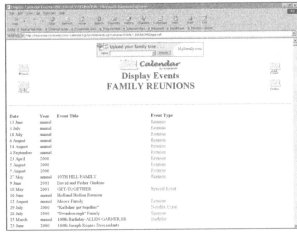

http://resources.rootsweb.com/~calendar

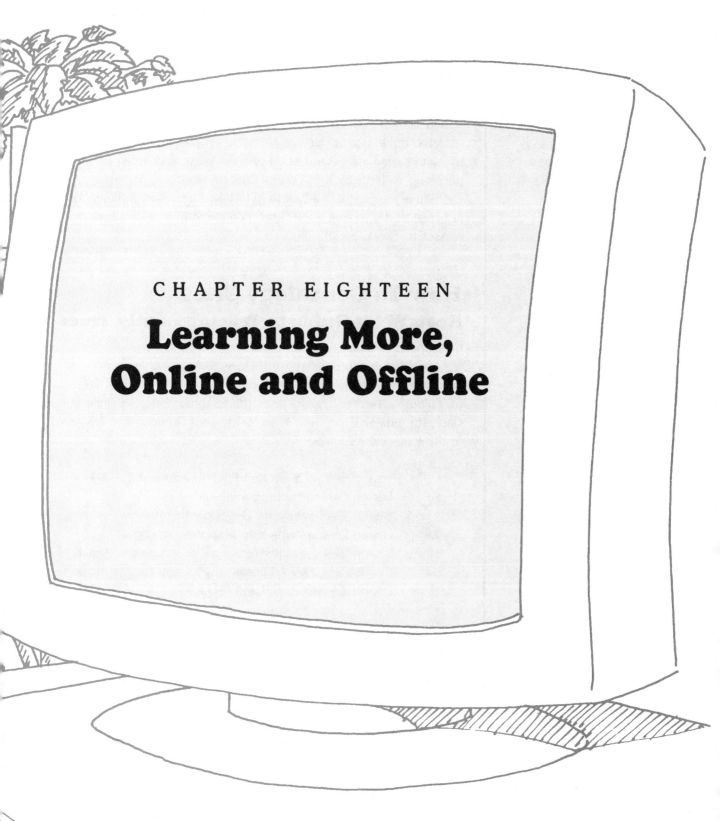

CHAPTER EIGHTEEN

Learning More, Online and Offline

A t this point in your research you may have your system nailed down and are happily accumulating records. However, if that's not the case, there's more help available online. A bunch of Web sites are just waiting to get you out of your current research doldrums, or perhaps help you get past that brick wall of trying to locate any record at all of your great-grandmother's parentage or birth back in County Cork, Ireland.

When you're stuck, it can help to take a refresher course. You just might have missed an archive mentioned in one of these classes that will save the day.

How-To Genealogy Sites
RootsWeb's Guide to Tracing Family Trees

www.rootsweb.com/~rwguide

RootsWeb has a great set of lessons to help you learn the basics of sound genealogical research; they apply to both online and offline research. The scope of the lessons, written by Julia M. Case, Rhonda McClure, and Myra Vanderpool Gormley, can be seen in the following examples:

Lesson 8—Why You Can't Find Your Ancestors
Lesson 15—Tracing Immigrant Ancestors
Lesson 19—Heraldry for Genealogists
Lesson 23—Exploring Your Scandinavian Roots
Lesson 26—Germanic Ancestors (Plus: Austrians, Dutch, Belgians, Swiss, Luxembourgers, and Liechtensteiners)
Lesson 29—American Land Records

RootsWeb also has several mailing lists devoted to genealogy instruction, where you can participate in the give-and-take atmosphere of the (virtual) classroom:

• GENCLASS-L@rootsweb.com—A mailing list for free genealogy classes offered by Diana Hanson (offerings cover Beginning, England, Ireland, and African-American with plans to add Iowa,

Germany, Scotland, and Hispanic). Additional information on these classes can be found on the Free Genealogy Classes Web page at *www.rootsweb.com/~genclass*. The list is open to anyone, both beginners and experienced researchers, who wants to ask questions on genealogy research.

- IIGS-UNIVERSITY-L@rootsweb.com—A mailing list for volunteers who are working on the International Internet Genealogical Society (IIGS) University project. Experienced researchers conduct classes for beginners and more experienced students in learning about the lives of their ancestors. This list is open to anyone who is willing to help the IIGS University grow. Additional information can be found on the University Web page at *www.iigs.org/university/index.htm*.

AOL Genealogy Forum's Beginner's Center

www.genealogyforum.com/gfaol/beginners.html

Even if you don't belong to AOL, you can get to this site for beginners. The GF has been able to create an excellent Web presence, thanks to the years of work of over one hundred forty volunteer staff members who have provided the Beginner's Tool Kit; Beginner's FAQ/Ask The Staff; The Five-Step Research Process; DearMYRTLE's Beginner Lessons; Internet Center: Getting Started; and Genealogy Forum Quick Start. There are also a set of "AOL Only" links: Beginners' Genealogy Chatroom; Genealogy Chat Schedule; Genealogy Course: Genealogy & Family History Centers. In the Genealogy Forum online chats, you can converse in real-time with hosts who are experienced genealogy researchers. Others provide support and encouragement if you'd like to venture out on the Web.

Some Online Reading
Genealogy.com's How-to Articles

www.genealogy.com/backissu.html

The same folks who provide the Family Tree Maker genealogy software and CDs have created a great collection of articles from a

Another Kind of Help: Random Acts of Genealogical Kindness

Look to the volunteers on this page— *http://raogk.rootsweb.com* for on-site research help when you just can't get there! Better yet, offer to volunteer once a month to help someone else! The volunteers for this site will, once per month, either videotape cemeteries, etc., or visit county courthouses in the county (or area of a country) they live. The cost to you would be reimbursement of costs incurred in granting your request (video tape, copy fees, etc.).

Evaluate!

"At some point you will have to evaluate the genealogical information you have found. If you are lucky, all your sources will provide the same data, but that just doesn't happen. Inconsistencies, discrepancies, and impossibilities in your sources will raise red flags signaling problems for you."

—Bill R. Linder,
How to Trace Your Family History,
Fawcett

variety of genealogy writers including: Karen Clifford; Myra Vanderpool Gormley; Kathleen W. Hinckley; Gary B. Hoffman; Rhonda McClure; Kory Meyerink; Michael Neill; Lyman D. Platt, Ph.D.; Donna Przecha; Edith Wagner; and Raymond S. Wright III, Ph.D. There are also book excerpts from genealogical publishing companies and how-to articles by Genealogy.com staff writers.

A Guide to Research

www.familysearch.org/sg/Guide_to_Research.html

This is the online version of the terrific booklet you can pick up at your local LDS Family History Center or the main Family History Library in Salt Lake City. It's a good one to share with a friend who might be thinking of getting into family history. The guide outlines the five basic steps of research: identify what you know about your family, decide what you want to learn about your family, select records to search, obtain and search the records, and use the information.

Some Offline Reading

Let's face it, whoever said computers would make us a "paperless society" was wrong. Genealogy proves it again and again, especially when it comes to good reference books and genealogy data CD-ROMs. Following is a selection of sellers specializing in genealogy books and CD-ROMs. Often books are available from the big online sellers like Amazon.com. But often the material is available only through a genealogy publisher.

If you're worried about purchasing by credit card over the Internet, then call the company's 800 number when available.

Genealogy Booksellers

- Ancestry.com (*www.shop.ancestry.com*) Here's where you'll find *The Source: A Guidebook of American Genealogy, Ancestry's Red Book*, and other essential reference works.

- Appleton's Books & Genealogy
  (*www.appletons.com/genealogy/homepage.html*) In a search for
  South Carolina, I received 183 hits, including these titles:

  *My Dear Mother & Sisters: Civil War Letters of Capt. A. B.
  Mulligan, Co. B 5th South Carolina Cavalry–Butler's
  Division–Hampton's Corps 1861-1865* by Olin Fulmer
  Hutchinson, Jr.

  *A Compilation of the Original Lists of Protestant Immigrants
  to South Carolina, 1763–1773* by Janie Revill.

  *A Guide to South Carolina Genealogical Research and
  Records* by Brent Holcomb.

  *Abstracts of the Wills of Charleston District, South Carolina
  1783–1800* by Carol T. Moore.

- Everton's Genealogy Supply Store
  (*www.everton.com/webcart/ep-store.htm*)

  In addition to the latest edition of *The Handybook for
  Genealogists*, check out their Magna Ruler to span long lines
  of type. A ruler is particularly useful with tabulated data as it
  serves as a linear guide. They also offer a Rectangular
  Magnifier with a 2 x 4 inch rectangular lens shape to study
  the small print on those old documents. Genealogists have
  been relying on this family-owned operation since 1947.

- Family Tree Maker (*www.familytreemaker.com*) is as renowned
  for its CD-ROM collection as it is for its genealogy software.
  Recent CD-ROM releases include:

  Colonial Virginia Source Records, 1600s–1700s (#510)
  *The Complete Mayflower Descendant and Other Sources,
  1600s–1800s* (#203)
  Early New England Settlers, 1600s–1800s (#504)
  Early Tennessee Settlers, 1700s–1900s (#511)
  Early Texas Settlers, 1700s–1800s (#514)
  The Encyclopedia of Quaker Genealogy, 1740–1930 (#192)
  Genealogical Dictionary of New England, 1600s–1700s (#169)
  The Genealogist's All-in-One Address Book (#115)

Do You Want to Write a Book?

"So often ambitious
researchers set out to do
comprehensive genealogies,
only to burn out in the
process of trying to produce
an overwhelming amount of
research and writing. If you
are compelled to do a book,
give yourself a break and
do a small book. If you survive the small one and are
still game, then go after a
telephone-directory size
production."

—Bill R. Linder, *How to
Trace Your
Family History*,
Fawcett

Genealogy as a Profession

There are many professionals who offer genealogical research services for a fee. The Association of Professional Genealogists is a good resource if you are considering a career in this research based field. Here are some tips:

Consider the demand for such services and your ability to organize and run a lucrative business.

Make sure you have access to all essential resources and information.

Decide if you want to have a specialization in the field.

Get certified and accredited through the Board of Certification of Genealogists (*www.bcgcertification.org*).

Be aware of the newest and most current developments in the field of genealogy.

- Genealogical Bookshop (*www.genealogical.com*) Recent additions from this genealogical publisher include:

  Web Publishing for Genealogy by Peter Christian
  In Search of Your Asian Roots: Genealogical Resources on Chinese Surnames by Sheau-yueh J. Chao
  1864 Census for Re-Organizing the Georgia Militia compiled by Nancy J. Cornell
  The Barbour Collection of Connecticut Town Vital Records. Litchfield (1719–1854) compiled by Debra F. Wilmes

- Heritage Books (*www.heritagebooks.com*) is known for reprinting in book and now CD-ROM format those old 1880–1922 county history books. Recent additions include:

  A Genealogical and Personal History of Bucks County, Pennsylvania by William W. H. Davis
  Prince George's County, Maryland, Genealogical Society Bulletin, Vols. 1–30, PGCGS
  Port Tobacco Times and Charles County Advertiser, Vols. 1–6 by Roberta J. Wearmouth. Contains the complete set of newspaper abstracts for southern Maryland, spanning the years 1844 through 1898 (originally published in book form by Heritage Books).

- Heritage Quest (*www.heritagequest.com*) is the place to order the scanned and enhanced census images on CD-ROM. One National Archives U.S. federal census on microfilm fits on each census CD-ROM. Heritage Quest also provides a document service, providing a photocopy of the requested item from their extensive microfilm collection.

- Picton Press (*www.pictonpress.com*) specializes in 17th-, 18th-, and 19th-century material: genealogies of Mayflower passengers; books on New England towns and settlers; and books on German-speaking immigrants from Germany and Switzerland to all of North America.

- Willow Bend Books (*www.willowbend.net*) has over eight thousand- four hundred genealogy books, maps, and CD-ROMs. A search for Tennessee resulted in 201 hits, including:

> *Tennessee Convicts: Early Records of the State Penitentiary*
>   by Charles A. and Tomye M. Sherrill
> *Tennessee Mortality Schedules 1850, 1860, and 1880*
>   by Byron and Barbara Sistler
> *Tennessee Divorces 1797–1858* by Gale Williams Bamman
>   and Debbie W. Spero

Book Loan Services

Researchers who are homebound or live too far from libraries with genealogy reference works will be happy to know about several book loan services:

Genealogical Center Library

http://homepages.rootsweb.com/~gencenlb/

Tony and Barbara established this Web site to spread the word about their book rental service. The fees are $25 membership per year including a complete catalog of titles. Patrons pay $3 per book plus postage and handling. Members may keep the book two weeks from receipt, and use handy preprinted address labels for returning each item.

New England Historic Genealogical Society

www.nehgs.org

When you join this society, you'll gain access to their 25,000-title Circulating Library to research right at home. It is the largest genealogical lending library available. Members may borrow up to three books at one time for a small fee. Books may be kept for two weeks from the time they are received.

Corroborate!

"Is what you know accurate? Most people would accept your testimony about your parents and brothers and sisters because you were an eyewitness to much of what has happened in their lives. But it is not so clear that your recollection would be good enough to document the vital events in your grandparents' lives. This brings us to an obvious but important rule in genealogy: although all statements must be documented, the greater the separation in time and place between a researcher and an ancestor, the more necessary it is to corroborate personal testimony with information from other sources."

—Ralph Crandall,
Shaking Your Family Tree,
Yankee Books

National Genealogical Society

www.ngsgenealogy.org

An NGS librarian, Dereka Smith, explains, "The National Genealogical Society provides a book by mail service to members. We have approximately twenty-five thousand books to circulate and all of them are listed in our online catalog. The catalog can be viewed by going to the NGS web site. Click on library, then on online catalog."

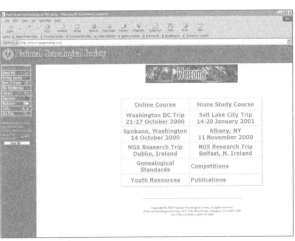

www.ngsgenealogy.org

The NGS charges $10/11/12 (depending upon where the borrower lives in the U.S.) for 2–4 books (depending upon their size) and that includes shipping. The borrower may keep the books for two weeks after receipt and must pay return shipping. They may return by book rate, which is quite inexpensive. NGS membership is $40 per year and includes subscriptions to both the *NGS NewsMagazine* and the *NGS Quarterly*.

A Great Look-up Service
Books We Own

www.rootsweb.com/~bwo

If you are looking for reference works on a specific state or country and need someone to look up an ancestor or topic, you'll appreciate Books We Own, a list of resources owned/accessed by ROOTS-L mailing list members. Volunteers look up genealogical information and e-mail or snail mail it to those who request it. Resource owners are volunteers with a limited amount of time and resources to spend looking up information. All 50 states are covered as well as most countries. Miscellaneous categories such as Medieval History and Religious Groups Worldwide are also in the Books We Own resources. See the list online.

CHAPTER NINTEEN

The Miracle of Microfilm

Ultimately, as you'll find or already know well, our online research must be augmented by original document research. Many of the parish records of christening, marriage and burial, court, land, probate, and immigration records are on microfilm.

When you visit the National Archives in Washington and ask to see federal census records, you'll be directed to look at the collection of microfilm rolls filed in numerous multi-drawer file cabinets. Military service and pension records microfilms are next to the census microfilms. In the back room you'll find passenger arrival lists and some naturalization records also on microfilm.

Microfilm, on a reel, and its less bulky cousin that comes in sheets, microfiche, have been the leading method of preserving old documents since the form was first developed in the late 1940s. Copies of microfilms can be purchased, rented, or viewed through National Archives field branches, and the LDS Family History Library in Salt Lake City. Also libraries such as the Allen County Public Library (Ft. Wayne, Indiana) and the Orlando Public Library have fantastic genealogy collections that include NARA census microfilms, etc. Such facilities also provide microfilm/fiche photocopy machines, enabling researchers to create a "hard copy" of documents pertaining to their ancestors.

The LDS Church began to microfilm records from churches and courthouses throughout the world when the impact of the WWII bombing of London demonstrated the vulnerability of documents already fragile due to age. If you'd like to know more about the process of storing microfilm in the "granite vaults" in the mountains of Utah, ask to view the out-of-print video *In a Granite Mountain* next time you visit the Family History Library in Salt Lake City or at a Family History Center near where you live.

Lately there has been a move to place scanned images from microfilm to CD-ROM and also the Internet. However, there has been much debate about the reliability of CD-ROMs and Web pages for storage, simply because the technology hasn't been around long enough to know how long it will last. In the late 1980s, the Eastern Division of the Bureau of Land Management determined that it was more cost-effective to scan its old land record books than it was to microfilm them. The BLM is now searchable online. A researcher who finds an ancestor listed in the BLM site can literally click to view and print the scanned image of the original land record. It would only be necessary to write to BLM in the rare instance where a certified copy of the record is required.

Locating Microfilm Online

You'll probably spend 80 percent of your offline genealogy research time reviewing microfilm and microfiche of the millions of records at the Family Library in Salt Lake City. There are over thirty-five hundred branch Family History Centers throughout the world where you can see the microfilm. The other 20 percent of your offline research time will be spent actually visiting those localities that haven't yet microfilmed their records.

Let's go through the process of locating a microfilm to view and photocopy an original document. The online Family History Library catalog indexes the following records contained on microfilm:

> Original census records
> Original courthouse will and probate books
> Original parish records of christening, marriage, and burials
> Original land records
> Original military service and pension files

Here's the process I followed online to locate microfilm of records for Chester County, Pennsylvania:

1. Go to the Family History Library Catalog—
    www.familysearch.org/Search/searchcatalog.asp
2. Click the Place Search button
3. Type in "Chester" (without quotes) in the Place field,
4. Click the Search button.
5. Click on Pennsylvania, Chester. (The "Chester list" includes around twenty localities, ranging from Nova Scotia to Idaho.)

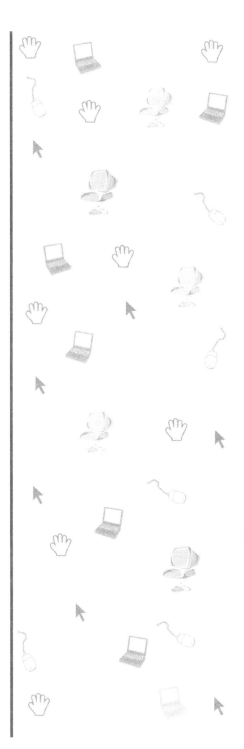

6. The screen lists topics or categories of books, microfilms, microfiche, etc., for Pennsylvania, Chester. Examples are:

    Pennsylvania, Chester—Bible records
    Pennsylvania, Chester—Bibliography
    Pennsylvania, Chester—Biography
    Pennsylvania, Chester—Biography—Indexes
    Pennsylvania, Chester—Business records and commerce
    Pennsylvania, Chester—Cemeteries

    Click the underlined hypertext at the bottom of the screen that reads "View Next Set of Matching Topics" and you'll see additional topics. The screens end with:

    Pennsylvania, Chester—Taxation
    Pennsylvania, Chester—Town records
    Pennsylvania, Chester—Vital records

7. If any of these Chester, PA topics or categories of information are what you need, you can click to get a more detailed list. I'm interested in locating probate records from the early 1700s for some family members who are said to have lived in East Goshen, Chester County, Pennsylvania. Since family historians always try to get the original document whenever possible, I'll see what the library has available and click on the hypertext "Pennsylvania, Chester—Probate records."

8. Of the 21 related titles under the category, I clicked on the likely entry for "Abstract of wills of Chester County, Pennsylvania Martin Jacob" and go to the next screen:

9. It would appear that I could just print out this list and take it to my local LDS Family History Center. There is one problem, however. While this short listing explains that Volume 1 covers 1714–1758, Volume 2 covers 1759–1777, Volume 3 covers 1778–1800, and Volume 4 covers 1801–1825, I don't know which microfilm has

Volume 1, the time period I require. For this I need to click the "View Film Notes" button, circled in red.

10. This is the page I print out to order the correct microfilm, although in this case the item is available on microfiche—which is even better. I can order the entire set, at 15 cents per fiche, and it will stay permanently in my local Family History Center. Microfilm can be rented for short-term, long-term, or indefinite loan. Microfiche, once ordered, is kept by the local center.

    The page I've printed has a "FHL US/CANADA FICHE" notation. This helps if you're planning to visit the FHL in Salt Lake City. It indicates that at the FHL you'd go to the floor for US/CANADA, then look in the collection of FICHE for microfiche number 6089197.

11. However, since I'm using the local Family History Center, I'll just take the printout with the fiche numbers listed, and the volunteer will help me fill out the order form. They'll notify me when the item arrives. You can usually make copies at a microfilm/fiche reader-printer in the center. If your local FHC is small and doesn't have duplication equipment, you can complete a photoduplication request form and send it to the Family History Library. The form is available at every FHC, because it is essential to document our research and cite our sources.

National Archives and Records Administration (NARA)

www.nara.gov/genealogy

- How to Use NARA's Census Microfilm Catalog—*www.nara.gov/genealogy/microcen.html*
- Microfilm Catalogs—*www.nara.gov/ngenealogy/#cats1*
- National Archives Microfilm Rental Program—*www.nara.gov/publications/microfilm/micrent.html*

Six thousand libraries throughout the U.S. subscribe to NARA's microfilm service. As an individual researcher, you can subscribe by

ordering the $25 start-up kit. Rental fees are based on a quantity discount, as follows: 1–4 rolls $3.25 each; 5–9 rolls $2.75 each; 10 or more $2.25 each. You'll add $3 postage and handling, and may elect to extend the use of the film for 30 additional days for an additional $3 per film.

To find which rolls you wish to order, access the online catalog. NARA microfilm catalogs online include those for:

> American Indians
> Black Studies
> Federal Court Records
> Genealogical and Biographical
> Immigrant and Passenger Arrivals

USGenWeb Census Images Online

www.rootsweb.com/~usgenweb/cen_img.htm

Once you find your ancestor in a census index, you can look to see if the census microfilm images are online at USGenWeb, as an alternative to renting or buying the microfilm.

Searching the "1890" for Pulaski County, Kentucky, for example, the site yielded the notation: "1890 Special Schedule, War of the Rebellion Survivors & Widows, Pulaski County, Kentucky" followed by: "Most of the 1890 population schedules were badly damaged by fire in 1921, and subsequently destroyed. None exist for Kentucky. However, most of the Special Military Schedules still exist, including those for Pulaski County, Kentucky."

When you get to the page, there is an alpha listing of names.

I clicked on "Patterson, Daniel" and was presented with the scanned image of the actual census page where Daniel is listed with the rank of private, Company H, 7th Kentucky Infantry.

Other columns on the census form list his date of enlistment, date of discharge, and length of service. The top of the page states the source of the document: "Pulaski Co., KY 1890 Special Schedule: War of the Rebellion Survivors & Widows, NARA Film M123, Roll 3. Donated to the USGenWeb Archives by V. J. Davis, Oct 1999." You can then print out the page to save this document for your files—or use it on your family Web site.

Buying Microfilm

Many Web sites we've already discussed—and that you've probably already visited—sell microfilm and CD-ROM records. There are advantages to owning microfilm: researchers who can't get to libraries, archives, or Family History Centers for one reason or another will buy them, and other researchers just seem to want to own the records themselves. Pretty handy, in fact, if you want to become a professional genealogist!

Of course, to read microfilm or a microfiche you'll need a machine. Microfiche and film readers are available at most libraries, or you can often pick these up cheap from the local school board or corporate auctions. Or check out eBay, where you're bound to find one. Whatever you do, check used sources before you buy one new.

Here's a sampling of sites offering genealogical records on microfilm:

Federation of Family History Societies

www.ffhs.org.uk/pubs/general.htm

In British genealogy, FFHS publications are essential to successful research.

Many British genealogical societies publish transcripts and indexes on microfiche rather than as printed books, or republish on microfiche when a book goes out of print. A comprehensive listing of transcripts and indexes of various census, parish registers, monumental inscriptions, miscellaneous records, with costs, all produced by FFHS members, has been compiled on microfiche. This is one of the most important county-by-county references to research aids in England, Wales, and Ireland. Includes some material pertaining to Australia, New Zealand, and Canada.

Heritage Quest

www.heritagequest.com/html/sourcedoc.html

For years, this company was known as American Genealogical Lending Library (AGLL) and many public libraries and avid

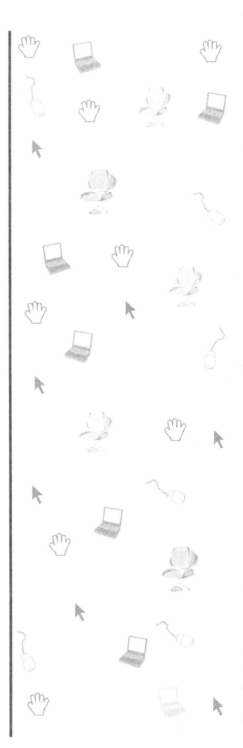

genealogy researchers belonged to it. Look through the HQ index to find an ancestor, make a note of the microfilm volume number and roll number. Then order it through Heritage Quest.

Categories from the catalog include: marriage records, military records, Native American records, other county records, selected state censuses, ship passenger lists, special collections, surname collections, vital records, and U.S. census records 1790–1920. Microfilms are available for purchase and through the rental program. Membership is $29.95 per year. Rent 10 or more rolls of microfilm at only $2.75 each or 1–9 titles for just $3.25 each. Keep them for 30 days. Reliable service from a name known and trusted.

Interlink Bookshop Genealogical Services

www.interlinkbookshop.com
Here we learn of the British Directories Project, an Australian initiative from Scriptorium Family History Centre, Melbourne. More than seven hundred fifty directories or sections of directories have been issued on microfiche. The years range from 1769 to 1936, for nearly all counties and/or cities of England, Wales, Scotland, and Ireland; overall, more than ten million names are included. Examples:

- *Name Index to Poor Law Settlement Papers, Essex, 1574–1865:* Full name index to over forty thousand individuals compiled from a database of those named in Settlement Certificates, Removal Orders, and Settlement Examinations.
- *Parish Census Listings, Essex, 1797–1831*—Transcription of more than sixty surviving returns completed by parish overseers for the first four official censuses. Index to over four thousand individual names.
- *Parish Census Listings Supplement 1641–1840*—A collection of unofficial lists of inhabitants and householders for the following parishes: Ardleigh, Bocking, Chingford, Colchester St. James, Earles Colne, Great Leighs, Halstead, Little Parndon, Terling, Toppesfield, Witham, Woodford. Most are early 1800s, full transcripts and index.

- *Jones Glasgow Directory 1789*
- *Directory of Forfarshire 1837*
- *Slater's Directory Ireland, Connaught, Munster, and Ulster 1846*
- *Pigot's Directory of Ireland, Dublin and Leinster 1824*

New Zealand Society of Genealogists

http://homepages.ihug.co.nz/~nzsg/Publications/fiche_main.html
Microfiche available under General records:

> *Bankruptcies in New Zealand 1881–1940:* An index
> *Bankruptcies in Canterbury NZ 1863–1880:* An index
> *Machinery Accidents 1879–1919:* An index
> *Masters, Mates & Engineers 1866–1921*
> *Mining Accidents 1879–1958:* An index
> *New Zealand Patents 1860–1890:* An index to applications
>   by New Zealand Residents
> *New Zealand River Drownings 1840–1887*

Other categories are cemetery, church, land, military, newspaper, shipping, wills and estates records.

Ancestor Spy

www.ancestorspy.com
This site offers over thirteen hundred titles offerings on CD-ROM and microfiche. Examples:

- *Couch Family History* by Benjamin C. Couch, written in 1888. Includes descendant chart, pedigree and family group sheets. Indexed. One microfiche.
- *A History of Presbyterianism in New England* by Alexander Blaikie, published in 1882. A handbook of religious history from the Presbyterian point of view, dating from the landing of the Pilgrims to the year of grace 1881. Indexed. Five microfiche, 512 pages.
- *List of Taxable Property in the County of Rowan, North Carolina, 1778.* Also Includes tax lists for 1784 by A. D.

Osborne, Clerk of the Court. Indexed by Annie Walker Burns. One microfiche.

- *The Descendants of Nathaniel Mowry, of Rhode Island, 1631–1878* by William A. Mowry, A.M., published in 1878. Contains eight generations. Indexed. Four microfiche, 343 pages.
- *Old Families of Louisiana (about 1608–1929)* by Stanley Clisby Arthur, published in 1931. Includes reprinted biographies of the Dimitry series of French and Spanish families as available. Also, English, Scottish, and Irish lineage. Indexed. Five microfiche, 432 pages.
- *History Of Royalton, Vermont with Family Genealogies 1769–1911* by Evelyn M. Wood Lovejoy. Begins with the early days of Royalton. Tells of the first settlers, Indian raids, social events such as husking parties and quiltings, churches, roads, the poor, the cemeteries, hotels, militia, and so on. Many names are mentioned in this history, giving genealogical information. Many illustrations.

Avotaynu Jewish Genealogy Microfiche

www.avotaynu.com/microf.htm

Jewish Genealogical Consolidated Surname Index. Lists some two hundred thirty thousand unique surnames and shows in which of 28 different databases each appears. three fiche, $10. Most of the microfiche indexes here are $5–$35. The entire collection of 121 fiche is $250.

Some of the databases available:

- *Jewish Cemeteries throughout the World.* Information on more than seventy five hundred cemeteries in seventy-nine countries. Two fiche.
- *Jewish Genealogical People Finder.* The latest (1995) version has three hundred thousand entries! Database of individuals that appear on family trees of Jewish genealogists. Twenty-two fiche.
- *Jewish Residents in Canadian Censuses: Montreal & Quebec City (1871–1901); Toronto (1861–1901); Western Canada*

(1861–1901); Canadian Maritime Provinces (1901); Greater Quebec Province (1871–1901). Five fiche.

- *Romanian Census Records.* Index to the census of Jews in 1824–25. 1852 census of Jews of Monesti. One fiche.
- *Birth Index for Buda (Hungary) Jewry 1820–1852, 1868.* Index to certain Jewish birth records of Budapest. Shows date of birth, child's name, father's name, mother's name including maiden name and, in some cases, date of death. Two fiche.
- *Noms des Juifs du Maroc Moroccan Jewish Surnames.* One fiche.
- *Index to the 1784 Census of the Jews of Alsace.* Documents some twenty thousand Jews who were enumerated in this census. In four sequences: by surname; by given name; by town; for married women, by maiden name. One fiche.
- *Galician Towns and Administrative Districts.* List of six thousand Galician towns and the administrative districts to which they belong. Two fiche.
- *Publications of the Jewish Genealogical Societies 1977–1990.* A set of most of the newsletters and publications of Jewish-American genealogy published between 1977 and 1990. Twenty-four fiche.
- *Index to Memorial to the Jews Deported from France.* Alphabetic list of fifty thousand surnames that appear in Memorial to Jews Deported From France. Shows surname and convoy number. One fiche.
- *Palestine Gazette.* List of over twenty-eight thousand persons, mostly Jews, who legally changed their names while living in Palestine during the British Mandate from 1921–1948. Six fiche.

Appendices

Appendix A: Research Guidelines from the National Genealogical Society

www.ngsgenealogy.org/about/content/committees/gene_stan.html

Standards for Sound Genealogical Research

Remembering always that they are engaged in a quest for truth, family history researchers consistently

- record the source for each item of information they collect.
- test every hypothesis or theory against credible evidence, and reject those that are not supported by the evidence.
- seek original records, or reproduced images of them when there is reasonable assurance they have not been altered, as the basis for their research conclusions.
- use compilations, communications and published works, whether paper or electronic, primarily for their value as guides to locating the original records.
- state something as a fact only when it is supported by convincing evidence, and identify the evidence when communicating the fact to others.
- limit with words like "probable" or "possible" any statement that is based on less than convincing evidence, and state the reasons for concluding that it is probable or possible.
- avoid misleading other researchers by either intentionally or carelessly distributing or publishing inaccurate information.

- state carefully and honestly the results of their own research, and acknowledge all use of other researchers' work.
- recognize the collegial nature of genealogical research by making their work available to others through publication, or by placing copies in appropriate libraries or repositories, and by welcoming critical comment.
- consider with open minds new evidence or the comments of others on their work and the conclusions they have reached.

Standards for Using Records Repositories and Libraries

www.ngsgenealogy.org/about/content/committees
Recognizing that how they use unique original records and fragile publications will affect other users, both current and future, family history researchers habitually

- are courteous to research facility personnel and other researchers, and respect the staff's other daily tasks, not expecting the records custodian to listen to their family histories nor provide constant or immediate attention.
- dress appropriately, converse with others in a low voice, and supervise children appropriately.
- do their homework in advance, know what is available and what they need, and avoid ever asking for "everything" on their ancestors.
- use only designated work space areas, respect off-limits areas, and request permission before using photocopy or microform equipment, asking for assistance if needed.
- treat original records at all times with great respect and work with only a few records at a time, recognizing that they are irreplaceable and that each user must help preserve them for future use.

- treat books with care, never forcing their spines, and handle photographs properly, preferably wearing archival gloves.
- never mark, mutilate, rearrange, relocate, or remove from the repository any original, printed, microform, or electronic document or artifact.
- use only procedures prescribed by the repository for noting corrections to any errors or omissions found in published works, never marking the work itself.
- keep note-taking paper or other objects from covering records or books, and avoid placing any pressure upon them, particularly with a pencil or pen.
- use only the method specifically designated for identifying records for duplication, avoiding use of paper clips, adhesive notes, or other means not approved by the facility, unless instructed otherwise, replace volumes and files in their proper locations, before departure, thank the records custodians for their courtesy in making the materials available.
- follow the rules of the records repository without protest, even if they have changed since a previous visit or differ from those of another facility

©1997 by National Genealogical Society; includes material ©1995 by Joy Reisinger, CGRS^{SM}

Standards for Use of Technology in Genealogical Research

Mindful that computers are tools, genealogists take full responsibility for their work, and therefore they

- learn the capabilities and limits of their equipment and software, and use them only when they are the most appropriate tools for a purpose.
- refuse to let computer software automatically embellish their work.

- treat compiled information from online sources or digital databases like that from other published sources, useful primarily as a guide to locating original records, but not as evidence for a conclusion or assertion.
- accept digital images or enhancements of an original record as a satisfactory substitute for the original only when there is reasonable assurance that the image accurately reproduces the unaltered original.
- cite sources for data obtained online or from digital media with the same care that is appropriate for sources on paper and other traditional media, and enter data into a digital database only when its source can remain associated with it.
- always cite the sources for information or data posted online or sent to others, naming the author of a digital file as its immediate source, while crediting original sources cited within the file.
- preserve the integrity of their own databases by evaluating the reliability of downloaded data before incorporating it into their own files.
- provide, whenever they alter data received in digital form, a description of the change that will accompany the altered data whenever it is shared with others.
- actively oppose the proliferation of error, rumor, and fraud by personally verifying or correcting information, or noting it as unverified, before passing it on to others.
- treat people online as courteously and civilly as they would treat them face-to-face, not separated by networks and anonymity.
- accept that technology has not changed the principles of genealogical research, only some of the procedures.

Standards for Sharing Information with Others

Conscious of the fact that sharing information or data with others, whether through speech, documents, or electronic media, is essential to family history research and that it needs continuing support and encouragement, responsible family historians consistently

- respect the restrictions on sharing information that arise from the rights of another as an author, originator, or compiler; as a living private person; or as a party to a mutual agreement.
- observe meticulously the legal rights of copyright owners, copying or distributing any part of their works only with their permission, or to the limited extent specifically allowed under the law's "fair use" exceptions.
- identify the sources for all ideas, information, and data from others, and the form in which they were received, recognizing that the unattributed use of another's intellectual work is plagiarism.
- respect the authorship rights of senders of letters, electronic mail and data files, forwarding or disseminating them further only with the sender's permission.
- inform people who provide information about their families as to the ways it may be used, observing any conditions they impose and respecting any reservations they may express regarding the use of particular items.
- require some evidence of consent before assuming that living people are agreeable to further sharing of information about themselves.
- convey personal identifying information about living people—like age, home address, occupation or activities—only in ways that those concerned have expressly agreed to.

- recognize that legal rights of privacy may limit the extent to which information from publicly available sources may be further used, disseminated or published.
- communicate no information to others that is known to be false, or without making reasonable efforts to determine its truth, particularly information that may be derogatory.
- are sensitive to the hurt that revelations of criminal, immoral, bizarre or irresponsible behavior may bring to family members.

©1993 and 2000 by National Genealogical Society. Permission is granted to copy or publish this material provided it is reproduced in its entirety, including this notice.

Appendix B: RootsWeb's Mailing Lists

Ethnic Groups

www.rootsweb.com/~maillist/ethnic/index.html

Our wonderful friends at RootsWeb.com provide perhaps the single largest collection of ethnic genealogy mailing lists. Here are selections from the Index. New lists are added all the time, so check online if what you're looking for isn't here. To subscribe online, just click on the link.

ACADIAN-CAJUN-L—A mailing list for anyone with Acadian-Cajun ancestry worldwide.

AFGS-AFGNEWS-L—A read-only mailing list for members of the American-French Genealogical Society (AFGS) or anyone interested in AFGS activities who would like an electronic version of the AFGnewS that is sent bi-monthly by postal mail to members. The AFGS is a genealogical and historical organization dedicated to the study and preservation of the French-Canadian culture. Additional information on the AFGS can be found on the AFGS Web page at *www.afgs.org*.

AFRICANAMER-GEN-L—A mailing list for the discussion and sharing of information regarding all aspects of African-American genealogy.

AL-AfricaAmer-L—A mailing list for anyone with an interest in African-American genealogy in Alabama. Additional information can be found on the Alabama African American Genealogy Web page at *www.rootsweb/~alaag/*.

ARIA-L—A mailing list for Australians and New Zealanders who are researching their Italian heritage, culture, and ancestry.

AMERIND-US-SE-L—A mailing list for those with a genealogical, historical, or cultural interest in the lost Indian tribes of the southeastern United States, in order to help the descendants of these scattered tribes to learn about their ancestors. The list will address small and "extinct" tribes like the Appalachee and Yuchi as well as those absorbed into larger tribes like the Cherokee, Creek, and Seminole.

ATTAKULLAKULLA-L—A mailing list for the discussion and sharing of information regarding the ancestors and descendants of Attakullakulla, Chickamauga Cherokee, also known as the Little Carpenter and White Owl, and related lines. Of special interest is information about lines in east and south Tennessee and northeast Alabama (i.e., Watts, Webber, Jordan, Siniard, Leach, Ford).

BAPTIST-ROOTS-L—A mailing list for anyone with a genealogical or historical interest in the Baptist church. Additional information can be found on the Baptist Church History & Genealogy Web page at *http://homepages.rootsweb.com/~baptist/index.html*.

BLACK-DUTCH-L—A mailing list for anyone who wants to help define the most common meaning of the term "Black Dutch."

BLACKWARHEROS-L—A mailing list for anyone with a genealogical or historical interest in Black Americans who were heroes during any war.

BRETHREN—For anyone who wants to exchange information and search for Brethren Roots (i.e., ancestors and families that are or were members the Church Group founded in 1708 near Swarzenau, Germany). The movement came to America mainly in two groups, one in 1719 and the other in 1729. This includes such church groups as Tunkers/Dunkers, Church of the Brethren, and German Baptists.

CHEROKEE-L—A mailing list for the discussion of Cherokee history and culture. Please use the related CherokeeGene mailing list below for genealogical discussions. Additional information can be found on The Cherokee Genealogy Page at *www.io.com/~crberry/CherokeeGenealogy*.

CHEROKEEGENE-L—A mailing list for anyone interested in Cherokee genealogy. Please use the related Cherokee mailing list described above for history and culture discussions. Additional information can be found on The Cherokee Genealogy Page at *www.io.com/~crberry/CherokeeGenealogy*.

CHOCTAW-L—A mailing list for anyone with a genealogical interest in the Choctaw Indian tribe in Oklahoma (McCurtain County and neighboring counties).

CHOCTAW-SOUTHEAST-L—A mailing list for anyone with a genealogical interest in the Choctaw Tribe of Native Americans. While the list will emphasize those who lived in the southeastern United States, especially Mississippi, all Choctaw researchers are welcome. Additional information can be found on

The Choctaw Genealogy Page at *http://freepages.cultures.rootsweb.com/~choctaw/*.

CORNISH-L—A mailing list for researchers of ancestors who are in Cornwall, England, or emigrated from Cornwall to the United States, Canada, Australia, New Zealand, or any other location. We are dedicated to tracing our Cornish ancestors and learning more about our ancestors' culture, occupations, and traditions (a companion list, CORNISH-GEN, exists for those with a stricter genealogy focus).

CORNISH-GEN-L—A mailing list for researchers who are in Cornwall or whose ancestors emigrated from Cornwall to the United States, Canada, Australia, New Zealand, or any other location. This list observes a strict genealogical focus (a companion list, CORNISH, exists for those with a broader approach allowing the discussion of many varied but Cornish-related topics).

CREEK-SOUTHEAST-L—A mailing list for anyone interested in the genealogy and history of the Creek Indians of the southeastern United States, and those living among the Creeks.

DEU-BALTISCHE-L—A mailing list for anyone who is interested in Deutsch-Baltische (Baltic German) genealogy. The languages for this list are German and English.

EARLY-NAZARENE-CHURCH-L—A mailing list for anyone with a genealogical interest in the early Nazarene Church.

EURO-JEWISH-L—A mailing list for anyone with a genealogical interest in the migration, history, culture, heritage, and surname search of the Jewish people from Europe to the United States and their descendants in the United States. (Note: This is Not a Religious discussion list).

EXULANTEN-L—A mailing list for anyone with a genealogical interest in the "Exulanten" who are the Protestants that were forced to leave Austria in the 16th–18th centuries. Additional information can be found on the Exulanten-L Mailing List Web page at *www.rootsweb.com/~autwgw/agsfrx.htm*.

FENIANS-L—A mailing list for anyone with a genealogical interest in the history of the Fenian Brotherhood and the Irish revolutionary movement that was formed in 1857 and continued on until the 1870s. Additional information can be found on The Fenian Brotherhood Web page at *www.public.usit.net/mruddy/fenian1.htm*

FIANNA-L—A mailing list for those who are researching Irish ancestry and history to discuss ways of improving their skills in searching for their Irish ancestors. Subscribers are welcome to post questions and information regarding sources and methods for Irish research. Specific questions on individual ancestors are beyond the scope of the list. Interested individuals may want to check out The Fianna: Irish Ancestry & History Research Web page at *www.geocities.com/heartland/meadows/4404/* and the Fianna Study Group Hideaway and Guide to Irish Genealogy at *www.rootsweb.com/~fianna/*

FIVECIVILTRIB-L—A mailing list for anyone who is researching the Five "Civilized" Tribes (i.e., Cherokee, Choctaw, Chickasaw, Seminole, Creek).

FPC-OTHER-FREE-GEN-L—A mailing list for anyone with a genealogical interest in Free Person of Color, Other Free, and/or Mulatto as reported by official records.

FRENCH-INDIAN-L—A mailing list for anyone with a genealogical or historical interest in the French and Indian War.

GEN-AFRICAN-L: Gatewayed with the soc.genealogy.african newsgroup for the discussion of African genealogy.

GEN-HISPANIC-L: Gatewayed with the soc.genealogy.hispani newsgroup for the discussion of Hispanic genealogy.

GEN-ITALIAN-L: Gatewayed with the soc.genealogy.italian newsgroup for the discussion of Italian genealogy.

GEN-ROOTERS—A mailing list for members of the Church of Jesus Christ of Latter-day Saints to share ideas and helpful hints on the "how-tos" of genealogy. To subscribe send a nicely worded message to Dianne Morris at azdee@aol.com containing a brief description of your Church affiliation and a request that you be added to the list.

GEN-SLAVIC-L—Gatewayed with the soc.genealogy.slavic newsgroup for the discussion of Slavic genealogy.

GERMAN-AMERICAN-L—A mailing list for anyone interested in genealogy related to German immigrants and their families *after* their arrival in America. Please note that this mailing list is not intended for discussions of genealogy materials, sources, and places in Germany since other mailing lists exist for these purposes. Rather, this mailing list focuses solely on the genealogy and families of these immigrants *after* they came to America.

GERMAN-BOHEMIAN-L: A discussion group for those interested in sharing information about the culture, genealogy, and heritage of the German-speaking people of Bohemia and Moravia, now the Czech Republic.

GERMAN-CANADIAN-L—A mailing list for the discussion of issues concerning the settlement of German-speaking immigrants coming from any-

where to Canada. The list is a forum for historical and genealogical questions, and sharing of information regarding Germans in Canada and their descendants.

GER-RUS-ARG-L—A mailing list for anyone with a genealogical interest in the Germans who migrated from Russia to Argentina. The language for the list is Spanish; however, postings in English or German are acceptable.

GRDB-L—A mailing list for the discussion of genealogy databases containing German-Russians and their descendants, being developed by the American Historical Society of Germans from Russia (AHSGR), and the village research coordinators that work with AHSGR.

HANDCART-L—A mailing list for anyone who has an interest in the genealogy, journals, and stories of the Pioneers of the Church of Jesus Christ of Latter-day Saints who settled in the Salt Lake Valley from 1847 to 1860.

HERBARZ-L—A mailing list for the discussion of Polish and Lithuanian heraldry, the history of the armorial clans, and the genealogy of noble families.

HUGUENOT-L—A mailing list for anyone with a genealogical interest in the Huguenots. The Huguenots were French Protestants from the 16th and 17th centuries, many of whom migrated to other countries due to religious persecution.

HUGUENOTS-WALLOONS-EUROPE-L—A mailing list for anyone with a genealogical interest in the research of Huguenots and/or Walloons in Europe. For the purposes of this list, Europe includes all of continental Europe as well as the United Kingdom and Ireland.

INTERRACIAL-GENEALOGY-L—A mailing list for anyone who is researching their interracial ancestry. Additional information can be found on the Interracial-Genealogy Mailing List home page at *http://freepages.genealogy.rootsweb.com/~lineaje/INTERRACIAL-L.html*

JEWISH-ROOTS-L—A mailing list for anyone interested in Jewish genealogy.

LDS-WARD-CONSULTANT-L—A mailing list for the use of ward and stake genealogy consultants and specialists of the Latter-day Saints (LDS) Church to exchange suggestions, guidelines, data, etc. related to their duties. This list is not sponsored by the LDS Church. Additional information can be found on the LDS-Ward-Consultants Mailing List web page at *http://homepages.rootsweb.com/~acwomack/LDS.htm*.

LUTHERAN-ROOTS-L—A mailing list for anyone with a genealogical interest in the Lutheran Church, both Evangelical and Reformed. Additional information can be found on the Lutheran Roots Mailing List Page at *http://homepages.rootsweb.com/~mdtaffet/lutheran-roots_list.htm*.

MADEIRAEXILES-L—A mailing list devoted to the research of Dr. Robert Reid Kalley's Portuguese Presbyterian exiles from Madeira, Portugal, who emigrated to Trinidad and then to Illinois (ca. 1846–1854). Postings regarding research of related exiles who settled in Trinidad, Antigua, St. Kitts, Jamaica, Demerara, etc. are also welcome. Additional information can be found on the Kleber Family Genealogy Web page at *http://homepages.rootsweb.com/~madeira*.

MCF-ROOTS-L—A mailing list (Maryland Catholics on the Frontier) for the discussion of descendants of Maryland Catholics who migrated first to Kentucky and then to other parts of the frontier. This was a planned migration and the first group left Maryland in 1785 with others following for the next 10 years or so. Many of the surnames are so intertwined that it is impossible to separate them and the families can be researched as one great big family, especially in Maryland and Kentucky. Additional information can be found on the Maryland Catholics on the Frontier Home Page at *http://bsd.pastracks.com/mcf*.

MELUNGEON-L—A mailing list for people conducting Melungeon and/or Appalachian research including Native American, Portuguese, Turkish, Black Dutch, and other unverifiable mixed statements of ancestry or unexplained rumors, with ancestors in TN, KY, VA, NC, SC, GA, AL, WV, and possibly other places.

MENNO-ROOTS-L—A mailing list for anyone with a genealogical or historical interest in the Mennonites.

METHODIST-L—A mailing list for anyone who is researching their ancestors who were of the Methodist faith. Additional information can be found on the Researching Your Methodist Ancestors Web page at *www.geocities.com/Vienna/Choir/1824/methodistresearch.html*.

METIS-L—A mailing list for Metis descendants, those who have mixed Native American and European (principally French) ancestry.

MORAVIANCHURCH-L—A mailing list for the worldwide Moravian Church, the oldest Protestant denomination. This list is for an exchange of Moravian records, genealogies, references, and historical information; especially in Europe and Colonial America.

NAOTTAWA-L—A mailing list for anyone with a genealogical interest in the Ottawa Indian Nation.

NATIVEAMERICAN-DELMARVA-L—A mailing list for anyone researching their Native American ancestry in Delaware, Maryland, and Virginia.

OH-AfricaAmer-L—A mailing list for anyone with an interest in Lower African-American genealogy in Ohio.

PADUTCHgenONLY-L—A mailing list for anyone interested in doing Pennsylvania Dutch genealogical research. This list is for genealogical discussions only. Additional information can be found on the Pennsylvania Family History Site at *http://homepages.rootsweb.com/~padutch/*.

PADUTCH-LIFE-L—A mailing list for anyone interested in discussing and sharing information and memories of the Pennsylvania-German people commonly called Pennsylvania Dutch. Topics include customs, everyday lives, recipes, and genealogy to give insight as to how our present-day lives are a continuation of our Penna-Dutch heritage. Along with serious discussions, you will find the not-so-serious ones in a spirit of good fellowship among Penna-Dutch cousins.

PGST-L—A mailing list for the discussion and sharing of information regarding the activities of the Polish Genealogical Society of Texas (PGST) and resources available for researching Polish ancestry. Additional information can be found on the PGST Web site at *www.pgst.org*

POCSOUTH-L—A mailing list (People of Color, South) to open a dialogue with African-American genealogists doing research in the 13 southern United States. "People of Color in Old Tennessee" is the forerunner project and information on this project can be found at *www.tngenweb.org/tncolor/*

PRESBYTERIAN-L—A mailing list for anyone with a genealogical or historical interest in the Presbyterian church including all Presbyterian denominations (e.g., A.R.P., U.S.A., P.C.A., etc.).

PreussenAmericans-L—A mailing list for anyone with a genealogical interest in Prussian immigrants to America.

QUAKER-ROOTS-L—A discussion group for anyone with an interest in their Quaker heritage. Our Quaker ancestors kept excellent records and documented their migration into new areas. If you find one Quaker family on your family tree, you probably have many more!

SDB-L—A mailing list for anyone researching ancestors affiliated with the Seventh Day Baptist church.

SEMINOLE-WARS-L—A mailing list for anyone with a genealogical interest in the Seminole wars.

SHAMROCK-L—A mailing list for those trying to find their Celtic/Irish roots and for Irish historic research.

THE-ROAD-L—A mailing list for anyone with a genealogical interest in the Scottish/Palatine (German) ethnic mix along the traditional "Philadelphia Road" in Pennsylvania, Virginia, North Carolina, and South Carolina.

Turkish_Jews-L—A mailing list for Sephardic Jewish genealogists with roots in the former Turkish Ottoman Empire including Turkey, Serbia, Greece, and Yugoslavia.

VOLHYNIAN-MENNONITES-L—A mailing list for anyone with a genealogical interest in the Mennonites from the Volhynia area, and surrounding areas, of old Polish Russia, now known as the Ukraine.

History Mailing Lists

www.rootsweb.com/~maillist/

1776-L—A mailing list for genealogical and historical research surrounding 1776 and the American Revolution.

ACWGREY-L—A mailing list for those trying to find genealogical information from the Southern States during the period of and around the American Civil War.

AMERICAN-REVOLUTION-L—A mailing list for the discussion of events during the American Revolution and genealogical matters related to the American Revolution. The French-Indian Wars and the War of 1812 are also suitable topics for discussion. Additional information can be found on The American Revolution List Web Page at *www.shelby.net/jr/amrev/index.htm*.

AMREV-HESSIANS-L—A mailing list for anyone with a genealogical interest in the Hessian soldiers (German auxiliary troops employed by King George III of England) who remained in America after the American Revolution.

ANDERSONVILLE-L—A mailing list for the descendants and interested historians of Andersonville, the Civil War's most notorious prison camp, to swap knowledge and research the lives of Union prisoners before, during, and after their time in Andersonville.

CIVIL-WAR-L—A mailing list for the discussion of events during the Civil War and genealogical matters related to the Civil War. Additional information can be found on the Civil-War List Homepage at *www.public.usit.net/mruddy/*.

CIVIL-WAR-IRISH-L—A mailing list for those with a genealogical interest in the Irish participants in the American Civil War and their descendants. Additional information can be found on the ALH-NACW Web page at *www.usgennet.org*.

CIVIL-WAR-WOMEN-L—A mailing list for those with who are researching women who served or assisted in the American Civil War. Additional information can be found on the ALHNACW Web page at *www.usgennet.org*.

CSA-HISTORY-L—This list welcomes Confederate States of America early history and culture, genealogy, migration trails, War of Secession, monuments, cemeteries, prisons, CSA regiments, Reconstruction, and other pertinent topics.

CW-POW-L—A mailing list for the discussion and sharing of information regarding the Civil War prisoner of war camps and prisoners of war, both Union and Confederate. This will include all aspects of the prisoner of war experience. Additional information can be found on the Brothers Bound Web page at *http://homepages.rootsweb.com/~south1/bound.htm*.

HONEYHILL-L—A mailing list for anyone with a genealogical or historical interest in the Civil War Battle of Honey Hill.

STATE-HISTORICAL-MARKERS-L—A mailing list devoted to the transcription of State Historical Highway markers and their relevance to the genealogical research community.

UNITED-EMPIRE-LOYALIST-L—A mailing list for anyone with a genealogical, cultural, or historical interest in the United Empire loyalists who came to Canada from the United States during and after the American Revolution. For more information please see the home page at *http://members.tripod.com/~firstlight_2/BNA.htm*.

USRW-BRANDYWINE-L—A mailing list for anyone with a genealogical or historical interest in the Revolutionary War Battle of Brandywine.

USWARS-L—A mailing list for anyone with a genealogical interest in the wars and military actions in which the United States fought. Not directed toward a specific war or military action. Additional information can be found on the USWARS GenConnect boards at *http://genconnect.rootsweb.com/indx/USWARS.html.*

USWARS-1800S-L—A mailing list for anyone with a genealogical interest in the "little" wars fought by the United States during the 1800s (e.g. Mexican War, Spanish-American War, Indian wars).

WARBRIDES-L—A mailing list for putting WWII war brides and their children in touch with others to share reminiscences.

WAROF1812-L—A mailing list for anyone with a genealogical and a historical interest in the War of 1812. This includes veterans of this war and all the battles from 1812 to January 1815.

WAROF1812-NC-L—A mailing list for anyone with a genealogical interest in the participation of North Carolina in the War of 1812. Additional information can be found on the North Carolina in the War of 1812 Web page at *www.rootsweb.com/~nc1812.*

Appendix C: Seventeen Ways to Jump-Start Your Research on the Internet

I've been updating and revising this list for five years in response to a dear friend who was about to give up on the Internet for genealogy research. He was overwhelmed by the myriad possibilities, so I designed this task-oriented list of things to do. He tells me it really jump-started his research!

1. Subscribe to these free e-mail genealogy newsletters:
    Ancestry Daily News—*www.ancestry.com*
    DearMYRTLE's Daily Genealogy Column—*www.DearMYRTLE.com/subscribe.htm*
    Dick Eastman's Genealogy Newsletter—*www.ancestry.com/columns/eastman/*
    Everton's Family History News—*www.everton.com*
    Family Tree Finders—send a blank e-mail message to: *join-family-tree-finders@gt.sodamail.com*
    RootsWeb Review & Missing Links—*www.rootsweb.com/~review/*

2. Search the Social Security Death Index (free):
    Ancestry.com—*www.ancestry.com/ssdi/advanced.htm*
    RootsWeb—*www.rootsweb.com*

3. Visit these sites indexing other sites on the Web:
    Cyndi Howells' List—*www.cyndislist.com*
    Genealogy Resources on the Internet—*members.aol.com/johnf14246/internet.html*
    Genealogy.com.—*www.genealogy.com* (formerly Banner Blue, Family Tree Maker, etc.)
    Juliana's List—*www.ancestry.com/ancestry/testurllinks/search.asp*

RootsWeb—*www.rootsweb.com*
SurnameWeb—*www.surnameweb.org*

4. Check out suppliers of charts and forms listed by Cyndi at *www.cyndislist.com/supplies.htm.*

5. Study PERSI Periodical Source Index for references to my ancestors, their ethnic background, and places they lived in genealogical magazines published since 1847: *www.ancestry.com/home/library/abtpersi.htm.* You can send away for a copy of the article if your local public library doesn't have the issue.

6. Visit USGenWeb sites to discover more about the states and counties where my ancestors once lived: *www.usgenweb.com.*

7. Join SURNAME or LOCALITY Message Group (free) by subscribing at RootsWeb: *www.rootsweb.com/~maillist.*

8. Search genealogy databases on the Web at:
Ancestry.com—*www.ancestry.com*
Genealogy.com.—*www.genealogy.com* (formerly Banner Blue, Family Tree Maker, etc.)
Everton's—*www.everton.com*
GenConnect—*genconnect.rootsweb.com/*
GenServe—*www.genserv.com/*

Note: Ancestry.com allows you to see the number of hits *before* typing in (fee-based) user name and password required to see the full document.

9. Order books through Amazon.com—*www.amazon.com.* Amazon often sells genealogy books for less (10–30%) than advertised by the publishers.

10. Visit historical sites such as:
George Washington's Letters Online—Library of Congress Web Site—*www.loc.gov*
History Channel—*www.historychannel.com/*
Tower of London Virtual Tour—*www.toweroflondontour.com*
Valley Forge Home Page—*www.valleyforge.org*
WPA Life Histories—*http://lcweb2.loc.gov/ammem/wpaintro/*

11. Visit national Web sites:
Canadian National Archives—*www.archives.ca/www/Genealogy.html*
General Register Office—Scotland—*www.open.gov.uk/gros/groshome.htm*
National Archives and Records Administration—*www.nara.gov/nara/nail.html*
National Archives of Ireland—*http://www.nationalarchives.ie/*

12. Check out dictionaries and translation services:
America Online's Dictionaries—*www.aol.com/webcenters/research/reference.adp*
German–English—*http://dict.leo.org*
Middle English Dictionary—*www.hti.umich.edu/dict/med/*
French-English Dictionary—*http://humanities.uchicago.edu/forms_unrest/FR-ENG.html*

13. View scanned images of original records:
Bureau of Land Management—*www.blm.gov/nhp/index.htm*
Hillsborough County, Florida Marriage Records, Index—*www.lib.usf.edu/spccoll/guide/m/ml/guide.html*
USGenWeb Census Project—*www.usgenweb.org/census/*

14. Visit online card catalogs and state library Web pages to prepare for a research trip, or borrow a book through interlibrary loan.
Library of Congress—*www.loc.gov*
Library of Virginia—*www.lva/lib.va.us*
National Union Catalog of Manuscript Collections (NUCMC)—
http://lcweb.loc.gov/coll/nucmc
State Library of North Carolina—
www.dcr.state.nc.us
WebCats—*www.lights.com/webcats/*

15. Find maps and use town locator services:
1895 U.S. Atlas Map—*www.LivGenMl.com*
Ancient Map Site—
www.iag.net/~jsiebold/carto.html
Color Land Form Maps—
http://fermi.jhuapl.edu/states/states.html
Gazetteers & Geographical Information—
www.cyndislist.com/maps.htm
MapQuest—*www.mapquest.com/*

16. Search LDS FamilySearch Online—
www.familysearch.org
Ancestral File (lineage database)
International Genealogical Index
Family History Library Catalog Online
SourceGuide Online

17. When all else fails, go surfing!
Hot Bot—*www.hotbot.com*
DejaNews—*www.dejanews.com/*
Dog Pile—*www.dogpile.com/*
Genealogy Gateway—*www.gengateway.com/*
GenSearcher—*www.gensearcher.com/*
Alta Vista—www.*altavista.com*
Newspapers—*http://ajr.newslink.org/*
Yahoo—*www.yahoo.com/*
InfoSeek—*www2.infoseek.com/*

Appendix D: Additional Resources
National Genealogical Libraries

Daughters of the American Revolution Genealogical Library
www.dar.org
Memorial Continental Hall
1776 D Street
Washington, D.C. 20540

Library of Congress Genealogy Reading Room
http://lcweb.loc.gov/rr/genealogy
Thomas Jefferson Building
1st–2nd Streets, N.W.
Washington, D.C. 20540

National Genealogical Society Library
www.ngsgenealogy.org
4527 17th Street North
Arlington, VA 22207

The Best State by State

ALABAMA
Florence-Lauderdale Public Library
www.library.florence.org

Mobile Genealogical Society Library and Media Center
www.siteone.com/clubs/mgs

ALASKA
Alaska State Library
www.library.state.ak.us

Alaska State Archives
www.archives.state.ak.us

www.library.yale.edu

ARIZONA
Arizona State Library
www.lib.az.us

ARKANSAS
Pine Bluff and Jefferson County
Library
http://pbjc-lib.state.ar.us/
genealogy.htm

CALIFORNIA
California Genealogical Society
Library
www.calgensoc.org

Fresno County Free Public Library
www.sjvls.lib.ca.us/fresno

Napa Valley Genealogical and
Biographical Society Library
www.napanet.net/~nvgbs

Paradise Genealogical Society
Library (Butte County)
www.jps.net/pargenso

Solano County Genealogical
Society Library
www.scgsinc.org

Southern California Genealogical
Society Library
www.scgsgenealogy.com

COLORADO
Denver Public Library
www.denver.lib.co.us

Pike's Peak Regional District
Library
http://library.ppld.org

CONNECTICUT
Godfrey Memorial Library
www.godfrey.org

Yale University Libraries
www.library.yale.edu

DELAWARE
University of Delaware Library
www.lib.udel.edu

DISTRICT OF COLUMBIA
Martin Luther King Memorial Library
www.dclibrary.org/mlk

FLORIDA
Palm Beach County Genealogical
Library
www.gopbi.com/community/groups
/pbcgensoc

State Library of Florida
http://dlis.dos.state.fl.us/stlib

GEORGIA
DeKalb Historical Society Reading
Room
www.dekalbhistory.org

Huxford Genealogical Society
www.huxford.com

HAWAII
Hawaii Mayflower Society Library
www.geocities.com/Heartland/Ridge/4602/index.html

IDAHO
Idaho State Historical Society
www2.state.id.us/ishs/index.html

ILLINOIS
Cook Memorial Public Library
www.cooklib.org/home.htm

Morton Grove Public Library
www.webrary.org

Newberry Library
www.newberry.org/nl/newberryhome.html

INDIANA
Allen County Public Library
www.acpl.lib.in.us

Noblesville-Southeastern Public Library
www.nspl.lib.in.us/nspl.html

Saint Joseph County Public Library
www.sjcpl.lib.in.us

IOWA
Iowa Genealogical Society Library
www.iowagenealogy.org

KANSAS
Midwest Historical and Genealogical Society
http://skyways.lib.ks.us/kansas/genweb/mhgs

KENTUCKY
Kentucky Historical Society Library
www.kyhistory.org

National Society of the Sons of the American Revolution
www.sar.org

LOUISIANA
Hill Memorial Library, Louisiana State University
www.lib.lsu.edu/special

Howard Tilton Memorial Library
www.tulane.edu/~html

MAINE
Brooksville Free Public Library
http://media5.hypernet.com/~BFPL/library.html

MARYLAND
Maryland Historical Society Library
www.mdhs.org/library/library.html

MASSACHUSETTS
American Antiquarian Society
www.americanantiquarian.org

Berkshire Athenaeum
www.berkshire.net/PittsfieldLibrary

www.kyhistory.org

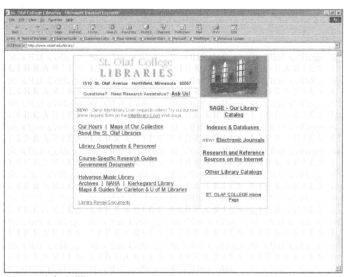

www.stolaf.edu/library

Boston Public Library
www.bpl.org

Massachusetts State Library
www.magnet.state.ma.us/lib

MICHIGAN
Detroit Society for Genealogical
Research
www.dsgr.org

State Archives of Michigan
www.sos.state.mi.us/history/archiv
e/archive.html

MINNESOTA
Heart O'Lakes Genealogical Society
www.angelfire.com/mn/HOLGS

Rolvaag County Genealogical Library
www.stolaf.edu/library

MISSISSIPPI
Harriette Person Memorial Library
http://library.msstate.edu/magnolia

Jackson-George Regional Library
System
http://jgrl.lib.ms.us

MISSOURI
St. Louis County Library
www.slcl.lib.mo.us

St. Louis Public Library
www.slpl.lib.mo.us

MONTANA
Cascade County Historical
Museum and Archives
www.mtgr.mtlib.org/www/library/
cchs.html

Montana State University Libraries
www.lib.montana.edu

NEBRASKA
Nebraska State Historical Society
Library
www.nebraskahistory.org

University of Nebraska Libraries
http://iris.unl.edu/screens/text.html

NEVADA
University of Nevada Libraries
www.library.unr.edu

Washoe County Library
www.washoe.lib.nv.us

NEW HAMPSHIRE
Dartmouth College Libraries
www.dartmouth.edu/~library/
thelibs/baker.html

New Hampshire State Library
www.state.nh.us/nhsl/index.html

NEW JERSEY
Monmouth County Historical
Association and Library
www.cjrlc.org/~mchalib

New Jersey State Library
www.njstatelib.org

NEW MEXICO
New Mexico Genealogical Society
www.nmgs.org

Rio Grande Valley Library System
www.cabq.gov/rgvls/specol.html

NEW YORK
Buffalo & Erie County Public
Library Special Collections
Department
*www.buffalolib.org/cl_*
collectdetails.html

The New York Genealogical &
Biographical Society
www.nygbs.org

The New York Public Library
(Humanities and Social Sciences)
www.nypl.org/research/chss/lhg/
genea.html

NORTH CAROLINA
Old Buncombe County
Genealogical Society
www.obcgs.com

State Library of North Carolina
http://statelibrary.dcr.state.nc.us/
iss/gr/genealog.htm

OHIO
Medina County District Library
Franklin Sylvester Genealogy Room
www.rootsweb.com/~ohmedina/
mclibrar.htm

State Library of Ohio
http://winslo.state.oh.us/services/g
enealogy/index.html

The Ohio Genealogical Society
Library
www.ogs.org

OKLAHOMA
Oklahoma Genealogical Society
Library
www.rootsweb.com/~okgs

Tulsa City-County Library
www.tulsalibrary.org/genealogy

OREGON
Genealogical Forum of Oregon
Library
www.gfo.org

Oregon Genealogical Society Library
www.rootsweb.com/~orlncogs/
ogsinfo.htm

University of Oregon Library System
http://libweb.uoregon.edu

PENNSYLVANIA
Carnegie Library of Pittsburgh
http://www.clpgh.org

Genealogical Society of
Pennsylvania Library
www.libertynet.org/gspa

The Free Library of Philadelphia
www.library.phila.gov/central/ssh/
waltgen/geneal1.htm

RHODE ISLAND
Providence Public Library
www.provlib.org

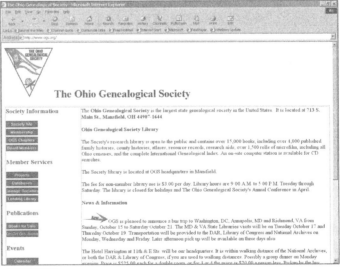

wwwogs.org

The Church's Family History Library (c 1988) houses the world's largest collection of genealogical records. More than 2,000 people come here daily to research their family histories. The five-floor library opened in Salt Lake City in 1985. Photographer: Marty Mayo

www.mormons.org/daily/family_history/library_eom.htm

The Clayton Library Center for Genealogical Research
www.hpl.lib.tx.us/clayton

UTAH
Family History Library
www.mormons.org/daily/family_history/library_eom.htm

www.familysearch.org
(This is an online service the library maintains)

University of Utah, J. Willard Marriott Library
www.lib.utah.edu

Rhode Island Historical Society Library
www.rihs.org

SOUTH CAROLINA
The Heritage Library
www.heritagelib.org

The South Carolina Genealogical Society Archives
www.geocities.com/heartland/woods/2548

SOUTH DAKOTA
South Dakota State Historical Society Library
www.state.sd.us/deca/cultural/arc_gene.htm

The University of South Dakota; I.D. Weeks Library
www.usd.edu/library/idweeks.html

TENNESSEE
Chattanooga-Hamilton County Bicentennial Library
www.lib.chattanooga.gov

Tennessee State Library and Archives
www.state.tn.us/sos/statelib/pubsvs/intro.htm

TEXAS
San Antonio Public Library
www.sat.lib.tx.us/central/texana.htm

VIRGINIA
Fairfax County Public Library
www.co.fairfax.va.us/library/virginia/varoom/menu.htm

The Library of Virginia
www.lva.lib.va.us/pubserv/genie.htm

WASHINGTON
Seattle Public Library
www.spl.org/humanities/genealogy/genealogy.html

Spokane Public Library
http://splnet.spokpl.lib.wa.us/subject/findingaids/genea.html

WEST VIRGINIA
Cabell County Public Library
http://cabell.lib.wv.us

Greenbrier Historical Society
Archives and Library
*www.greenbrierhistorical.org/
archive.html*

WISCONSIN
Milwaukee Public Library
www.mpl.org

The State Historical Society of
Wisconsin Library
www.shsw.wisc.edu/genealogy

WYOMING
Cheyenne Genealogical Society
www.wyomingweb.net/genealogy

Laramie County Library System
*http://library.gowyo.org/special_
collections/gen_intro.htm*

International Web Resources

AUSTRALIA
Flinders University Library
www.lib.flinders.edu.au

State Library of Queensland
www.slq.qld.gov.au

State Library of Tasmania
www.tased.edu.au/library

The National Library of Australia
www.nla.gov.au

CANADA
Halton Hills Public Library
*www.hhpl.on.ca/library/hhpl/
hhpl.htm*

National Library of Canada
*www.nlc-bnc.ca/services/
genealogy/gnlogy-e.htm*

Toronto Public Library
www.tpl.toronto.on.ca

University of Calgary Library
www.ucalgary.ca/library

IRELAND
National Archives of Ireland
www.nationalarchives.ie

SCOTLAND
Angus Archives
www.angus.gov.uk/history/archives

The Scottish Genealogy Society
www.scotsgenealogy.com

SWITZERLAND
Center of Genealogical Research
www.genealogyrsch.com

www.scotsgenealogy.com

Appendix E: Genealogy Abbreviations

For online definitions and glossaries see:

Family Search Glossary—
www.familysearch.org

Cyndi's List of Dictionaries & Glossaries—
www.cyndislist.com/diction.htm

BLW—Bounty Land Warrant

BT—Bishop's Transcript (parish registers).

c., ca.—circa (about)

cert.—certificate, certified, certain

ch.—child

chn—children

chr—Christening

d/o—daughter of

do.—ditto

fgs—family group sheet

FGS—Federation of Genealogical Societies.

FHL—Family History Library, the genealogical library located in Salt Lake City, Utah, sometimes referred to as the "Mormon" genealogy library.

FHC—Family History Center, one of thirty-five hundred-plus local branches of the main FHL Salt Lake City, Utah Family History Library.

FPC—Free Person of Color

GEDCOM—Genealogy Data Communication file Created as a generic export file by most mainstream genealogy programs so that the data can be imported by researchers into their existing database of names/dates/localities, notes.

intestate—an ancestor's estate is probated without a will

LDS—an abbreviation for the Church of Jesus Christ of Latter-day Saints. Sometimes the Family History Library is referred to as the "LDS library" and its microfilms as "LDS microfilm #."

m., md.—married

m/1—married first

m/2—married second

N.A.—Native American or North America

N.S.—New Style date (Gregorian calendar)

nunc.—nuncupative (oral, as opposed to written)

n.x.n.—no Christian name

P.C.—Privy Council

PS—Patriotic Service

relecta—widow

relectus—widower

twp.—township

VR—vital record

wd—warranty deed

Appendix F:
Selected Bibliography

This is my list of great genealogy books. If not found at the library, you might consider purchasing these basic reference works for your home library. URLs are cited if the book can be ordered at a genealogy site. Sometimes it just helps to curl up with a book like *The Source* and find different ways to combat your research brick walls.

Baxter, Angus. *In Search of Your British and Irish Roots.* 320 pp., Indexed. (1994), 1999.

——. *In Search of Your European Roots.* 304 pp., (1994), 1999. *www.genealogical.com*

——. *In Search of Your Canadian Roots.* (3d ed.) 400 pp., Indexed (1994), 2000. *www.genealogical.com*

——. *In Search of Your German Roots.* 122 pp. (1994), 1999. *www.genealogical.com*

Bremer, Ronald A. *Compendium of Historical Sources: The How and Where of American Genealogy.* (1998). *www.everton.com*

Carmack, Sharon DeBartolo. *A Genealogist's Guide to Discovering Your Female Ancestors: Special Strategies for Uncovering Hard-To-Find Information About Your Female Lineage.* 260 pp. (1998). Betterway Pubns.

Cole, Trafford. *Italian Genealogical Records.* 265 pp. (1995) *www.ancestry.com*

Colletta, John Philip. *Finding Italian Roots: The Complete Guide for Americans.* 128 pp.(1993). *www.genealogical.com*

Croom, Emily. *The Genealogist's Companion and Sourcebook.* 227 pp. (1994). Betterway Pubns

Dollarhide, William. *America's Best Genealogy Resource Centers.* 139 pp. (1998). *www.heritagequest.com*

Dollarhide, William. *The Census Book: A Genealogists Guide to Federal Census Facts, Schedules and Indexes.* 83 pp. (1999). *www.heritagequest.com*

Eichholz, Alice. *Ancestry's Red Book: American State, County, and Town Sources.* 858 pp. Rev edition (1992). *www.ancestry.com*

Everton, Lee, ed. *Everton's Handbook for Genealogists.* 9th ed. 619 pp. (1999). *www.everton.com*

Filby, P. William. *Bibliography of American County Histories.* 449 pp. (1985), 1987. *www.genealogical.com*

Fischer, David Hackett. *Albion's Seed: Four British Folkways in America.* 946 pp. (1989). *www.amazon.com*

Gouldrup, Lawrence P. *Writing the Family Narrative.* Set includes book 157 pp. (1998). and workbook 168 pp. Workbook edition (1998). *www.ancestry.com*

Greenwood, Val D. *The Researcher's Guide to American Genealogy.* 3d ed. 676 pp. (2000). *www.genealogical.com*

Grundset, Eric G. and Steven B. Rhodes. *American Genealogical Research at the DAR, Washington, D.C.* 180 pp. (1997). *www.dar.org/*

Hatcher, Patricia Law. *Producing a Quality Family History.* 286 pages. 1997. Ancestry, Incorporated; *www.ancestry.com*

Hone, E. Wade. *Land and Property Research in the United States*, 600 pp. (1998). *www.ancestry.com*

Kempthorne, Charley. *For All Time: A Complete Guide to Writing Your Family History.* 150 pp. 1996. Heinemann

Kirkham, Kay. *The Handwriting of American Records for a Period of 300 Years.* (1973). *www.everton.com*

Klein, Reinhard. *Family History Logbook.* 224 pp.. 1997. Betterway Pubns

Meyerink, Kory, editor. *Printed Sources: A Guide to Published Genealogical Records.* 800 pp. (1998). *www.ancestry.com*

Miller, Olga K. *Migration, Emigration, Immigration*, vol. 1 & vol. 2. (1981). Everton Publishers. *www.everton.com*

Mills, Elizabeth Shown. *Evidence! Citation & Analysis for the Family Historian.* 124 pp., Indexed. (1997), 1999. *www.genealogical.com*

Neagles, James C. *U.S. Military Records: A Guide to Federal and State Sources, Colonial America to the Present.* 441 pp. 1994. Ancestry Press. *www.ancestry.com*

Newman, John J. *American Naturalization Records 1790–1990: What They Are and How to Use Them.* 127 pp. (1998). *www.heritagequest.com*

Ryan, James G. *Irish Records: Sources for Family and Local History.* 860 pp., *www.ancestry.com*

Schaefer, Christina K. *Genealogical Encyclopedia of the Colonial Americas.* 830 pp., Indexed. Illus. 1998. *www.genealogical.com*

——. *Guide to Naturalization Records of the United States.* 439 pp., (1997), 1999. *www.genealogical.com*

——. *The Center: A Guide to Genealogical Research in the National Capital Area.* 160 pp., Indexed. Illus. 1996. *www.genealogical.com*

——. *The Great War: A Guide to the Service Records of All the World's Fighting Men and Volunteers.* 1998. *www.genealogical.com*

——. *The Hidden Half of the Family: A Source Book of Women's Genealogy.* 310 pp., Indexed. Illus. 1999. *www.genealogical.com*

Sperry, Kip. *Reading Early American Handwriting.* 289 pp. (1998). *www.genealogical.com*

Stanek, Lou. *Writing Your Life: Putting Your Past on Paper.* 179 pp. 1996. Avon Books.

Szucs, Loretto Dennis. *They Became Americans: Finding Naturalization Records and Ethnic Origins.* 260 pp.,(1998). *www.ancestry.com*

Szucs, Loretto Dennis, and Sandra Hargreaves Leubking, eds. *The Source: A Guidebook of American Genealogy.* 846 pp. Revised edition (1997). *www.ancestry.com*

Tepper, Michael. *American Passenger Arrival Records*, updated ed. 144pp. (1993). *www.genealogical.com*

Thomas, Frank P. *How to Write the Story of Your Life.* 1989. Writers Digest Books

Thorndale, William, and William Dollarhide. *Map Guide to the US Federal Census Records.* 445 pp., Illus. (1987), 2000. *www.genealogical.com*

Q

Quaker studies, 141

R

Ragan, Robert, 172
Railroad information, 133
Reading
    offline, 242–45
    online, 241–42
"Read-only" mailing lists, 170–71
Records
    available on computer, 8
    birth, 50, 53, 96, 111
    cemetery, 56, 58
    citizenship, 58
    computer, 8
    court, 58
    death, 51, 53
    divorce, 51
    draft, 68
    drawing information from home, 23–24
    English, 81
    extracted, 71
    immigration, 62, 65
    kinds of, 197–98
    land, 132–33
    local, 52
    manumission, 97, 103
    marriage, 51
    military, 66, 68, 96
    naturalization and citizenship, 63–64
    personal, 198, 199
    post-slavery, 97–98
    preservation of family, 29
    probate, 58, 60
    religious, 55, 59, 96
    state, 50–52
    of your records, 177
Records libraries/repositories, standards
    for using, 260–61
Reference.com, 155
Relatives, asking for genealogy information,
    24, 26, 196–98
Religious records, 55
    African Americans in, 96
    centralized, 59
Reunions, announcing online, 238

ReunionTips.com, 237
Rhodes, Steven B., 142
Rightside-up triangle or pyramid, 3
Riverside Keystone-Mast Photo Collection,
    119–20
Roots Cellar, 46
Roots (Haley), vii, ix, 94–95, 98
RootsWeb, 40–41, 47, 74, 162, 212, 225–26,
    241, 269
    GenConnect, 157–58
    Guide to Tracing Family Trees, 240–41
    mailing lists, 166, 168–69, 262–2697
    Social Security Death Index at, 76
RootsWeb Review & Missing Links, 172, 269
RootsWeb Surname Helper, 90–91
RootsWeb Surname List (RSL), 40
Rosado, Mike, AOL Hispanic Genealogy
    Group Web page, 108
Runs With Ponies' Search for Our Elders,
    106–7

S

St. Catherine's House, 137
Sanborn Map Company, 133–34
San Francisco Bay Area Jewish Genealogical
    Society (San Mateo, CA), 105
Saxony Court Records Project, 82
Scandinavian patronymics, 86–88
Schomburg Center for Research in Black
    Culture (New York City), 97
Schweitzer, George K., 72
Scottish surnames, 90
Scrapbooks, 24
    materials of, as source for life story,
    220–21
Scriptorium Family History Centre, 254
Search engines, 18, 19
    comparing different, 20
    Find option, 21
    genealogy, 21
Search LDS FamilySearch Online, 271
Semidivine descendent, claiming, 23
Semi-private journal, 203
Semi-public journal, 203–4
Service records, 66
Ship passenger arrival lists, 62–63
Short, Ken, 127

Shtetl Seeker site searches, 133
Siler Rolls, 106
Sill, Sterling, 214
Sinko, Peggy, 143
Slave Data Collection, 99
Slavery and genealogy, 96–97
Slides as source for life story, 220
Slovenian Genealogy Society, 151
Smith, Dereka, 246
Snapshots as source for life story, 220
Social Security Death Index, 76
Société Généalogique Canadienne-
    Française, 151
Society of Arcadian Descendants, 151
Software, genealogy, 27–28, 161–62, 177,
    180–84
Sons and Daughters of Pioneer
    Rivermen, 148
Sons of Confederate Veterans, 148
Sons of Union Veterans of the Civil War, 148
Soundex system, 51, 54–55, 133
SourceGuide's Germany Research Outline, 21
Standards
    for sharing information with others, 262
    for sound genealogical research, 260
    for use of technology in genealogical
    research, 261
    for using records libraries/repositories,
    260–61
Stark, Gene, 76
State libraries, 271–76
State records, 50–52
    birth, 50, 53
    death, 51, 53
    divorce, 51
    marriage, 51
Steps to Native American Genealogy, 107
Surname Resource Center (SRC), 92
Surname Ring Center, 92
Surnames, 56, 84, 86. *See also* Names
    discussion forums on, 92, 159
    European, 85
    medieval sites, 89–90
    message groups for, 270
    online help, 90–92
    Scottish, 90
    websites for, 90

Notes